Eighteen Words to Sustain a Life

Eighteen Words to Sustain a Life

A Jewish Father's Ethical Will

חי

BY
David Patterson

CASCADE *Books* • Eugene, Oregon

EIGHTEEN WORDS TO SUSTAIN A LIFE
A Jewish Father's Ethical Will

Cascade Books
An Imprint of Wipf and Stock Publishers
199 W. 8th Ave., Suite 3
Eugene, OR 97401

www.wipfandstock.com

PAPERBACK ISBN: 978-1-6667-5093-5
HARDCOVER ISBN: 978-1-6667-5094-2
EBOOK ISBN: 978-1-6667-5095-9

Cataloguing-in-Publication data:

Names: Patterson, David, author.

Title: Eighteen words to sustain a life : a Jewish father's ethical will / by David Patterson.

Description: Eugene, OR: Cascade Books, 2023

Identifiers: ISBN 978-1-6667-5093-5 (paperback) | ISBN 978-1-6667-5094-2 (hardcover) | ISBN 978-1-6667-5095-9 (ebook)

Subjects: LCSH: Judaism—Doctrines. | Holocaust, Jewish (1939–1945)—Moral and ethical aspects. | Good and evil—Religious aspects. | Philosophy and religion.

Classification: BS1225.52 .P40 2023 (print) | BS1225.52 (ebook)

06/23/23

For Miriam, Rachel, Jacob, Aaron, and Julia

Contents

Preface

Why Eighteen?

חי

Why eighteen? The *eighteen* in these eighteen words that sustain a life comes from the Hebrew word *chai*, which means "living," "alive," and "life." Made of the letters *chet* and *yud*, which have numerical values of eight and ten respectively, *chai* is equal to eighteen. Therefore Jews often give *tzedakah* or "charity" in dollar amounts that are multiples of eighteen. The sages tell us that *chai* corresponds to the eighteenth word in the Torah, which is *merachefet* or "hovering," as when God hovered over the face of the deep in the instant before creation. It is, they say, a "touching and yet not touching," where God simultaneously hovers over each of us and instills us with his life-giving Presence. Yes, my children, he is at once near and far. Like these eighteen words I here offer you, this hovering points to the delicate balance between the revelation of God's Presence in our lives and the concealment of that Presence. But there is more, my children. There is always more.

The letter *chet*—with a value of eight, which is one *more* than seven—signifies the infinite and the eternal, what is *more* than all there is, beyond the space-time reality that came into being during the seven days of creation. Indeed, mathematicians signify infinity with the lazy eight, the symbol ∞. What sustains life originates with the infinite and the eternal, as designated by the letter *chet*. It is not to be found in the space-time world around us. Rather, it is above and beyond us. The Talmud tells us that in the time of the Messiah, the seven-stringed harp that was played in the temple will have eight strings, signifying the ultimate merging of above and below. We circumcise a male infant on the eighth day and thus draw the light of the Holy One into the life of the child. The Chanukah candles burn for eight days, signifying the Light of Torah that emanates from the temple into this world.

Life's first movement into this world begins under the *chupah*, which is *chet-pey-hey*. The *chupah* resembles the letter *chet*. Standing under the *chupah*, we are taught, the bride and groom affirm the power of *chet* to bring life into this world. It is the power of drawing God, the "Life of Life" or *Chai HaChayim* into this world. May these eighteen words, the meaning of *chai*, enable you to draw the Life of Life into this world.

And the *yud*, with a value of ten? The secret of the *yud*, say the sages, is the secret of the ability of the Infinite to contain the finite within himself. It is also the mystery of the ability of the finite to contain the Infinite. Where there is *chai* or "life," the finite is embraced by the Infinite One, the Holy One. Hardly more than a dot suspended in midair, the *yud* represents the humility that alone enhances life through living for the sake of another. *Yud* means "hand," the helping hand that we extend to our fellow human being. These eighteen words that sustain life should lead you, my children, to extend a hand to another. In that offering of the hand lives the hand of God in his boundless giving and sustaining of every life.

Yud is the first letter of the Divine Name, *yud-hey-vav-hey*. As the smallest of letters, it signifies the Divine humility, from which creation unfolds. With a value of ten, it invokes both the Ten Utterances of Creation and the Ten Utterances of Revelation, without which we have no life, no meaning, no redemption. There were ten generations from Adam to Noah, to draw a measure of righteousness into the world that would save a remnant of the world, and then ten generations from Noah to Abraham, to draw the covenant into the world. A *minyan* consists of ten, the number of Jews required to gather for prayer to bring holiness into this realm. Says the Talmud, "there are ten synonyms for prayer, ten synonyms for song, ten synonyms for martyrs, ten spiritual functions of the heart," and so on. And Yom Kippur, when we plead for our lives and the life of our soul, falls on the tenth day of Tishrei. There are other, deeper, more mystical meanings of the letter *yud*, which I shall not go into, though the temptation to do so is great. For now, let be said that, as the world is made of ten, so is meaning made of ten, so is the soul made of ten. Attached to the *chet* that is the infinite, the eternal, to make the word *chai*, this letter draws truth and meaning and life from the upper worlds into this world.

So you see, my children, how I arrived at the number eighteen for the eighteen words that sustain a life. You will also see how each of these eighteen words is interwoven with all the others. You will encounter themes and variations on themes, repetition of themes, where each repetition introduces a new perspective on what I here bequeath to you. Hopefully, you will see how these eighteen words might sustain a life, the *chai* that is life. My hope is that these eighteen words will impart to you, my children, some deeper understanding of this one word: חי.

Note: All biblical translations are my own.

An Avenue into This Ethical Will

"Place these words upon your heart and within your soul . . ."

—Deuteronomy 11:18

A WILL NORMALLY LISTS the worldly goods a person has accumulated to enumerate how they might be divided up and passed on to his or her heirs. I have very little in the way of worldly goods, but, with God's blessing, I have perhaps attained some measure of an understanding of the Good, some portion of wisdom, some measure of what is meaningful, to pass on to you, my heirs, my beloved children. And it cannot be divided up. As the great sage Hillel once said, blessing does not come to what can be weighed, measured, or counted. May this ethical will be a blessing upon you.

Plato once said, "Each of us, neglecting all other studies, should seek after and study this thing: the ability to distinguish the life that is good from the life that is bad." The good life is not something we enjoy—it is something we rejoice in. There is a difference: we kick back and enjoy, but we rise up and rejoice. Rising up as a soul on fire, we affirm the dimension of height, the Truth of the Most High, without whom we never live but only hope to live. Know that there is no flame more life-affirming than Torah. Made of black fire on white fire, it is our most precious inheritance. It is the inheritance that I here offer to you. Learn to think in terms of Torah, and the Torah will think from within you—the Torah will *think* you. It will burn within you and light your path. Know God, and you will be known by God. You will know the love and the awe of God. God will lay claim to you, summon you, bless you, and comfort you. There is no greater blessing, no inheritance more sublime.

In the Torah God summons us to choose between good and evil, life and death, commanding us to choose life. This does not mean that we must choose to stay alive, since, in the end, no one gets out alive. No, God summons us to learn how to distinguish the life that is good from the life that is bad. For the life that is good sanctifies life and attests to what makes life *matter*. But how are we to make such a distinction? My prayer is that these eighteen words will come to your aid in times when the distinction may not be so clear. So I leave you with my inheritance of these eighteen words to help you through times when you may wonder what, indeed, *matters*. Life is made of such moments of decision. It is made of the choices we make in the light of having already been chosen, already laid claim to.

What, then, you ask, is an ethical will? What makes it a will, and what is ethical about it? Writing an ethical will for our children and grandchildren is an ancient Jewish custom, as old as the ethical will that Jacob left to his children, when he gathered them around his bed as he lay dying, to offer them his blessing and his last words of wisdom, words charged with an ethical injunction. It is as old as the wisdom Moses left to his people, when they were about to enter the Land of the Covenant and he was about to enter the upper realms. As Moses prepared for his passing, God blessed the Israelites with one last commandment, the 613th commandment, which is to write a Torah scroll; here God refers to the Torah as a *shir*, a song or a poem. Learn to sing, my children. Write poetry. Poetry makes you human. Through poetry you may restore meaning to words emptied of meaning. Through poetry you may for a moment lend an ear to the thin voice of silence that comes from above and from within. As Ralph Waldo Emerson once said, blessed is one who knows that Within and Above are synonyms.

We sing, we compose poetry, precisely when words fail, when we must impart extraordinary meaning to ordinary words. The language of silence and the substance of language—that is what poetry and prayer are. That is what the Torah is: poetry and prayer. For the teachings of Torah are made not only of the words but of the silences between the words. And so what follows throughout this volume is my prayer, my Torah, my teaching in words and in the silence between the words, in poetry and prayer and stories. Yes, stories. We are taught that if you would know the One who spoke and brought heaven and earth into being, you must know the stories, the *Aggadah*. God creates by telling tales. Memory is made of those tales, both our memory of God and God's memory of us. And in memory, as the Baal Shem Tov, founder of Hasidism, teaches, lies our redemption from meaninglessness. What threatens human life is neither suffering nor even evil. It is *meaningless* suffering, meaningless evil. It is the meaninglessness that comes with the loss of memory. And in our lives, memory is among the first things that we lose.

There are a couple of words in Hebrew for "inheritance." Indeed, I shall frequently turn to the Holy Tongue throughout this ethical will. In the Holy Tongue is to be found the will's ethical aspect. Hebrew is the language of Torah—holy not because it is the language of Torah, but it is the language of Torah because it is holy, the language of God. When one of you was very small, you once asked me, "What does *Adonai* mean?" I replied that it is a Hebrew word we use to refer to God. After a pause, a bit puzzled, you answered, "I thought every Hebrew word refers to God." From the mouths of babes. Listen to your babies. Wisdom and Torah abide on their untainted smiling lips, even as they babble. That babbling is not the "unknown tongue," as it is sometimes called; no, it is the Holy Tongue, and language that at times only a mother can understand, for no one loves as a mother loves. One of the great Hasidic masters once observed: "Have you ever noticed how a baby will lie in the crib and babble away? The great sages of the world could not decipher what the babe is saying. But his mother enters the room, and she knows precisely what the little one is trying to say."

That babbling is a form of praying. We are taught that only the prayers of little children reach the ears of God, for their lips are untainted by sin. So teach your children the prayers. It is crucial.

The Hebrew words for "inheritance"? One is *nachalah*, which is a cognate of *nachal*, or "river," something that flows naturally and without effort. Another word for "inheritance" is *morashah*, which means to acquire or receive through our own enduring effort. The inheritance I leave you in this ethical will and testament is a *morashah*. Receiving the inheritance couched in these words will require energy and effort, something that each of you, I know, embodies and exemplifies. I place them in your hands; I commend them to you. What will you make of them, my beloved ones? Take the will for what it is worth. Dwell upon it. Challenge it. Do not just accept it out of hand. Take it in hand and examine it, reflect upon it. Wrestle with it, as Jacob, Son of Isaac, wrestled with the Angel, with God himself.

A will is a testament and a testimony bequeathed to our heirs. In the case of an ethical will, we hand down to our heirs the teachings that have shaped our lives, despite all our failures to live up to those teachings. There lies the true treasure that I have to pass on to you. The higher the teaching, the more common the failure. Do not despair of your efforts that fall short, for despair has a way of paralyzing us, draining us of every effort. As one of my teachers, Elie Wiesel, once told me, only God can begin, but it is given to us, as a profound blessing, to begin again. It does not take much to live up to a lower standard. Indeed, there is no life, no meaning, without the higher standard that we have forever *yet* to attain, without the summons from the Most High, who commands us to be holy as he is holy, a summons we can never fully live up to. It is an injunction to be forever *more*, as we are commanded to love God with all our "mores," *bekol-meodekha*—as we are called forth to *live* with all our "mores." There, in the *more*, lies the ethical in the ethical will. For the ethical is *more* than all there is, an incursion of the eternal into time, of the holy into the mundane. Indeed, there is nothing more mystical, more mysterious, than the mundane. Which, my children, means: acquire a capacity for wonder. I'll never forget the day when one of you discovered the sky, looking up in rapt wonder. Indeed, when you look for wonder, that is where to look: to the sky. Or into the eyes of your newborn, as it happened with me. For everything to be found in the heavens is gathered into those eyes, as they take their first look at this world below.

The ethical in an ethical will lies in its testimony to the Good that sanctifies life from beyond life. Be assured, my children, there is a beyond that forever abides in our midst, here and now. Commanded to choose life, we are commanded to choose the Good. *HaEl HaTov*, the God who is the Good, chooses us prior to all of our choices. That is what makes our choices *matter*. Note well: God is a Who, and not a What, not a concept or an idea but a living Presence who becomes present in the simplest act of goodness. There will be times when you may ask: Where is God? The answer: he is right here, in your act of loving kindness, in your good word offered to another, in the cheerful countenance with which you greet another. If he seems to be absent, it is up to us to make him present by opening a door through which he many enter. Such an act lies above all in having *time* for another: time is the portal through which God makes his entry into this realm. The only time we have, the time of our lives, unfolds in having time for another. Otherwise we merely mark time, kill time, do time, or waste time. That is where the Good, the ethical, is manifest: in offering up the time of our life for the sake of the life of another, in welcoming the other person simply by saying, "What can I do for you? How can I help you?" The ethical inheres in this saying of *Hineni!*, "Here I am for you!"

I am approaching the time when I shall join Moses in the upper worlds. I have spent my life trying to sound the depths of the "big questions," seeking God, who, indeed, is in the midst of the question, the *el* in *shelah*. Throughout this endeavor I have sought out the wisdom of the ages and the teachings of the sages. And yet, as the great Talmudic teacher Rabbi Eliezer once declared, when I turn to my teachers, I am like a dog lapping at the sea. Of course, I am no Rabbi Eliezer. Nevertheless, I turn to my teachers, who even now look over my shoulder, in order to pass along a small measure of their wisdom to you, and all wisdom begins with a question. In ancient times the great sage of the Talmud, Rabban Gamliel, would begin his encounters with his students by saying, "Ask!" And he would end by urging them, "Go and ask further!" So my counsel to you is: ask questions. Do not be afraid of wondering why. For the Holy One himself abides in that wondering, in that why: in every cry of "Why?" God himself cries out.

Do not be afraid of questions; be more afraid of fixed formulas and ready answers. They have a way of settling matters, of settling accounts that, in truth, can never be settled. To be a human being is to be unsettled, to have your accounts forever unsettled. To be a human being is to bear one responsibility *more*. Once again, there, in the *more*, lies your humanity. For to be a human being is to be forever summoned to be *more*, to do *more*, and, by doing, to hear and understand *more*. Thus, when the Israelites were gathered at Mount Sinai and asked if they would live by the Torah they were about to receive, they answered, "We shall do and we shall hear." We shall act, and through our action, we shall try to understand. I am reminded of a scene from Dostoevsky's *The Brothers Karamazov*. The rational intellectual Ivan puts a question to his brother Alyosha, a young man of faith: "How am I to love life if I do not know its meaning?" To which Alyosha answers, "It is only by loving life that you can ever hope to understand its meaning." And yet, to love life is to know what there is to love, what there is to fear, and what there is to fear *for*. There lies the wisdom that makes a life.

I think I have been blessed not so much with wisdom as with the ability to recognize it in people who are truly wise, like Salieri, who could recognize the genius in Mozart but did not possess it himself. I have been blessed to count among my teachers some of the renowned sages of my time, people whom I have been blessed to know personally and to learn from: Joseph Brodsky, Elie Wiesel, Emil Fackenheim, Sir Martin Gilbert, Rabbi Adin Steinsaltz, Yechiel De-Nur, Chaim Gouri, Franklin Littell, Alan Rosen, and others, both renowned and otherwise. There was the beggar I encountered on the streets of Paris who held out one arm for alms, her face buried in the other. The sight of her made me shudder. Then there was the man, an African American, who stopped to give me a ride when I was hitchhiking in Oregon years ago, desperate to get home. When he left me at my doorstep, I told him, "I really appreciate it." He answered, "I know you do, brother. I know you do." And he drove on.

But more than these, I count among my teachers those who count themselves among my students. As one of the great sages of the Talmud once said, I learned much from my teachers, even more from my colleagues, but I learned most of all from my students. And even more, infinitely more, I say to you, my children, I have learned from you: you have always been my dearest, most profound teachers. Gazing into your infant eyes, my eyes were suddenly filled with wisdom, if only for a fleeting moment: I knew the meaning of life, why we live and why we die, what we live and die for. And so in this ethical will I bequeath to you what I have received from you.

I have been blessed to engage the teachings and the texts of the millennia-long Jewish tradition and testimony that inform this last will and testimony, only a fraction of which find their way into this ethical will. So far I have published forty books in the course of my journey, and I feel that

I may have just one more book in me: this book, this ethical will. Not that I am out of ideas—no, just the opposite: each idea leads to half a dozen others, so that I have much more yet to pursue, much more to bequeath. Nevertheless. Whether God grants me that strength remains to be seen. But the time grows near. I enter the autumn of my life with more questions than ever, but also with some measure of clarity, thanks be to God.

The first thing that I am absolutely clear about is that I love you, my children, with all my heart, all my soul, and all the "mores" with which I have to love. With this testimony, this ethical will, I leave you with whatever wisdom I may have gleaned from my lifelong endeavor to question, to understand, to realize something of what sustains a *life*. I leave you with my words of love, my children, for there is no wisdom without love. You must choose life, my children and grandchildren. With this will and testament, with this reflection on what constitutes a meaningful life, I hope to help you in that choice, to help you understand what you are choosing and what is at stake—in the light of your having been chosen.

"The Word is everything," my beloved teacher Elie Wiesel once said. "Through the Word we elevate ourselves or debase ourselves. . . . How would we pray without it? How would we live without it?" Through the Word, he said, we "plumb the unfathomable depths of being." And so I consign to you these eighteen words: eighteen, the numerical value of *chai*, the Hebrew word meaning "life" or "living." You will find some of the teachings I have started with here recurring in our journey through these eighteen words. Indeed, I take this will to be not only a kind of prayer but also a kind of symphony, replete with repeated themes and variations on themes, with each variation, each repetition in its context, shedding light on the other. I have selected these words from the 171,146 words in the English language because an understanding of these eighteen words will impart an understanding of all the other 171,128 words. If you weigh them and ponder them, they will unearth the silence and the meaning of every word, the silence of all tongues. And so I leave you these eighteen words and my reflections on these words as an inheritance.

Word

In contrast to the Hellenistic breakdown of the world into the categories of animal, vegetable, and mineral, Jewish teaching divides the stuff of our reality into four components: mineral (*domeh*, literally "silent"), vegetable (*tzomeach*, "that which grows"), animal (*chai*, meaning "alive"), and human being (*medaber*, that is, a "speaking being"). These levels of creation are based on the teaching that all of creation issues from the Divine Word, with every level instilled with the Word. Because all that *is* derives its being from the Divine Word, Adam did not name the animals—he *read* the names of the animals, as it is written in the Hebrew, *vayikra*: so great was his wisdom that he could perceive the Divine Word of which they were created. That is the wisdom to which you must aspire: you may not be able to read the names as Adam did, but the names that go into the creation are there. The best way to begin to decipher them is to study Hebrew. Those names, those Hebrew words of which creation is made, are a key to meaning, both in the world and in your life. Take a look at my book *Hebrew Language and Jewish Thought*, and it may tell you something about the words that comprise your precious soul, as well as the wisdom harbored in the Holy Tongue.

Inanimate matter is called *domeh*, not because God is silent but because at that level of creation, the Word is most muted, as if it were created with a barely audible Divine whisper, for even at that level there is Divine utterance. Even at that level there is a faint trace of what we term *nefesh*, which is the soul in its physical aspect. You can hear it if you fall silent. Yes, in order to hear the word, you must learn how to be silent. Only then can you listen closely as you gaze upon the silence of the starry night sky, the majesty of the mountains, the lushness of the forests, the starkness of the desert, or the vastness of the sea. Each of these wonders is precisely that: a wonder, instilled with the infinite. All of these wonders are embodied in every word. Herman Melville once said that water and meditation are forever wed. Cast your eyes upon the waters about you, the waters that surround the earth, above and below, and meditate. There is a close bond between Torah and water: in water there is Torah. In water, as in Torah, lies the source of all life. There is no life without water. The word for "water" is *mayim*. It is the meaning of the letter *mem*, with a value of forty, the number of days required for the revelation of the Word of Torah, four times ten, as Moses ascended through the ten levels of the four worlds to stand before the Holy One. Water harbors this mystical teaching. And it harbors the mystery of the Word. One day you will understand.

All rivers run to the sea, and yet the sea is never full, as the wisest among us, Kohelet, has said. The river is the soul. The sea is its source. The sea is the Word. That is why the sea is never full: the source is as infinite as the dearness of the soul that issues from it. The soul is made of the Divine Word, to which no response is adequate, because its depth and its meaning are as deep as the sea. And so the word summons yet another word. And another. And another, as inexhaustible as the meaning found in the Torah. As inexhaustible as the dearness that shines in the innocent eyes of our little ones. Yes: innocence is inexhaustible. And mystical.

Because the human being is a *medaber*, a speaking being, the spoken word constitutes the essence of the human being. If we come into being through the Word of the Holy One, our being is also sustained—or threatened—by our own words, inasmuch as our words, like fire, can heal or harm ourselves and others. Because a human being is a speaking being, life is not about *me*: speaking the word implies the presence of two, one who speaks and one who is addressed. Therefore whatever life I have is never *my* life, any more than my words are mine alone. I do not make up words, but rather I am *made up* of words. The word is not like the blood that courses in my veins but like the air that I breathe, the air of generations, as I move into the between space that constitutes my relation to another. In this speaking and listening that opens up through the word life unfolds. The soul is mended by what it restores, and it suffers what it inflicts, beginning with the words that issue from it. Therefore when you speak, let your words be words of healing and kindness, a saying of: "Here I am for you." And let your silence teem with presence: to be present is to be *with*.

Before every class I teach I utter a prayer from the Psalms: "O Lord, open my lips, that I may sing your praise." It is a prayer that we say three times a day, as we begin the Eighteen Benedictions (yes, eighteen) at the center of the liturgy. Let the words that come forth from your lips be a song of praise, gratitude, and testimony. For every time you speak you teach others, whose precious souls are placed in your care. What will be your teaching? What will be your care?

What, then, does it mean to say that the human being created in the image and likeness of the Holy One is a *medaber* or a *speaking* being, endowed with the word? It means, first of all, that the image and likeness of the Holy One, the very essence of who we are, lies in the word. Where the Hebrew text of the Torah relates that God breathed a *nishmat chaim*, a "living soul," into the dust he gathered to create the first human being, in the Aramaic Targum Onkelos renders it as God breathed the word into the human being to create a "speaking spirit" or "a spirit endowed with the word," *l'ruach memalla*. The early medieval sage Saadia Gaon teaches that through the "luminosity" it received from God, the soul "came to be endowed with the power of speech." The word is light, a reflection of the light brought into being through God's first word: "Let there be light." It illuminates not only the path to which we are called but also the ways in which we illuminate a path for others. The *mitzvah* is the candle, and the Torah is the light, as it is written in the Proverbs. The stars *have* light only inasmuch as they *give* out light, and so it is with life: we have only as much life as we give. So yes, indeed, the Torah is light and light is Torah: it delineates not only the horizon of the event but also its meaning.

Let your words be endowed with luminosity and light, not only for your own sake but for the sake of those whose lives are attached to yours. Let your words open the eyes of others to the meaning they hunger for. Endowed with a capacity for speaking the word, we are endowed with a capacity for creation and destruction, wielding powers that the Creator himself has placed in our hands and in our mouths. As God was about to speak, when his spirit "hovered" over the face of the deep, in his "hovering," in his *merachefet*, he "hesitated." Indeed, the angels tried to talk him out of it, as if to say, "This is going to hurt you. Because your word, the word of creation, is spoken with infinite love, you will suffer for it: there is no loving without suffering. And because you are the Infinite One, your suffering will be infinite." Do not, my children, let God regret his creation. Let your words assure him that his creative Word was not in vain. Each time you open your mouth, he is listening to you. Make your words into prayers. Be his Witnesses. For if you are not his witnesses through the words you speak, he is not the God who spoke and brought all that there is into being. If you are not his witnesses, he, the One who loves you beyond measure, will suffer beyond measure. Prove the angels wrong with your words.

So, my children, be careful before you give utterance to the word. Bear in mind the words of Mar, son of Ravina, spoken in the Talmud: "My God, guard my tongue from speaking words of evil and my lips from speaking words of deceit." This is the teaching on the *lashon hara*, or the "evil tongue." The Talmud compares speaking evil to shedding blood and deems it a denial of God himself. Your lips, your tongue, and your mouth decide the condition of your soul because they decide the actions of your hands. When you speak, see to it that your every word is an expression of love and goodness. I repeat: your words can harm, or they can heal. See to it that your words are healing words, truthful words, words that uplift and reassure, for in the end nothing is more harmful than deceit. The capacity for the word arises from God, and not from some meaningless evolution; we receive it from the breath that God breathes into us, from the *neshimah* that is our *neshamah*, our very soul.

Elie Wiesel once related to me a story from his youth, when he worked as a journalist in France. During those early years of his calling, a rabbi, his teacher, asked him what he did for a living. Wiesel answered, "I am a writer." The rabbi was shocked, scandalized. "A *writer*!?" he retorted. "Don't you know that words create and destroy worlds? And you have the temerity to take yourself to be a *writer*!?" The word is the most exciting of all discoveries, and the most terrifying, my teacher once said. Through the word, he said, God created heaven and earth, and through the word humankind is destroying it. Just look at the unbridled lies spread throughout the so-called social media, Twitter, and Facebook, not to mention the pronouncements of politicians and newscasters. Tweeting is the opposite of speaking, and Facebook is the opposite of the face. Do not be a party to that destruction. Get off of Facebook, Twitter, and all the other sanctioned assaults on the word. We see it at work everywhere, from cancel culture to book burnings. And, as the poet Heinrich Heine prophetically said a hundred years before the Holocaust, when you begin by burning books, you end by burning people. When you begin by canceling words, you end by canceling people—by any means necessary. The cancel culture is a culture that would obliterate the soul. Do not be a party to that assault on the soul, on your own soul.

Elie Wiesel always identified himself as a Vizhnitzer Hasid. Altogether familiar with Hasidism and the mystical tradition, he knew very well what the rabbi was saying. "For everything is in the word," said my teacher Elie Wiesel. "It is enough to arrange certain syllables, to form certain sentences, speak certain words according to a defined rhythm, to be able to lay claim to celestial powers and master them." Yes! He knew very well the Talmudic teaching that our words and deeds create angels for good or for ill, and the angels we create go out into this world and ascend to the upper realms to do their work. According to this Talmudic teaching, the angels ascending the ladder in Jacob's dream are the angels we have created through our deeds and, above all, through our words. See to it, my children, that your words create good angels who will go into the world and ascend into the heavens. Your words have an impact on humanity, on the angels and God himself, that exceeds your field of vision.

A tale about the nineteenth-century Hasidic master Rabbi Avraham Yaakov Friedman of Sadigora comes to mind. "Know that God never leaves off speaking to us," he taught his disciples. "Not only in the works of nature does He call out to us but also in the works of humanity."

One of his disciples, however, had some trouble with this teaching, especially when he looked around and saw the state of the world. "Rabbi," he said, "you have told us that God addresses us and teaches us in all things. But when I look at the new inventions that have come into the world, I cannot see anything of value to be learned from them. The railroads foul the air with their smoke and their noise. The telephone removes us from the face of our neighbor. And the telegraph reduces words—the most holy of things—to mere dots and dashes. What can God possibly be teaching us through these things? What is he saying?"

The rabbi answered, "Even through these new inventions the Holy One speaks to us. In this, too, there is Torah. The railroad, for instance, teaches us that a moment's hesitation will cause us to miss everything. The telephone teaches us that what is said here is heard there. And the telegraph? Here we have perhaps the most important lesson of all. The telegraph teaches us that every word is counted—and charged. And so even in these new and strange inventions God addresses us."

Yes. Counted and *charged*: there is One who listens to every word we utter, who counts every word that issues from our lips, and asks us, "What was that you said? What was that you failed to say? Did I hear you say, 'Here I am for you'?" No words are more precious than these. These are the words that are counted and charged.

Another story, a story about human words told by Elie Wiesel in his memoir, his first book, *Night*. After Eliezer and others had completed their initiation into the camp and were gathered in the block for their first night in Auschwitz, the young Pole in charge urged them to "have faith in life, a thousand times faith. By driving out despair, you will move away from death . . . . And now, here is a prayer, or rather a piece of advice: let there be camaraderie among you. We are all brothers and share the same fate. The same smoke hovers over all our heads. Help each other." And then we come to Wiesel's comment: "The first human words." These are human words because they are words that are bound to meaning and therefore words that affirm the bond between one human being and another. Let your words bind you to another and thereby drive out despair, for you and for others: the word is the one antidote to despair. And any alleviation of your despair lies in the alleviation of the despair of another, in helping another, if only through your words.

These are human words not because they belong to a system of signs but because they attest to the sanctity of human relation. They create good angels. Like I said, they are words that retain their bond with meaning, for a word's tie to meaning lies in its capacity to draw one human being closer to another, and not in its semiotic function within some language game. As an assault on the soul, the Holocaust was an assault on the bond between human and human engendered by the word. "There is no word for this offense," Primo Levi wrote, "the demolition of a man," for the demolition of a man, of a human being, is precisely the demolition of the word. Where the word has meaning it harbors a commandment and a connection, not between signs but between souls. In our own time words have been reduced to empty, vacuous, and insidious sound bites and slogans, torn from any ultimate or absolute meaning that transcends the system. Words have become weapons and lies, for lies are always used as weapons. With this tearing of the ultimate from the word there has been a corresponding tearing of sanctity from the human being, a move that begets and justifies violence. Do not be a party to that tearing.

So ask yourself: Do my words bring me closer to this person, or do they drive a wedge between us? Ask yourself, my children: Are the words I utter human words, words of love and friendship, words that help rather than harm? Do the words I utter open my ears and heart to another, or do they blind me to the face and render me deaf to the outcry of the other human being? Only where meaning is bound to the word, only where the word binds us each to the other, are we able to *hear* the word.

Coming from God, the word harbors a mystery, even in the midst of the mundane. As I have said, there is nothing more mysterious, no greater source of awe and wonder, than the everyday, precisely because the everyday is made of the word. You say, "Hello," and you make someone's day, affirming the wisdom of the Talmud's dictum that we must greet everyone with a face full of joy. If you would align your soul with your words, just offer someone a hello. It can work wonders. Literally.

The Hebrew word for "word" is *davar*, which also means "thing": first we have the world of words, and then the world of things falls into place. As for what sort of world it is, that lies in what sort of words we utter. It may lie in a welcoming hello, or it may lie is a skeptical scowl. In just one simple word we realize that the word is the domain of mystery, without which no soul can live. Make your hello mean *Hineni*, "Here I am for you." For through the silent eyes of the other person God casts his silent eyes upon us and puts to us the question put to the first human being: "Where are you?"

"The space between any two words," Professor Wiesel asserts, "is vaster than the distance between heaven and earth. To bridge it you must close your eyes and leap." Yes, that leap is itself a bridge. And: "The task of man is to be a blank between the words, a messenger, a link between God and man, between man and man, between present and past." To fashion the bridge between word and word is to forge the bridge between human and human—through a leap. A kind word is a leap that can save a soul, beginning with your own. Every kind word bespeaks the message that we messengers are charged to deliver: that is why you *matter*—you matter because your words matter. The leap of faith is a leap from one word to the next, and not a leap of belief or of acceptance of what we do not understand. If you understand nothing else, understand this: in every word there abides mystery and meaning, realization and revelation. The meaning of the word is already given, by the grace of the Holy One who breathes the word into us to bring us life. Be sure that your words vibrate on that breath and reverberate into the world. For that is why you have been created and sent into this world.

Yes, revelation . . . In Hebrew we do not speak of the Ten Commandments revealed to Moses. We speak of the *aseret hadibrot*, the "Ten Words," uttered at Mount Sinai. Wherever the word is tied to the meaning with which God instills it, it is tied to the mystery, to the revelation, of a commandment. To speak the word is to receive and to respond to a commandment: when God speaks, he speaks in the imperative. The words we speak resound with an imperative addressed to us by our own lips. Let your words, my children, be spoken in response to the Commanding Voice of the Holy One.

The prophet Hosea tells us that, as we betroth ourselves to God, we shall know him, a teaching that we affirm when we lay *tefillin* each morning. To know God is to know the word, and to know the word is to know what must be done. Where there is word, there is mission, and the fulfillment of the mission for which you are created, my children, lies first of all in a vigilance over the words that escape your lips. And yet, a word uttered is the dead flesh of meaning. Each word that is bound to meaning calls forth another word, word generating word: the decisive word, the word in which our humanity inheres, is the word *yet* to be uttered. There is no such thing as having the last word, and there is no greater betrayal of the word than the drive to have the last word. For the One who has the last word hears every word, counts every word, even the word uttered only in the heart. Remember that.

To be a good guardian of the word, a vigilant guardian of your lips, is to be a good guardian of your hearing. The Talmud teaches that we have earlobes so we can use them to plug our ears against lies and evil words, words of slander. Again, to watch over the word is to watch over and cultivate a capacity for careful *listening*. And so we have the prayer that we utter upon rising and upon lying down, the prayer that frames the days of our lives, the prayer with which we end our lives: the *Shema*, which is a summons from on high to *listen* to the words we encounter both from above and here below.

To hear "hear, O Israel, *HaShem* our God, *HaShem* is One" is to hear the outcry, the pain and the suffering, the loneliness and despair, from the lips of our fellow human being. In that cry lies the cry of our suffering God, the God who suffers because he loves. We are endowed with the word not only so that we may speak, but also so that we may hear and respond with the one word that defines who we are: *Hineni!*, "Here I am for you!" So once again I return to my behest: cultivate, my children, a capacity for the utterance of the word *Hineni!* There lies our capacity for hearing.

I am reminded of yet another story, a story about Mother Teresa, the story of how she was led to leave her convent in India. She was on an outing with a group of nuns setting out for a prayer retreat, when she passed by a beggar crying out, "I am thirsty." The cry of the beggar seized her soul. A Hasidic master once declared, "I am afraid of nothing, but the cry of a beggar makes me shudder." And so the young nun shuddered.

Upon her return from the retreat, Teresa went to the priest in charge of the convents and asked to be allowed to leave the cloister, but she did not want to leave the order. At the time such a thing was unheard of. The priest told her to take some time to think it over, and he, too, would give it some thought. A year later she returned to him and repeated her request. He expressed his doubts, when finally she pleaded with him, "But don't you understand? God has spoken to me." Taken aback, the priest replied, "Oh, really? God spoke to *you*? And what, pray tell, did he say?"

And she answered: "I am thirsty."

The thirst and hunger that devastate the soul of the beggar devastate the soul of God himself, the One who has breathed his soul into us in the Word of Torah, as it is written. The first word spoken at Mount Sinai was *Anokhi*, an acronym for *Ana nafshi ketavit vehavit*, or "I shall give my soul to you in writing." When the Israelites were gathered at Mount Sinai, the Holy One uttered just one word, *Anokhi*, I, but that word contained all the words that we speak, to spread his glory throughout the world, a light unto the nations. And so, as God gives us his soul through the word, we are summoned to listen and to hear the word.

Mother Teresa exemplified what it means to *listen* and to *hear*. This Catholic nun teaches us, as Jews, the meaning of the *Shema*. And so Mother Teresa left the convent with only what she could carry. Having no means, no plan, she set out like Abraham, without knowing where she was going, to carry out her first mission with what means she had: it was to hold in her arms those who were dying, silently, in the streets of India. To know the word, to know how to listen, is to know how to listen to this silence. And how to speak the word, silently, in the act of a loving embrace: to have a capacity for the word is to have the capacity for just such an embrace. Dostoevsky once said, "I know of nothing higher than the embrace. What, with your philosophy, would you offer in return?" A speaking being is an embracing being, even—or especially—as the other human being is breathing his last breath, the breath upon which the word vibrates, even in its silence. Here, in the moment of an embrace, we glimpse the mystery of eternity.

In the act of embrace the word finds its bond with meaning. Only where word and meaning are of a piece can we find deliverance from the rising waters of the abyss. The word for the "ark" that carried Noah over the deep is *tevah*, a word that also means "word." It was the word that sustained and suspended Noah over the face of the deep. God commanded Noah to make a "skylight" or a *tzohar* in the roof of the ark. The Baal Shem Tov explains that *tzohar* means not only "window" but also "light," so God is commanding us to draw light (*tzohar*) into each word (*tevah*) we speak. The meaning we connect with the word is the light that we draw into life in a sanctification of life. What was the night in the Kingdom of Night made of? The darkness that remains when the word is drained of meaning, drained of the light of the *tzohar*. As the waters of the deep rise and the darkness of night descends, our only hope for deliverance lies in the light of meaning within the word, in the skylight to the upper realms opened in the ark *from above*. The dimension of height that sanctifies life, indeed, is manifest in the bond between word and meaning, which is a bond between human and human, between human and the Holy One.

So we have a sense of why we must watch over our words. To watch over your words, my children, is to watch over a certain silence, the silence of the *alef* that is hidden in every word, like a *tzohar*, the silent letter that harbors the meaning of the word. Before you speak, listen, not only to what you hear but to what might find its way to your lips: what is the word lurking in your own silence? It is not just a matter of thinking before you speak but of *listening* before you speak. It is "by probing silence that I began to discover the perils and power of the word," says our teacher Professor Wiesel. To know how to speak is to know how and when to remain silent and to probe the silence. The Talmud tells us that God himself is announced by a great silence: God himself listened before he spoke, and in his listening he commands us to listen. He listens to his creation, to us, and above all to himself. Hence we have the teaching from the Talmudic sage Shimon ben Gamliel: "I have found nothing better for a person than silence." In order to know how to listen and to learn, to know how to receive the word that sanctifies life, you must know how to be silent, how to wrap yourself in a listening silence. Do not think that this is such an easy thing to do. How often, when listening to another speak, do we ponder what we might say next? How often are we tempted to interrupt? Even when we lie on our bed at night, our soul finds it difficult to fall silent.

By the same token, says Professor Wiesel, "the words you strangle, the words you murder, produce a kind of primary, impenetrable silence. And you will never succeed in killing a silence such as this." That silence devolves upon us with the exile of the word, which is the exile of the Divine Presence, of the *Shekhinah* herself. For she, says the Zohar, is the source of speech. As the word goes into exile, so does meaning, so does humanity, and the *Shekhinah* follows her children into exile. Exile is precisely the exile of the word. It is exiled in our heart, in a place where words escape us. And yet the words that escape us, words of joy and sorrow and longing that have a life of their own, are the most needful. That is why when such words stir in our heart, we turn to poetry and prayer.

Professor Wiesel was deeply taken with the notion of the word in exile, which in Jewish tradition is the exile of the *Shekhinah*. Why does she accompany us in our endeavor to restore meaning to the word? Because she knows that only with that mending of the word can there be a mending of the world and a dwelling place for her children, a dwelling place for God himself. Indeed, her name *Shekhinah* means "one who dwells." And so God allows his *Shekhinah* to leave him and to suffer in his name, suffer the exile of the word, the *galut hadibur*, with his children. When the word is in exile, everything is in exile, because the being and essence of everything rests upon the word. Blessed, therefore, is one who unites his words and his silence with the words and silence of the *Shekhinah*. How do we do that? Through prayer. Get into the habit of praying, my children. Make your poetry into prayer. Get into the habit of making your words poetic, my children. We are never so careful with our words as when we are composing a poem or a prayer. Weigh and listen to ever word that proceeds from your lips, every word that vibrates on your breath.

Rebbe Nachman of Breslov once invoked the teaching that Just Men obey the word of God, adding that this should be read differently: Just Men *make* the word of God, that is, Just Men compose the language with which God creates his universes by returning the word to its meaning, which, as we have seen, lies in our loving tie to the other human being. Prophets transmit the word of God, said Rebbe Nachman, but Just Men conceived it. There, in the word, lies their justice, their righteousness. They often conceived it in the form of tales, for the tales we tell transmit the ineffable that otherwise eludes utterance. And Rebbe Nachman is known as the storyteller of Hasidism.

The integrity of the word lies in storytelling. Tell your children stories, my children. When you lie down to put your little ones to bed they will surely ask you to tell them a story. So tell them a story about when you were little. Maybe you will tell them a story about me? Or about my mother? Yes, your children will ask you, as you asked of me: "Tell me a story." For in their innocent souls they know the truth of these words I bequeath to you now.

We are taught that all of creation is sustained by the thirty-six righteous individuals who live in every generation: they live for the sake of returning the word from its exile, for the sake of returning to the word to its meaning. And they are all storytellers. The People of the Book? Not exactly: the People of the Word. The People of the Tale. That is who we are. The next time you are in synagogue, my children, note well the care taken for the words of the Torah scroll, the *Sefer Torah*, which is made of poetry and tales. The scrolls are meticulously written by a scribe skilled in calligraphy, a righteous person, who undergoes elaborate rites and rituals each time he dips his pen into the inkwell. The scrolls are handwritten, because, even though they proceed from the mouth of God, they are received by the hand of Moses, who, in turn, places these words in our hands, making it very nigh unto us to *do* it, to impart meaning to the words of our mouth through the actions of our hands. That is where the word comes to life: not on our lips but in our trembling hands.

When the words of the Torah are chanted aloud—not read but *chanted* and intoned according to the trope, which brings out the meaning of the words—there are at least two individuals entrusted with the task of following every word, to see to the integrity of the utterance of every word. Before and after the reading, the scrolls are carried through the congregation, to signify that these are indeed the words that bind each member of the community to the other. Upon the completion of the public reading of these words, the scrolls are held up for all to see, with at least three columns visible, as if to say, "See for yourself what you have just heard. See, hear, and heed. Draw them into your heart. For they have been placed in your hands."

And so I place these words, this inheritance, in your hands, my children, beginning with these reflections on the word. Have faith in the word. For without faith we are not human.

Faith

What does faith mean to a Jew, indeed, to any human being? If faith is about redemption or salvation, it is not *my* salvation: faith is never about *me*. No, for a Jew, as for any human being, faith is about the other human being, about humanity and its destiny. It is about the redemption that the Messiah brings through the realization of a certain covenantal relationship: it is about the Messiah. Rebbe Pinchas of Koretz, a disciple of the Baal Shem Tov, teaches that to be a Jew is to bind your destiny to the destiny of the Messiah. Therefore faith is about taking on a responsibility for waiting and working for his coming, about opening up a portal through which he may enter this realm, even as he is in the midst of this realm. For our sages teach us that the Messiah is among us in every generation, standing next to us, calling out to us. Faith is faith in that presence yet to come and that is yet already here, a response to that presence that has been here all along.

If God is *Ehyeh Asher Ehyeh*, "I Shall Be Who I Shall Be," as he identified himself to Moses, a human being is "I *am not yet* who I shall be." Faith lies in the *am not yet*, and not in some acceptance, acquiescence, or belief in things I cannot understand. Faith opens up the dimension of time that inheres in the *am not yet*, which is the dimension of meaning, the dimension of human relation: the other human being is the future. It lies in the truth that there is always something or someone *more* I must become by meeting one responsibility *more* to my fellow human being. Recall what I have taught you already, and let's take it to another level: invoking this "more," this "am not yet," God commands me to love *bekol-meodekha*, "with all your 'more,'" as we affirm twice a day in the *Shema*, in the "Hear, O Israel" prayer. The *more* with which I love—the "am not yet" that I am—is a messianic more. Thus we have the Jewish teaching that in addition to a trace of the soul of Adam, every soul harbors a spark of the soul of the Messiah, the Anointed One of the house of David. Indeed, say the sages, the letters of Adam's name, the *alef-dalet-mem*, signify Adam, David, and Messiah.

The teaching that the Messiah is with us in every generation and that his advent is at every moment possible stems from the Talmud. One day the sage Rabbi Yehoshua ben Levi asked Elijah when the Messiah would come, and the prophet directed him to a leper at the gates of Rome, saying, "Ask him yourself." Rabbi Yehoshua walked up to the leper and asked, "When will you come?" And the Messiah answered, "Today"—that is, "Today, if you heed the Voice of *HaShem*." And Yehoshua ben Levi walked away in dismay over a generation that is deaf to the Voice. It is said, however, that if he had simply helped the Messiah disguised as a leper to bind his wounds, the Messiah would have made his appearance, despite the wayward generation in which he lived. If the advent of the Messiah is at every moment possible, we are the ones who must have enough faith to make it happen. Indeed, according to the Talmud, the question of whether we anticipated and worked for the coming of the Messiah—whether we had faith in his imminent advent—is one of the four questions that God puts to us when we stand before the heavenly tribunal. It is a question concerning whether we have kindled the spark of the messianic soul within ourselves, the spark that would ignite our soul with the flame and the passion of faith.

Perhaps the most famous of Maimonides's Thirteen Principles of Faith is the twelfth, the affirmation of *Ani maamin beemunah shlemah beviat haMashiach; veaf al pi sheyimanmeah, im kol zeh achakeh lo bekol yom sheyavo*: "I believe with complete faith in the coming of the Messiah; even if he may tarry, no matter what, I shall await his coming every day." That is, I believe despite the evidence of the eyes and the knowledge of my understanding, despite my despair and desperation. I believe in spite of the pretensions of my righteous indignation and my illusory ego: faith requires the annulment of the ego and self-righteousness. I believe, therefore, no matter how foolish the belief may seem, even to myself—especially to myself. For to have faith is not so much a matter of belief as it is a way of understanding and *hearing* the world *differently*, an understanding emptied of the presumptions of the self that is nothing more than a self-deception.

The Baal Shem Tov relates a story about a deaf man who was once passing through a village. He happened to walk by a house where there was a wedding celebration. He looked into the windows and saw the wedding guests dancing, but he could not see the musicians who were playing the music. "This must be an insane asylum," he concluded, "with all of these people leaping and whirling about." He thought they were mad because he could not hear the music. In the eyes of those who have no faith, faith appears to be a kind of madness. Do not be afraid of having the deaf think you are mad, my children. One of Dostoevsky's characters declares: "I have a plan: to go mad!" His plan was to have faith, to take up a mad struggle for possibility, for an opening to an upper realm whose gates are otherwise closed. Where might we find the keys to unlock those gates?

"When the enemy has gone mad," says Elie Wiesel, "he destroys. When we go mad, we sing." We sing and dance to the music that only the faithful can hear, with passion, fervor, and joyous intensity. And the keys are placed in our hands and on our lips, through poetry and melody, both of which, like faith, come from above.

Recall another tale about the Baal Shem Tov.

As the story is told, the Baal Shem appeared to his son Reb Hersh one night in a dream. His son asked him, "How, Father, can I serve God *bee-munah shlemah*, with complete *faith*? What does complete faith look like?"

The Baal Shem climbed a mountain, went to the edge of a cliff, and cast himself into the abyss, crying out, "Like this!"

Again the Baal Shem visited his son in a dream, and again Reb Hersh asked: "How am I to serve God with *complete* faith?"

This time the Baal Shem appeared to him and was suddenly transformed into a mountain of fire. As he erupted into a thousand flaming fragments, he shouted, "Like this as well!"

What does the leap into the abyss have to do with erupting into a mountain of fire? What can this mean to you, my children? If faith is made of the fire that burns on the edge of the abyss, where lies the abyss?

It is said that the great French philosopher Blaise Pascal used to move his chair a little forward and to the right whenever he would sit down, because he feared the abyss yawning over his left shoulder. The abyss yawns over our left shoulder and over our right. It is all around us, but we are blind to it, even as we sit in our chairs that rock along its edge. Faith is required to scoot the chair a little further forward, the faith that leads us to elude the abyss. Or better: it lies in learning how to dance on the shifting ground, as the abyss of despair and desperation yawns. Only faith can dance along the brink of the abyss. For faith is even more dizzying than the abyss. Faith ignites the soul with an impatient passion. If the soul is the candle of God, as it is written in the Scriptures, it burns with the fire of faith. If the soul is the lamp and the Torah is the light, again, as it is written, it is the light that emanates from the enduring flame of faith, from the intoxication and the mystical madness of faith. As the fires of faith rise up, the soul rises up to God, the One who is a Consuming Fire. In faith we fall—upward.

Here is another Hasidic tale of faith, this one about Rebbe Barukh of Medzebozh: It is said that a man languishing in the paralyzing grip of despair once came to him, begging him for deliverance from the darkness of his depression. In his desperation the man had delved into the dangers of the hidden knowledge of the Kabbalah, but for naught. Standing at the fiftieth gate in the ascent to the upper realms, he cried out to the Rebbe, "Where am I to go now?" And the Rebbe answered, "Beyond the fiftieth gate lies not only the abyss but also faith—and they are one next to the other." Faith begins beyond the fiftieth gate, the gate of *Binah*, of understanding, as the Kabbalists teach us. The root of *Binah* is *ben*, or "between": it is the between space of relation, where faith unfolds, the space between above and below, between God and human, between human and human. Such understanding does not come from within you but only from beyond you. And yet that beyond abides within. That is why we pray for faith: it comes from the One in whom we long to have faith. It is a prayer from the heart for an opening up of the heart.

The faith we seek is not only a faith in God—it is a faith in humanity, again, despite the evidence of the eyes, the evidence of the slaughter bench of history. All too often the world remains silent in the face of atrocity, as you surely know. And yet, as you go through life, you will encounter random acts of loving kindness. And you will randomly engage in such acts. The philosophers are fond of invoking the problem of evil, according to which there is no way a loving and all-powerful God can abide the evil all around us. Therefore, they would have it, evil is inexplicable, and there is no God. But I have found that the goodness we encounter in people is even more inexplicable. It runs radically counter to the much vaunted "laws of nature," the culture of looking out for Number One. And yet, there it is, what I call the problem of goodness. In the end, the Number One whom we must look out for is the Holy One—that is where faith will lead you: to look out and watch over God himself, who perhaps is not so almighty after all, who is perhaps as helpless as an infant, and if we do not watch over him in faith, he will die. Yes: God can die, die to us. Faith is the lifeblood of God.

Which brings me back to Maimonides. Not only shall I "await" the coming of the Messiah, who will engrave the love that is Torah into every heart, but I shall "expect" it, which is another meaning of *achakeh*, as if he might come at any instant, with the performance of *this mitzvah*, *this* good word, *this* good deed, for the messianic aspect of my soul lies in this messianic responsibility: to have faith is to have this responsibility, to be already chosen for it, an "already" that is a readiness. Faith means: I am *ready*. Therefore faith means not only that one day he will come; it means that one day he was there, already calling out to me, in the *Ayekah?!*, in the "Where are *you*?!," the outcry and the question put to the first human being. There lies the *emunah shlemah*. It is as if you were awaiting the arrival of a beloved guest, going to the window every minute to see if he is here, getting your house in order for his arrival, with a "*Hineni!* Here I am for you!" Faith means *Hineni!*

So how can anyone believe with *complete* faith? After all, faith, it seems, is like the weather: sometimes we see by the light of sunny skies, and sometimes it is overcast, and things are not so clear. The answer: this Twelfth

Principle is not a declaration—it is a supplication: *may* I believe with complete faith, help me to believe, so that I may hasten the coming of the Messiah, when our every act will be an act of loving kindness, so that I may align my soul with his, in the expectation of his coming upon my next act of loving kindness. For the wholeness of such complete faith can come only from the God who is whole, who is One. That is the meaning of the *Shema*: "Hear, O Israel, *HaShem* our God, *HaShem* is One." Each act of loving kindness bears within it a glimpse of the Messiah whom we *expect* at every moment. To live is to live with this expectation: to live is to live in faith, as faith lives in this expectation. But it lies in even more.

Jewish thinking about "faith," about *emunah*, entails much more than matters of belief or the acceptance of a doctrine. Indeed, doctrine is irrelevant and undermining to faith. It is not reducible to the assent of the understanding to what is believed or something we fall back on when reason fails, as if reason were the high court of truth. No, my children. In addition to "faith," *emunah* means "conscientiousness," "honesty," and "trust." In the Talmud, for example, a person who does not keep his word is called a *mechusar amanah*, literally "one who is lacking in honesty" or "one who is lacking in faith"; each amounts to the other. The mystical tradition defines "faith" as *devekut*, that is, as a clinging to God that lies in a devotion to one's fellow human being—there is no clinging to God apart from the embrace of the other human being. Hence to embrace another human being, to feed the hungry and give drink to the thirsty, is an act and a realization of faith. From the standpoint of the Jewish teaching that is central to your inheritance, my children, there is no question of faith or deeds; each is a manifestation of the other. Faith, then, implies a certain character, a certain condition of the soul, which in turn implies living in a loving relation with other people, and not just with God. Just as thought is an emanation of the God who "thinks" us, so is faith an emanation of the God who commands us, with complete faith in us: only God can believe *beemunah shlemah*. God is not the object of belief; rather, he is the subject who, in the wholeness of his faith, summons honesty, truthfulness, character. Yes, faith—faith in us—is an issue for God himself. Let us merit his faith in us.

Looking at other meanings of *emunah*, we notice that the cognate verb *aman* is to "foster" or "bring up"; *neeman* is to "be educated," as well as to "be found true" or "trustworthy," and the adjective *amun* means both "faithful" and "educated." With this ethical will, with this prayer, I pray that I may somehow educate you further, that I may further bring you up and elevate and consecrate your precious souls. I pray that you may be found true and trustworthy. As for being educated, that lies not in the degrees you earn—I know many uneducated people with PhDs—but in the teaching, that you live. The Hebrew word for "education" is *chinukh*; it also means "dedication," as in the dedication of the Temple, as well as "sanctification," as in the sanctification of a home. To be educated, therefore, is to have a capacity for sanctifying life. There lies any true knowledge that we may attain: to know is to live, and to live is to have faith.

When Levi Yitzchak of Berditchev was a youth studying with the Maggid of Mezeritch, he was once returned home for Passover. His father asked him, "So tell me: what have you learned in Mezeritch?"

To which Levi Yitzchak answered, "I have learned that God is in the world."

And his father, indignant, retorted, "But everyone knows that." And he called over their maid, who was serving them their Passover meal, and he asked her, "Is God in the world?" And she answered, "Why, of course."

Triumphant, his father declared, "There. You see? Even our maid knows that."

To which Levi Yitzchak replied, "She says. But I *know*." For Levi Yitzchak had received an education in Mezeritch.

Faith is a way of knowing what cannot be otherwise known. How is this knowing that exceeds all knowledge to be attained? Not through access to more information but through attaining a deeper realization of what *matters*. Faith lies in being open to the word and the teaching, to the plea and the outcry of another. Faith lies in this listening. It lies in a listening openness, especially when no Voice is heard. It is, therefore, not a matter of belief in things unseen by the light of reason, which is a darkening of the light. No, my children, it exceeds mind and intellect: it is wisdom. There is no faith without wisdom and no wisdom without faith. It is not about knowing the attributes of God, a vain and pointless intellectual exercise that theologians indulge in. No, it is about knowing that God is in the world, in the midst of his creation, right here in front of you, moving over the face of the deep that yawns over your left shoulder. Faith is not the opposite of disbelief. You will have your moments of disbelief. In fact, nowhere in the Torah do we read about doubting God: there is no biblical Hebrew word for "doubt." There is rebellion against God and the worship of false gods, but nothing about doubt. Rather, faith is the opposite of folly, the complete reversal of our deadly isolation within the illusory ego. It is the opposite of taking ourselves to be like God.

We are created in the image and likeness of God. Yes: in his image and likeness. And we can be created in the image and likeness only of the One who we are *not*. Faith begins where the ego ends. There is no room in the soul for faith and ego. The Hasidic master Menachem Mendel of Kotzk teaches that to have faith is to have a disregard for self-regard. It comes with the realization, says Abraham Joshua Heschel, that we live in the house of another, that God is in the world and that we live in *his* house. Therefore, Heschel teaches, the assertion that "I believe in God" cannot mean that I, in my individual autonomy, accept the fact of his existence. That would suggest that I come first, and then I accept God into my life. No. It is the opposite. It is a matter of trying to find my way into God's life, as it unfolds in this world, in the endless and relentless wait and working for the coming of the Messiah. I do not "believe" in God, as someone might believe in the tooth fairy. If I am able to believe in God, it is because he believes in me, has already chosen me, for the path of faith. It has nothing to do with belief.

Truth, wisdom, and goodness happen through me. Torah enters the world through me, as an *event*. For the wisdom that is faith—and the faith that is wisdom—is made real through interaction. The interaction engenders the faith, and the faith engenders the interaction: *naasei v'nishma*: "we will do, and we will hear," as the Israelites cried out at Mount Sinai. We will act and we will be instilled with faith, wisdom, and understanding. It is an interaction that unites the Divine Name into One, as it is written in the Zohar: "The essence of the mystery of faith is to know that this is a complete Name. This knowledge that Y-H-V-H is one with *Elokim* is indeed the synthesis of the whole Torah, both the Written and the Oral, for 'Torah' stands for both, the former being symbolic of Y-H-V-H and the latter of *Elokim*." In other words, my children, faith means imparting flesh and blood to the teachings of Torah through deeds of Torah. Faith is an unfolding, an overflowing of sanctity into the world, from within the world and beyond the world. Remember that.

So to have faith does not mean "I believe in God." It means, "Here am I, Your servant, ready to serve," ready to enter a service that is the opposite of servitude, that redeems me from the servitude and the madness of the world. Stated differently, to have faith is to know your name, in which is inscribed the meaning and the mission of your life. It is to live in a "covenant," which is a meaning of the cognate *amanah*, and to live in a covenant is to live not just with a particular belief—which may wax and wane—but according to the *mitzvot*, through which we enter into a partnership with God to create a world where the Messiah may become manifest: *Ani maamin beemunah shlemah beviat haMashiach*. There lies the meaning of faith and covenant: entering into a covenant, through the actions of Creation and Revelation, God declares to us, "Help Me, through your faith, to bring about the Redemption! Help Me to have faith in the redemption that only you can bring!"

Understood in terms of covenant, faith becomes an issue for God as well. In the psalms, for example, we declare that God accomplishes his works *beemunah*, "through faith," and that he judges the nations *beemunato*, "in his faith" or, as it is often translated, "in his truth." Each morning upon waking we affirm in the *Modeh Ani*, "I give thanks," God's "great faith" in us for returning us to life and sending us on another day's mission: it is this truth that returns us to life, and, as Nachman of Breslov has said, "the only way to attain faith is through truth." Jewishly understood, faith entails truth, relation, understanding, partnership, readiness, judgment, and more. It entails a daily gratitude for God's faith in *me*, even though I have failed him day after day. The question that haunts us, my children, is not how we can have faith in God after beholding all the evil in the world. No, it is how can God have faith in *me*, as the one chosen to confront the evil and to rejoice in his Name, his trust, *his* faith, after beholding the evil that his children have perpetrated in the world. So you see, once again, faith is an issue for God as well. And being created in his image and likeness is what makes faith an issue for us.

Elie Wiesel once told me that it takes three hundred years to produce a single scholar. If that is so, it takes millennia to produce a single person of faith. Professor Wiesel was once asked how he could go on believing after all he had seen. And he answered, "Will three thousand years of the faithful end with *me*?" Just so: will it end with *you*? Will you stand idly alongside the blood of the Jewish martyrs that soaks the ashen earth that we tread? What will you say to them when they ask you, "What have you made of us?" For faith in God is a faithfulness to the dead: each is inextricably bound to the other. Perhaps no prayers are uttered with greater faith than the prayers of the Yizkor, prayers that one day before long you will say for me. When you say those prayers, that *Kaddish*, please remember this teaching I bequeath to you.

In the creed-based traditions, such as Christianity and Islam, a religious person or a person of faith is called a believer. In Judaism he or she is called a *yare HaShem*, one who has attained a profound love and awe of God, an awe steeped in the wisdom attained in *emunah shlemah* through study, prayer, and acts of loving kindness. Chief among these actions, according to the Hasidic master Nachman of Breslov, is having children, children who bear the names and the responsibilities of those of us who have preceded them. Perhaps when the Holy One blesses you with children, you will name one of them for me, Avraham David ben Avraham. Once again, "the Hebrew word for 'faith,'" Rebbe Nachman notes, "is *emunah*. Turn the letters into numbers, and the gematria is *banim*—'children.'" Where there is faith, there are children. For where there are children there is a future we await and an action we have yet to perform. Have children, my children. And if you cannot have children, embrace the children in your lives as if they were your own. For your children will teach you the meaning of love, which is the meaning of faith.

Rabbi Abraham Isaac Kook drives home this connection between faith and love. The two come together, he taught, in the light that is the soul. "The Torah is the love," he teaches us, "and the *mitzvot* the faith." Every performance of a *mitzvah* is an act of faith, an act of connection. Faith is about making a connection, between human and God, *ben adam leMakom*, and between human and human, *ben adam lechevero*—faith in God and faith in humanity are of a piece. The actions that bind each of us to the other are of a piece. To believe, then, with perfect faith in the coming of the Messiah is to take up the stance that Rav Kook describes and prescribes: it means living according to the *mitzvot*, loving our fellow human beings, and striving for a deeper understanding of Torah, not through the acumen of our mind but through the works of our hands. Just how urgent that striving can be, we discover in the aftermath of the Shoah.

Rav Kook did not live to witness the singular horrors of the Shoah. Although his teachings can certainly inform our post-Holocaust Jewish understanding of the event, in its post-Holocaust contexts faith in the coming of the Messiah must be understood from other, unprecedented perspectives. You, my children, live in a post-Holocaust era, an era of growing oblivion. The survivors are passing on, even as those of us who knew them are passing on. But, says the Baal Shem, just as oblivion is at the heart of exile, so is memory at the heart of redemption, the messianic redemption that comes with complete faith. Faith becomes faith in memory and testimony. Cling to that faith, my children. Cling most stubbornly.

In the Talmud Rabbi Yochanan says that the Son of David will come in a generation that is either altogether righteous or altogether evil; Yehuda Hanasi maintains he will come in a time of catastrophe. Jews find it difficult to imagine a catastrophe greater than the Shoah. Shall we then abandon our faith in the coming of the Messiah, since he has tarried too long? Shall we jettison the trust and the covenant, the learning and the integrity, that make faith what it is? In his book *Faith After the Holocaust*, Eliezer Berkovits has a response to this question. He turns his gaze to the Jews who entered the gas chambers with the words of the *Shema* on their trembling lips. That image challenges the faith of those of us who were not there, making a facile faith into what Berkovits call a "vulgarity." But the rejection of faith on the part of the "sophisticated intellectual" who casually dismisses faith altogether, he declares to be an "obscenity." As for those who lost their faith in the shadow of the crematoria, he deems their disbelief "holy."

How can disbelief be holy? It can be holy because, as we have seen, faith is not reducible to belief. Here holy disbelief is not so much an absence of faith as it is the presence of outrage in the midst of faith. For there are times when the Holy One himself seeks our outrage, even with him. He wants us to confront him, to wrestle with him, as Jacob wrestled with the angel and thus earned the name of *Yisraél*, meaning "one who strives with God and humanity." Only faith can sustain such a confrontation. Indeed, as someone who was once a wrestler, I can tell you that when you wrestle with someone, you get really close to him. Like Abraham, Moses, and Job, we draw closest to God through the questions we put to him. To live with faith is to live with questions, in our clinging to God, our *devekut*.

Once again we see why after Auschwitz the wait for the Messiah is an impatient wait, an outraged wait, a wait made not only of doing but also of questioning, doing that itself is a form of questioning. That is where we encounter God, as we have seen: in the question, in the *shelah*, at the center of which is *el*, or "God": God lives in the question. Faith lives in the question. A question concerning what? Not the truth of Torah. No, it is a question put to the God of the Covenant precisely in the name of the Covenant of Torah; it is a confrontation with the One who—if one dares to speak such words—seems to have abandoned his Torah and his faith in us. Remaining in the Covenant, we remain within the relation of faith, and we have good reason for our outcry; abandoning the Covenant and surrendering our faith to circumstance, we have no grounds for complaining, which, outside of the Covenant, amounts to little more than pretentious whining. If we abandon the Torah—if we abandon our faith—then the outrage and the question become sheer vanity, as does everything else. If we abandon the Torah, the outrage and the question amount to no more than self-serving, indignant, intellectual arrogance. Only when we adhere to Torah does God adhere to Torah. And only when we adhere to Torah *beemunah shlemah* are we in a position to argue with God, as the Torah commands us to do. Only then are we in a position to open up the gates of prayer.

Prayer

A WORD OF CONFESSION and perhaps a prayer: There have been times in my life when I lost sight of what matters, when I have strayed from the path to which I have been called. You, too, may go through such times. The one thing that brought me back was prayer. Every morning for years—as some of you know—I wrapped myself in the prayer shawl and laid *tefillin*. As long as I remained faithful to my prayers, my prayers remained faithful to me and kept me on the path of my calling. For a time I strayed. I began to think, fool that I was, that I could accomplish so much more if I did not spend the hour or more each day that the morning, afternoon, and evening prayers required. Yes, "spend," as if the time spent in prayer were some sort of misguided business transaction, forgetting for a time the truth that we do not *spend* time in prayer—we *gain* time. So I left off with saying my morning, afternoon, and evening prayers. The return to prayer, the *teshuvah* that we pray for in the Eighteen Benedictions, was difficult at first. It required some discipline. It required thinking in different terms. But as I once again cultivated those prayers, I found my way back: thinking in different terms, the prayers began to think through me. And I realized the redemptive meaning of prayer. Without it I have no path. Without it I am not human.

Cultivate the habit of whispering a prayer when you rise up in the morning and lie down at night. Any prayer, really. *That* you pray is as crucial as *what* or *when* you pray, provided it is, indeed, a prayer, and not a way of asking for favors or entering into negotiations. God does not haggle or *handel*. Enter your waking consciousness with prayer and slip into your dreaming subconsciousness with prayer. Each morning God returns our *neshamah*, the soul that is our speaking being, from the upper worlds to this world, so that the first words we speak upon waking should be a prayer. At that moment, as God sends us on yet another mission, he breathes a prayer into us, as he breathed a living soul into Adam, and so we pray a prayer of thanksgiving upon waking: *Modeh ani*—I thank you. Know that the prayers we utter each morning impart meaning to the words we speak each day. Without prayer words have no meaning. Remember the Divine spark of the *alef* that abides in every word? That *alef*—the Divine silence of the *alef* that stirs in every word—is the prayer that is in every word. The *alef* that unlocks the meaning in the word also unlocks the gates that allow the *Shekhinah* into this world: without prayer there is no meaning because without prayer there is no Divine Presence.

The Koretzer Rebbe taught that, just as the shofar lies empty and silent until we raise it to our lips and blow, so no human being can lift up her voice in prayer, unless the *Shekhinah* prays through her: we are the *Shekhinah*'s shofar. We are her prayer. As she breathes into us the breath of life, the breath that God breathed into Adam, we emit the cry of joy and thanksgiving that is prayer. Indeed, the Baal Shem Tov maintained that prayer and the *Shekhinah* are of a piece. We think we stand before God to address our prayers to him, but that is not exactly the case, because the prayer itself is Divine: it has a living Presence of its own. It is not only we who address our prayers to God, but he addresses his prayers to us through our own prayers. In prayer, not only do we cry out to God, but God cries out to us: through prayer the Holy One seeks us out and lays claim to us. It is a means of hearing and heeding God's constant outcry, morning, afternoon, and evening, his cry of *Ayeka!?*

Through prayer, therefore, we do not speak to God—God speaks to us, and we answer him, for he has forever *already* spoken to us, declaring, "Hear, O Israel," through our own lips. Thus we begin the *Amidah*, the pinnacle of our prayers, with a prayer from the Psalms: "O, Lord, open my lips, and I shall sing your praise," even as we pray in silence, the "inner light," the *or pnimi*, of the soul is burning within us. The life of the living presence within the soul is determined by whether or not the *alef*—the silent meaning and meaning of silence—can find a place within our words. And that is determined by our ability to pray. If we come into being through an utterance—through a prayer—of the Holy One, our life is also sustained by the utterance of our prayers. Entrusted with the care of our souls, we are entrusted with the marriage of word and meaning—through prayer. Without prayer, the soul loses its living presence. Without prayer, the soul loses its *face*.

Notice that we ask God to open our lips before we pray *in silence*. Why do we ask God to open our lips, when we are about to pray in silence? This prayer that precedes the prayer calls upon God to do more than open our lips: we ask God to open up our "languages," for the word *sfatai*, "my lips," also means "my languages." Which "languages?" The language of the Divine silence and the language of our own utterance; these two languages form our two "lips." When these two languages come together, word is tied to meaning, abiding as it does in the silence of all tongues. "Prayer," says the Zohar, "does not consist in the audible voice nor is the voice prayer. Prayer consists in another Voice attached to the voice which is heard. It thus behooves a man to pray silently, to pray with that Voice that is inaudible." The person in prayer asks God to help him make heard the "silent Voice" that is "the supernal Voice from which all other voices proceed." What is the silent Voice from which all other voices proceed? It is the voice of the *alef* that precedes the *beit* in the first utterance of creation. It is the *alef* that abides silently in every utterance, in every word. At every instant God renews the deeds of creation, and we participate in that renewal through prayer.

Taking hold of us as we open our lips, the prayer sets a task before us: to pray is to be commanded to act, to perform a *mitzvah*, which makes the *mitzvah* itself, the deed enacted, into a prayer. Prayer is a mode of hearing in the midst of response and a response that is a hearing. Prayer alone can transform the silence of what appears to be Divine muteness into Divine eloquence, found not in the fire and the thunder but in the "thin Voice of silence," in the *kol demamah dakah*, that spoke to Elijah in his fervent longing for God. In the fervor and the longing that is prayer we realize that the thundering revelations of the great religious traditions are essentially the same as the quiet ones that happen all around us at every instant. In prayer God is drawn into a dialogue in which even his silence is a summons and a reply. Prayer is, as I have said, the substance of language, and the language of silence: without prayer, neither utterance nor silence has any meaning. The silence that has no meaning is the silence of a blank emptiness, deaf and mute, the silence that underlies all genuine horror. It is the silence of the infinite spaces that terrified Pascal.

As you lie upon your bed at night, my children, and the silence looms around you, know that it is not empty, deaf, or mute. It overflows with the Word of the Holy One, who listens to you even as he speaks to you, even as sleep somehow eludes you. That is when you must pray the night prayer: "Lie upon your bed and speak within your heart and then fall silent." Fall silent so that you may listen. And hear him listening. Can you hear him listening?

In the instant before the revelation at Mount Sinai, we are told, creation itself fell silent: no chirping of the birds, no lowing of the cattle, no bellowing of the beasts. That deep silence was the sound of creation listening, of God listening, waiting to hear the words that will issue from our lips. Yes, speak the words of prayer within your heart and then fall silent, making your silence, too, into a prayer, and you will hear him listening. And, for a moment, he will hear your silence. Then sleep, as the night prayers summon us to sleep. Dream, and you will hear him speak, for he addresses us in our dreams. Dream, and you will perhaps hear me speak, even after I seem to be gone, for I shall visit you in your dreams. You will know the wisdom of the night prayer we utter from the Psalms: "Speak within your heart and then fall silent." Then listen.

When you rise in the morning, begin your waking hours with the *Modeh Ani*: "I give thanks before You, living and sustaining King, who has speedily returned my soul to me, so great is Your faith in me." Notice that in the *Modeh Ani* we do not call upon God by any of his Holy Names, because the thanksgiving of the morning prayer transcends any naming of God. If we call upon him only as You, it is because *You* is one of the names of God. Recall the prayer we say on the Sabbath: *Atah hu Elokeinu*, "The You is who You are, our God." In every You we encounter the Eternal You. In every You abides the You of prayer. Let your precious soul begin her return to the light of day with this prayer of gratitude. Prayer transforms a life into a cry of gratitude, even in the midst of outrage and suffering, gratitude not for the suffering but for the truth that it *matters*.

By now you can see that prayer is not about submitting requests in the hope that they will be answered. There is no cliché more empty or misguided than the assertion that God answers prayers, but sometimes the answer is No. In contrast to the Greek *deomai* and the Latin *precari*—words for "prayer" that imply supplication, entreaty, and pleading—the Jewish *tefillah* is associated with decision, thought, analysis, and judgment; its cognate *naftulim* means "struggles" or "wrestlings," so that here prayer is not a petition submitted for oneself but an encounter for the sake of others, for the sake of God himself—at times adversarial, as when Jacob wrestled with the angel at Peniel. That wrestling is a teaching concerning prayer. And his prayer was "answered" when the angel blessed him with the name *Yisrael*, "he who strives with God."

When a Jew places his *kipah* upon his head, wraps himself in his prayer shawl, and lays his *tefillin* on his arm, it is as though he were suiting up for a confrontation or a contest, gathering his thoughts, girding his heart, focusing his concentration for the encounter. One thing I can compare it to, *lehavdil*, is when I used to suit up for a football game. I wrapped my ankles and wrists in tape, like laying *tefillin*, put on the pads, like donning a prayer shawl, and my helmet like a *kipah*, mentally gathering myself for the collisions that were about to come, eager to enter the fray, adrenaline rushing through me like a fire. Once suited up, in fact, I used to say a prayer. Cultivate that same rush when you pray. Adrenaline is the elixir of passion, and passion, *kavanah*, fuels the prayer. That is why we have preliminary prayers: we pray to get ready to pray, as the players warm up to get ready for the engagement.

The *kipah* is a *kaf*, which is the palm of a hand, the palm of God's hand on our head, like a loving father watching over us, as if to say, "I am right here," both as a comfort and as a caution. Jews who never otherwise wear a *kipah* wear one when praying. Wrapping ourselves in the fringes of the prayer shawl, we wrap ourselves in the Light of the Holy One, the Light of the Torah, that constitutes the very essence of prayer. You recall the meaning of the fringes. The numerical value of *tzitzit* is 600; add to that the eight threads and five knots, and you have 613, the number of the commandments in the Torah, the number that signifies Torah herself. Wrapped in the fringes, we are wrapped in Torah, as the Israelite kings used to wrap themselves in the Torah scrolls whenever they went out to confront the enemy. Here the prayer is not that we may conquer the enemy but that we may not forget the Torah, which can get lost in the project of conquest. If there is an enemy to conquer, it is the enemy within, the ego.

Laying the Word of Torah on our arm, we call upon the Torah to guide our hand; placing it between our eyes, it becomes the lens through which we behold creation. As we wrap the strap of the *tefillin* around our finger, we repeat the words of the Prophet Hosea: "I betroth myself to Thee forever, in righteousness and justice, in loving kindness and compassion, I betroth myself to Thee in faith." In that faith (recall what I have taught you about faith), before we pray, we declare, "I take upon myself the commandment to love my neighbor as myself," in the realization that whoever I am and whatever my prayers might mean lie in that loving relation to another human being, whether neighbor or stranger. Especially the stranger. Praying in preparation for prayer is praying rooted in this realization that there is no relation with God without our relation to this human being standing here and now before me, crying out to me. If I do not extend to him or her my hand wrapped in *tefillin*, then may my *tefillin* rot on my left hand, my right hand lose its cunning, and my tongue cleave to the roof of my mouth.

In the *Shulchan Arukh*, the Code of Jewish Law, the question arises: When is it light enough to put on *tefillin*, since we lay *tefillin* only in the light of day. The answer: when it is light enough to behold the face of the other human being. If you cannot see the face of the other human being, you have no business seeking the face of God in prayer, no hope of approaching the Holy One if you are blind to the holiness emanating from the face of your neighbor. For only in the face of our fellow human being do we glimpse a trace of the holiness of God. Therefore we give *tzedakah*, charity, even as we pray. I have been in a Hasidic house of prayer in Jerusalem for services, when those preparing to pray would lay out coins in front of them to give *tzedakah* to people who would pass through the congregation to collect alms. Both phenomena—prayer and charity—are laden with mystery and mystical meaning. Each is as impossible as it is commonplace. For both prayer and charity entail a *cheshbon nefesh*, an "accounting of the soul," that requires an unnatural, supernatural forgetfulness of the self for the sake of another.

Abraham Joshua Heschel once said that prayer may not save us, but it makes us worth saving, and perhaps now we can see why. It also makes God worth saving. If prayer is for the sake of redemption, it is for the redemption of God himself, and not merely of ourselves and others. The words of prayer are the keys that unlock the gates of prayer. Opening those gates, we allow God to enter his creation, where he longs to dwell with his *Shekhinah*. And we are the ones who make that dwelling possible. We do not pray *in* the name of anyone; we pray *for the sake of* the Name of the Holy One. Which is to say: prayer is for the sake of the *Knesset Yisrael*, the "community of Israel," for the sake of the *Shekhinah* in exile, as well as for all humanity: what befalls Israel befalls all humanity.

So you see, my children, there is much more at stake in our prayers than what we might think. When God places the word and the silence of prayer in our mouths, he places an infinite responsibility for an infinitely precious humanity in our trembling hands. As Dostoevsky stated it, each is responsible for all, and I more than the others. Therefore we pray not only with our mouths but also with our hands. The prayers through which we declare our love for God must be echoed in our words and deeds of loving kindness toward others. They must be reflected in our compassionate eyes and our attentive ears. Otherwise they are not prayers.

Entrusted with prayer, we are entrusted with our very humanity and therefore the humanity of all. Humanity derives from sanctity, and sanctity derives from prayer. It is not a question of belief; prayer precedes belief and overtakes nonbelief. Do not wait until you believe before you take up your prayers; if you wait until you believe, you may never get around to praying. Sometimes prayers must be said *despite* our nonbelief. During the Shoah the Jews were turned over to an anti-world, in which everything conspired to undermine all belief, all humanity, a realm of nonbeing in which everyone was *ferociously* alone, as Primo Levi says. Levi also once said that he refused to pray in Auschwitz because to pray there, in the Lager, would have been blasphemy. And yet Levi's refusal to pray was itself a prayer, an outcry to God.

Filip Müller, a survivor of the *Sonderkommando*—those Jews who were forced to work the gas chambers and the crematoria of Birkenau—recalls a man who, like him, languished in the depths of the belly of the beast. His name was Fischl, who, because he had no *tefillin*, would mime the ritual of wrapping the *tefillin* around his arm and head. Had Fischl gone mad? After all, it seemed to be sheer madness to pray in that place awash in the stench of burning Jews and covered in a relentless rain of the ashes. Nevertheless, Fischl's fellow inmates followed his example, wrapping invisible *tefillin* around their arms in their prayerful outcry to the One who was as invisible as the *tefillin*. The tighter they wrapped those leather straps that only the heart could see, the closer their tie to him, even in his absence. If the Absent One ever found his way into that unearthly domain, it was through those prayers, with those invisible *tefillin*. Never was there a more resounding outcry to the Invisible One.

Elie Wiesel relates a similar incident, recalling the day when, somehow, one of the Jews obtained a pair of *tefillin*, whose owner, no doubt, had already ascended into the heavens in a pillar of fire and a cloud of smoke. These *tefillin* retained a trace of his prayers, for they contained a remnant of his soul, and his prayers had flowed forth from that soul. Wasting no time, Wiesel and his fellow Jews lined up to lay the *tefillin* and to say the blessings, despite the risk they were taking—but with a difference: Each time one of them took his turn, he pronounced the blessings with indignation, praying in spite of himself, in spite of God, declaring that even if God did not merit their prayers, nevertheless they would pray. Nevertheless!

And so they prayed—*despite*. They prayed because the prayer that arose from within them emanated from the One to whom it was offered, as though it had a life of its own: the prayer found its way to their lips, as Eliezer prayed in *Night* to the God in whom he "no longer believed" that he may never abandon his father, as Rabbi Eliyahu's son had done. They prayed because, just as others beheld Fischl's invisible *tefillin* in the prayer offered to the Invisible Silent One, so did they hear a silent summons arising from the *tefillin* they held in their hands. We are taught that, wearing his *tefillin*, the Jew resembles the letter *alef*, which, you recall, is the prayer that abides in every word. The *alef* is made of three letters: a *yud* above, a *vav* down the middle, and a *yud* below. Donning his *tefillin*, the Jew lays on his head the *yud* above and on his arm the *yud* below, with his body—yes, his very body—in between forming the *vav*. These three letters have numerical values that add up to twenty-six (*yud* =10, *vav* =6, and *yud* =10), the value of the Four-Letter Name of the Holy One. If in Auschwitz God was hanging on the gallows, as Wiesel says in his memoir *Night*, he was also there in the Jews wrapped in their *tefillin* as they whispered their desperate, defiant prayers.

There were Jews in Majdanek who said their prayers during the High Holy Days under the threat of death. Their death camp caps served as yarmulkes, as they stood in front of their plank bunks and softly mumbled the sacred prayers, lest the guard might hear them. Lest God might hear them? This reminds me of a story that my teacher Emil Fackenheim related about a group of Jews gathered in a synagogue to pray in an unnamed city in Nazi Europe. Suddenly a pious Jew stealing his way through the city's streets burst through the door, and, in a loud whisper said, "Shhhh, Jews! Do not pray so loudly! God will hear you! Then he will know that there are still some Jews left alive in Europe!" Not "the Nazis will hear you," but God might hear you, as if he were the enemy. Still, he does not say, "Don't pray." He says, "Do not pray so loudly. Pray silently." And yet the silent prayer, like the silent scream, is the prayer that cries out the loudest, precisely because there are times when God seems to be deaf to our prayers. And so they prayed.

If Jews prayed in hiding, afraid for their lives—if Jews prayed in a place of red, reeking death, knowing that they were next—who are we *not* to pray in the luxury and security of our homes and synagogues? They had no homes: living in hiding, in a ghetto, or in a camp, *every Jew in Nazi Europe was homeless.* They had no synagogues: their synagogues had been either desecrated or burned, often with Jews inside them. They had no Torah scrolls, even though Jews ran into burning synagogues to save the Torah scrolls. Fackenheim once said to me, "The Nazis compared the Jews to rats. But rats do not run into burning buildings to save Torah scrolls."

These Jews prayed under the unblinking gaze of the Angel of Death, the Angel with a Thousand Eyes, because without their prayers these Jews would have indeed been dead—inside. Without these prayers God is dead—inside. Without their prayers—without *our* prayers—the Nazis attain their victory, over you and over me, over humanity. You, God, turned our grandparents over to death? You laid claim to these children, to these mothers and fathers devoted to you, who taught your prayers to their children and for that their children were marked for death? No matter: our memory will return us to life and you as well, with all our pain, with all your infinite suffering! You would reduce our bodies, our teaching, *your* teaching, to ashes? Then we shall fetch from those ashes the fire that ignites our prayers. We shall dance, like souls on fire, in remembrance of the flames that consumed other souls, in remembrance of Rebbe Leib, son of the great Maggid of Mezeritch, who cried out to his fellow Jews, "Your dancing counts for more than my prayers." Through prayer, my children, you can transform your life into a dance, even as the ground shifts beneath your feet. You can transform your dancing into prayer.

Another story inherited from the other planet: One night in Birkenau, a group of one hundred Hasidic rabbis danced by the terrible light of the crematoria, their prayers transformed into dance, praying as they danced. Mengele himself had ordered them to dance. He had wanted to humiliate them by forcing them to dance a jig. They danced, but it was *their* dance, the dance that the Hasidim are known for. Infuriated, Mengele ordered them to sing, and sing they did, chanting the *Kol Nidrei*, the prayer that ushers in Yom Kippur, the holiest day of the year. They sang not in obedience to Mengele but in an embrace of *Kiddush HaShem*, in a sanctification of the Name who summoned their prayer. They sang their affirmation of the one God, who alone determines the absolute prohibition against murder, even as they were about to be murdered. Without this prayer—without prayer *as such*—there is no prohibition against murder: if we are forbidden to murder, it is because we are summoned to pray, morning, afternoon, and night. Should these rabbis consigned to the flames have rejected God? Will *we* now reject him?

No: if they had rejected him—if we reject him—the Nazis would have their victory both over the rabbis and over God. Perhaps, on the other hand, their piety was itself a show of defiance. No one can say for certain. What is certain is this: prayer turns mockery into devotion, just as it turned prison caps into yarmulkes. It turns death into life, meaninglessness into meaning, and thus recovers a trace of the Holy One, who himself was and is consigned to death. It is not enough to learn Torah: we must pray Torah by dancing Torah, singing Torah. Only by thus becoming Torah can we ever hope to receive it. For if we do not have Torah, we do not have prayer, and if we do not have prayer, we do not have God: the Nazis would then have achieved their aim. We live in that aftermath. When the wind blows in a certain direction, you can *smell* the burning bodies of Israel.

We do not have to delve into the depths of Auschwitz in order for prayer to become an issue. All we have to do is walk out our door and into the street. I know that at least one of you has walked the halls of St. Jude's Hospital. Setting foot in those halls is enough to both summon you to pray and to stir in your prayer a moment of doubt and despair. But do not despair, my little ones. Despair is the enemy of prayer. Despair is the playground of the Evil One. For prayer affirms the holiness of both the human one and the Holy One, without whom none of the suffering matters. Do not for a moment assume that the Evil One does not exist. One of my teachers, Rabbi Adin Steinsaltz, once told me that the Evil One has convinced us that he does not exist, so that he may be free to go about his work uninhibited. Among the greatest obstacles to stand in the way of his freely doing his work is prayer. The prayers that we utter in word and in deed create hosts of angels that hold the Evil One at bay.

Which brings me back to the *mitzvah*. According to Jewish teaching, the response to prayer is not God's reply to a request but our engagement in action. Prayer in the form of a deed is part of our dialogue with the Holy One: what we *do*, we *say* to God. A *mitzvah* is not just a good deed; it is a *commanded* deed, and the reward for doing a *mitzvah* is that we shall do another *mitzvah*: *mitzvah goreret mitzvah*. Just so, each prayer we utter calls forth another prayer. The Talmudic sage Rabbi Chanina teaches that one who acts because he is commanded is greater than one acts without being commanded, because the commandment, the *mitzvah,* is a *tzavta*, a connection to God and humanity. Therefore the Nazis' project of killing God required the obliteration of the *mitzvah* and the connections it creates through the obliteration of prayer.

That is why they criminalized prayer, deeming it an act of sabotage, as the diarist from the Warsaw Ghetto Chaim Kaplan attests. Note well: the Nazis deemed prayer *an act of sabotage.* Why? Because prayer, and prayer alone, affirms the divine, transcendent authority behind the commandments, particularly the commandment that prohibits murder. The Nazis understood that they could not kill God without killing the commandment, and they could not kill the commandment without killing prayer: just as the *mitzvah* is itself a prayer, the prayer is itself a *mitzvah.* Therefore, if they did not burn them to the ground with Jews inside, they transformed houses of prayer into latrines, stables, and scrap depots. The assault on the synagogue is an assault not on a building or a space but on the commandment and the encounter between God and the soul that characterizes prayer. It is an assault on God. You do not have to look far to see that the assault on God, prayer, and the commandments continues. It is in the woke culture, the cancel culture, critical race theory, and other movements all along the political spectrum.

Just as he declared God and prayer to be one, the Koretzer Rebbe taught that "God and Torah are one. God, Israel, and Torah are one." Waged against Israel, God, and Torah, the war against the Jews, then and now, is a war against the *mitzvah*, against the prayer in the form of the deed, and against places of prayers that might be made into deeds. Thus we have the mission of the millennial German Reich and its heirs: to kill God by killing prayer. Elie Wiesel once declared to me that the problem of our generation is that we have lost the capacity for prayer. But what does having a capacity for prayer entail? Wherein lies the task that I here and now bequeath to you, my children? For the inheritance I pass along is just that: a task. Is it about faith? Learning? Acts of loving kindness? Yes, of course. But there is more: it is about prayer.

The great medieval sage Bachya ibn Paquda describes prayer as the "service of the heart." When God commands us to love him with all our heart, he is calling us to prayer. The heart is the seat of passion and of an understanding that only the heart can attain: the heart alone can perceive the truth, because as Antoine de Saint-Exupéry once said, only the heart can see rightly—what is essential is invisible to the eye. But what is invisible to the eye is audible to prayer. The Hebrew word for "heart" is *lev, lamed-beit,* the last and the first letters of Torah. To love with all the heart—to pray—is to love with all the Torah we are made of. And so in the time of the Messiah the truth of Torah will be engraved into the heart—engraved, and not just inscribed, engraved, so that the substance of the heart will be one with the substance of Torah and of prayer. Made of Torah, we pray. We pray and we listen. We pray and we learn: praying, we learn Torah. Praying, we become who we are.

As I write these lines, one of you is very sick. And my heart aches, aches with prayer: yes, sometimes prayer aches. Nothing too serious, God willing, but in need of prayer. Will prayer bring you healing, my little one? I do not know. Prayer sends out angels of healing, who may do their work of bringing you a *refua shlema*, a complete healing, the angels asking all the while if it is God's will that you be healed, the angels pleading, demanding, that it may be God's will. And so these words that I bequeath to all of you are themselves a form of prayer. The inheritance I pass along to you in this ethical will and testament? A prayer.

If it is to be an inheritance, you must pass it along to your children: you must teach your children to pray, teach them the prayers, beginning with the *Shema*. As the Maggid of Dubno has taught, only the prayers of the little ones reach the ears of God, for their lips are untainted by sin. That, too, is why the Nazis targeted the children first, slaughtering more than 85 percent of the Jewish children of Europe. *Yes!* More than 85 percent! They rendered entire areas void of Jewish children, having sent entire transports consisting only of children to the gas chambers: they wanted to render God deaf to the prayers of the Jews. Just as only the prayers of our children reach God's ears, so only the breath of our children sustains all of creation, as it is taught in the Talmud. Emptied of children, creation is emptied of prayer, of God, turned over to the chaos and void of the abyss. So emptied, creation is emptied of meaning.

Meaning

A HUNDRED AND FIFTY years ago Fyodor Dostoevsky wrote a story called "The Dream of a Ridiculous Man," a tale that you, my children, should all read and ponder. The "ridiculous man," whom others regarded even as a madman, opens his tale by saying that he was haunted by the terrifying thought that *nothing matters*, that it is all a sham, so much game playing, utterly vain and meaningless. It drove him to suicide—or an attempted suicide (read the tale). Meaninglessness negates life and leads either to suicide or to murder. Meaning sustains life, as bread sustains the body: meaning is the bread of life.

But where are we to look in our search for meaning? "Vanity of vanities, all is vanity," says Kohelet in the opening lines of Ecclesiastes. "There is nothing new under the sun." Yes, the sages tell us: there is nothing new under the sun, because meaning lies beyond the sun, beyond the heavens and the earth. That is where we must look for meaning: into the upper realms, into the heights that elude the eyes.

My children, there may be moments when you lie awake in the dead of night and the bulwarks crack. In those terrifying moments what passes for life appears to be made of just so many props, like in some sort of contrived, cosmic theatrical production, false, fake, and unreal, all of us parading about in some sort of absurd costume, following a contrived script, pretending to be other than who we are, without knowing who we are, children lost in a haunted wood, who have never been happy or good. As you follow the news and social media, inundated with the fashions and the fads of the day, you sense that something is wrong. At times, I know, it seems that everything is vanishing and vacuous. I know. And so I write to you now, I write to you this *iggeret*, this lengthy letter, this ethical will. And I say to you here and now, hear and heed me: *your life is not meaningless*. You know your father would not lie to you.

Yes, at times it seems that we live in an age of fear and hatred, of anxiety and alienation. From reality shows that are utterly unreal to murderers who pass for martyrs, from talk shows that say nothing to the horror that no longer horrifies, our lives are awash in a not-so-quiet desperation. We rush from thrill to thrill, from drug to drug, from sleep to sleep. But our sleep is troubled by recurring dreams of aimless wandering and frantic entrapment, of missed appointments and failed attempts, of places and faces at once familiar and strange. Unable to find release, we search for a word to name this fearsome longing and thus bring it under control. And yet we tear meaning from words. Unable to analyze, we grope for answers. And yet we dread the truth. Unable to find peace, we long for quietude. And yet we cannot endure the quiet. Why? Because there, in the silence of our solitude, we collide with the faint rumble of meaninglessness.

We grow afraid and surround ourselves with noise, so that we do not have to endure the silence that lurks beneath the near and anonymous drone of the abyss. We wake up in the morning, and, instead of saying the *Modeh Ani* or some semblance of it, we immediately turn on the television or the radio and poison ourselves with the sound of drivel. We go out into the world, but the noise of the world is not enough for us, so we insert our ear pieces and don our headphones, so that we may have our own noise. We fill outer space—the infinite silence of those empty spaces, where no one can hear you scream—with satellites and transmission devices, so that we may have more noise. We must never run out of noise; the neon lights must never go out, the Muzak must always play. To be sure, there has never been an age noisier than ours. Or emptier.

The more we search for a sign that might give voice to some meaning in the world, the more we collide with a sound and a fury signifying nothing. Confined to our own island of being, we slip a message—an outcry—into a bottle and cast it upon the deep and wait . . . . We travel to the Wall in Jerusalem and slip a note, a prayer, into the cracks between the stones, the cracks in the seemingly sealed ears of the Holy One, as I once slipped the residue of a wall from an Auschwitz gas chamber between those stones. I all but expected the wall to collapse under the weight of the cries buried in the walls of the Auschwitz gas chamber. The residue of the screams that inhabited that wall should go into the tenuous mortar of the Western Wall, of the Kotel. And so I inserted those cries into the Wall. But nothing washed back: there was no response but the silence of the Jerusalem stone, as I stood upon the shore of this port city on the sea of eternity, with nothing but the rumbling roar of emptiness washing back. And yet . . .

The dictum that terrified Dostoevsky—namely that nothing is true and everything is permitted—is now glorified by intellectuals who run from one postmodern mania to another and barter the serious for the superfluous. We live in a time—as perhaps in every human era—of a hunger in the soul, a hunger for meaning. Indeed, we are living in the midst of a "meaning famine." I know you have felt it. As the body needs bread, so does the soul need meaning. And our souls are starving. The soul is starving for the Torah that is its substance and its sustenance: the soul is made of Torah, made of the letters and the language of the Holy Tongue. Emptied of Torah—emptied of the Holy Tongue of any and all of our traditions—our lives are emptied of meaning. What would you trade for Torah? What would the crowd offer us in return? Prosperity? Popularity? Pleasure? The tragedy of the Jews of modernity is that so many have traded their Torah for a seat at the table of their murderers.

Study Hebrew. Study the words. Study the letters. Study just one letter. In a single letter you can discover the meaning of who you are, the meaning of your life. Said the thirteenth-century kabbalist Abraham Abulafia, in the letters of the Holy Tongue lies the root of all wisdom and knowledge, and wisdom lies in knowing the meaning of who you are. As I have said, Hebrew is the Holy Tongue not because it is the language of Torah; rather, Hebrew is the language of Torah because it is the Holy Tongue. It is not the means or the medium of revelation; rather, it is part of the revelation itself. Hebrew is not just one language among many. It is the eloquent silence that precedes and reverberates throughout all tongues, the Word that was before the word. It is the language that imparts meaning to language. It is the truth of language and the "language of truth," the *Sfat Emet*. When God spoke and brought heaven and earth into being, his pronouncement in the Holy Tongue broke into seventy sparks, and from each spark there emerged one of the seventy languages of the seventy nations. From each spark the lamp of meaning was ignited: it burns within every language, within the silence of all tongues.

Made of Divine Utterance, all of creation speaks. Beneath the anonymous rumbling of being lives—yes, *lives*—a murmur of holiness, a faint echo of the Holy Tongue, that tries to pierce the noise, a message that struggles to get through the indifferent din, a presence that longs to breach the rumbling silence. The very sense that something is wrong is a manifestation of the soul that cries out from the depths of our being. The soul made of the Holy Tongue is made of those depths and that disturbance: it is the deep that calls unto deep, the silence that cannot endure the silence, the stirring of the ineffable word that longs for utterance.

The Hebrew word for "meaning," "sense," or "significance" is *mashmaut*, from the root *shama*, which means to "hear." Like language, meaning is first of all *heard*; like language, meaning *addresses* us, summons us, commands us. To live as a human being is not so much a matter of speculation, introspection, or getting in touch with your feelings, as it is a mode of hearing and responding. To have a sense of meaning in life is to have a sense of hearing something or someone calling out to us, *with a desperate love and longing*, as God cried out "*Ayeka?!*"—"How could you?! Where are you?!"—to Adam. The first question put to the first human being harbors a commandment couched in an outcry addressed to each of us at every instant. Indeed, the most fundamental of all the commandments is *Shema*, "Hear!" Why? Because to receive a message is to hear a calling and follow a path. There lies the meaning of our lives and the measure of our days.

As the word *shema* suggests, meaning is about understanding and heeding, for understanding comes with heeding. It enters the listening heart, and suddenly we realize that the one we longed for, the life that eluded us, had been there all along, sitting in our lap and hugging us around the neck. The meaning of our lives announces itself in the smiling faces of our little ones, of *your* little ones, my children. In the midst of the collision with meaninglessness we seek the face of life, even as we fear that life may be faceless. We seek life's face because we strain to hear a voice: the word arises from the face, and the face is revealed in the word, even when no word is spoken, even—or especially—in the babbling of an infant. Stepping before the countenance, we hear the word and encounter meaning; stepping before the face, we receive a summons to which we must respond, "Here I am for you," if we are not to be swallowed up by the faceless silence.

Know this, my children: no soul comes into the world without a calling, and every soul is therefore *indispensable to all of creation*. Some of you, as I pen these lines, are still in your infancy. Yet even in your infancy you answer this call—with a smile that teems with holiness and meaning, a smile that opens up a path to redemption for your parents and grandparents. The Talmud tells us that we should greet everyone we meet with a cheerful countenance, because a smile, a simple smile, announces the truth that life is meaningful and dear. A simple smile can transform a life, even save a life. And each of you, my children, has a smile most beautiful, a smile that has given my life meaning.

The Jews are chosen to proclaim to humanity that every human being is chosen for a meaning and a mission that no other human being can assume. I look into your smiling faces, my children, and the revelation of this chosenness is there, in your heavenly smile, still harboring the trace of the angel who touched your lips as you entered this world. For the antisemites, the fear is not that life is meaningless but that it is meaningful. That is why they target the children first. They hate the Jews for turning them over to the meaning that is infinite, the responsibility that is infinite, for there is no meaning in life without this *infinite* responsibility. Therefore the account is never settled. Where there is meaning, there is *more*: more to say, more to do, more to answer for. Where there is meaning there is the *meod*, the "more," that came into being upon the creation of the human being on the sixth day, which God declared to be *tov meod*, good and *more*. Where there is meaning there is a loving *bekol meodekha*, with all your "mores," as the *Shema* summons us to love God. It is the meaning not only for which we live but also for which we die. It is the meaning that makes life life and death death. It is the meaning of meaning.

The sense of hearing born of a sense of meaning is a sense of direction. To have meaning is to have direction. The word for "direction" in Hebrew, *kivun*, is a cognate of *kavanah*, another word for "meaning"; *kavanah* also means "purpose" and "devotion." We long for a sense of purpose, for someone to whom we may devote our lives, for whom we may give up our lives: meaning lies in the realization that we have someone to die for. As we give to another person we become a sign of the dearness of the other person; becoming such a sign is the only way we take on significance or meaning.

Think of the moment when you held in your hands your newborn, just five seconds old, as she gazed for the first time upon this world. Suddenly you are a sage. Suddenly you know the meaning of life, what to love, what to fear, and what to fear for. So it happened with me upon the birth of two of you. So it happened with two of you upon the birth of your babies. So it may happen one day when, God willing, your babies bear babies of their own into this world. And so among the blessings we say at a *brit milah*, a "circumcision," is that the baby boy may one day stand under a *chupah* with his bride and, with God's blessing, bring souls into this world. And the baby girls? With God's help they will one day become a mother, as two of you have. Having become a mother, each of you knows that there is no greater blessing, no deeper meaning, than the meaning and blessing embodied in a mother. For there is no love in this world like the love of a mother. That love is an emanation from another world, from the upper worlds. Thus the mothers, too, were targeted in the days when that Night descended upon creation.

In the names your parents have conferred upon you and that you have conferred upon your little ones there abides a "remembrance and a name," a *yad vashem*, and with that remembrance comes a responsibility: meaning, like identity, lies in that responsibility. We do not make up names for our babies. No. Granting us a moment of prophetic insight, God allows us, mothers and fathers, a realization of the name he uttered when he created this soul. And so you, my children, are named, and your children are named with names that harbor meaning. Determining who we are and the purpose of our lives has nothing to do with dreams or obsessions, no matter how magnificent. Rather, the meaning of our lives is inscribed in the name that gives us life, the name with which we are blessed, the name of which our souls are made, and in which our destiny is inscribed.

A cognate of *kavanah*, the word *mekhuneh*, drives home this point; for *mekhuneh* means "named," "called," and "designated." To have meaning is to be singled out *by name* for this task that no one else can perform, even—or especially—if it appears to be a dangerous task. To have a name, again, is to have meaning. The summons that each of us receives in life—the summons that defines the meaning of life before it is lived—consists of our name. *That* is what we struggle to hear when we thirst for meaning, for *mashmaut*: the Divine calling out to us *by name*. This calling out is a questioning, often to the point of interrogation and even accusation. The issue of meaning, then, concerns a certain indictment that goes to our identity: to have meaning is to be accused, to be questioned, by a heavenly court. There is no meaning without reckoning. What, indeed, would life be without a reckoning, an answering, an accounting? It would be a horror.

According to a teaching from our tradition, when we die and lie in the grave, the Angel of Death comes to us and asks us a question to see if we are prepared to enter into the presence of the Holy One. The question is the same for all of us, but for each of us the answer is different. The question is: What is your name? But what does it mean to know your name? It means, first of all, that you know the name of your mother and your father: you are a son or a daughter, a *ben* or a *bat* of someone. It means knowing something about the sacred inheritance entrusted to your care. It means knowing how and when to answer when you are called by name to the task, to the meaning and the mission, that only you can carry out. To know your name is to know the meaning of your life. And it takes a lifetime to know your name.

Once we hear this calling inscribed in our name—once we have a sense of meaning—we must summon from within ourselves the devotion required to follow it. This brings us to another word derived from *shama*: *mishmaat* or "discipline," which is necessary to the pursuit of the "more" and therefore to any meaning that our lives may have. *Discipline* is an unpopular word. The fashionable fixation on a "safe space" reflects a longing for a space empty of responsibility and discipline; it is therefore a space of meaninglessness and aimlessness, of languishing and longing. Here we discover the modern delusion that to have meaning is to be safe, when to have meaning is precisely to be vulnerable. Discipline, my children, is essential to having a sense of meaning and mission, for accomplishing the mission for which you are created, because it is essential to coming out of the "safe space" we have contrived. It is essential to pursuing the "more," to the *meod* at the heart of meaning.

In our pursuit of the "more" that is meaning, we long to do more than hear: we long to understand, a point that is reinforced when we consider some words derived from *hevin*, the verb to "understand." The noun "understanding" that corresponds to the verb is *binah*; the related word for "meaning" or "sense" is *muvan*, which also means "understood." At the core of *binah* is *bein*, a word that means "between," suggesting that meaning or understanding is something that arises *between* two. And so we realize that the empty silence surrounding us is the sound of our own solitude; we realize that meaning in life is about our relation to another. Where meaning in life is concerned, we long to do more than understand—we long for the depth and dearness of a relation to another: we long to love. Recall the words of Alyosha to Ivan in *The Brothers Karamazov*: "It is only by loving life"—by loving another—"that you can ever hope to understand its meaning." In the revelation of meaning, we come to a realization of what there is to love and what must be done. It is a moment of knowing God, for to know God is to know what there is to love and what must be done. And so life is not simply about what we do but about what *more* must be done, what is *yet to be* done. In this *yet to be* we discover the dimension of meaning: it is time.

To receive the revelation from the Holy Tongue is to be charged with a sacred mission: having heard, we are now enjoined. This is where life becomes life *time*, which is the future time that opens up all time. Living *now* means having something to live *for*, so that life assumes a *direction* determined by a *devotion*. Direction and devotion constitute the *yet to be* that fosters meaning in life. Made of this *yet to be*, time is the presence of meaning in life; just as the word is the vessel of meaning, so is it the vessel of time. The other human being, to whom we offer a word of kindness, is the future. Hence the Name of the Holy One—the Tetragrammaton *yud-hey-vav-hey*, from which all meaning and all of creation are derived—contains all the tenses of time: *hayah* or "was," *hoveh* or "is," and *yihyeh* or "will be." As it is written in the *Sefer Yetzirah*, "All that is formed, all that is spoken, emanates from one Name." All that emanates from the Name has meaning because the Name is the vessel of all time and the source of every name. Time is the presence of God in the realm of space. And the presence of God is the foundation of meaning.

If the Holy Name contains the mystery of time, meaning lies in a simple act of giving. Where there is holiness, there is giving. Where there is giving, there is meaning. And so we have the following teaching concerning the revelation of meaning in the Holy Name: The first letter in the Name, the *yud*, represents a coin. The first *hey*, with a numerical value of five, denotes the five fingers of a hand that is about to give the coin to another in an act of loving kindness. The *vav* connects the hand to the body, and, with the value of six, it moves in the six directions of physical space to create a connection with another person. The second *hey* is the hand that receives the gift. The five that receives and the five that gives add up to ten, which is the value of the *yud* that is the gift itself. Thus, it is written in the Zohar, "he that gives charity to the poor makes the Holy Name complete as it should be above." If meaning in life requires holiness, it demands this giving that is revealed through the Holy Name. For holiness and meaning lie precisely in this mystery of giving; indeed, what is given is what has been received: *meaning*.

Not an answer but meaning. Nothing undermines meaning like fixed formulas and ready answers. To live a meaningful life is to live a life of questioning and of being questioned. And so it happens that having a sense of meaning comes with losing a sense of understanding. There are times when the sense of meaning, of what *matters*, undermines our understanding. As Elie Wiesel has said, there are times when we must lower our eyes and *not* understand. As one of his characters once cried out with regard to the horrors that the Jews endured during the Shoah, "if their suffering has no meaning, it is an outrage! And if it has meaning, it is an even greater outrage!" You recall the problem that Ivan Karamazov had with the suffering of the children: "If the suffering of a single child is the price of salvation, then I say that salvation is not worth such a price! I return my ticket!" But meaning cannot be purchased. It can only be given, *despite* the failure of the understanding. It can only be *lived*. There is always a certain "and yet" attached to meaning. Wiesel's character and Ivan Karamazov speak the truth. And yet . . .

Where there is meaning, there is wonder and mystery, the mystery of meaning itself. Whereas magic is a sleight of hand, mystery is an offering of the hand. One would manipulate the world; the other sanctifies the world. You seek meaning in your life? Extend a helping hand to another human being, as God extends his hand in Michelangelo's famous image of the creation of Adam. Look at the painting. Ponder it. Notice how the outreached hand of God is desperately seeking the limp hand of Adam. Human life has meaning because God is forever in search of the human being, reaching out to us, as the hand of the woman begging in the streets of Paris reached out to me years ago, her face buried in her other arm.

The meaning of life lies in the mystery of creation. The mystery of creation is that Some*one*, not some*thing*—through a movement of *love* and *longing*, and not from the necessity of cause—appears from nothing to bring all *this* into being. The creation *ex nihilo* is, as it were, God's creation of himself from the *Ain Sof*, from the Nameless "Infinite One." The world he creates from himself is filled with Divine sparks. Just so, he creates the human being—the human *who*—from his own *Who*. If I am someone, I am nothing without this the pre-originary Someone; if I am a *who*, I am nothing without the Divine *Who*. And he is asking at every instant about *who* I am. Indeed, every instant is made of his asking. It is as though God were constantly saying to each of us, "Let Me have a word with you: what have you done with My word?" Which means: "*Who* are you?" The mystery of meaning and the meaning of mystery lie in the *Who*. And it therefore lies in the *You*.

There can be no mending of meaning apart from a sense of the absolute, a sense of something holy at stake in that mending. If there is no absolute meaning—if nothing is *holy*—then meaning can be neither wounded nor mended; it can only shift from one context to another as it assumes one narrative over another. Such meaning is meaningless. If meaning does not derive from the absolute, then silence is simply a blank and prayer is nothing more than a psychological salve. But silence is not a mere blank. The fact that the soul is traumatized by the emptiness of silence and by the meaninglessness of idle talk tells us that silence is not a mere blank. The fact that the soul is so traumatized, moreover, tells us that the absolute or the holy is indeed part of the soul, if only as the thing that is missing or broken.

And so, my children, know that even in the dark night of the soul, when the bulwarks crack and meaning eludes you—even in the quiet terror that overtakes you when everything seems meaningless—there is meaning. Know, too, that I am with you, silently crying out to you, "Here I am for you." And to say to another, "Here I am for you," is to speak the truth.

Truth

One of the things most essential to sustaining a life, my children, is a capacity for distinguishing the difference between truth and lie. The truth engenders and nourishes life; the lie threatens life. Nor is it such a simple matter to distinguish between the two. The lie is always pleasing to the eye, else it would not be so insidious, so tempting: there is nothing more attractive, more seductive, than the lie and its promise to know and thus to be in control, to manipulate and appropriate. The serpent of old offered up to Eve the lie that the fruits of the Tree of Knowledge would make her like God, and those fruits were pleasing to the eye. They were pleasing to the eye because they promised to make her the voice of Divine judgment. Echoing the lie of the serpent, the religious fanatic, claiming to be like God and speaking for God, invariably claims to derive the truth from heaven.

The false promise of knowledge is not only that knowledge is power but that truth is determined by a will to power, so that not only will you know good and evil, but you will determine, through power, what is good and what is evil and therefore who will live and who will die—like God. Not, however, like the God who is loving and long-suffering, quick to forgive and slow to anger, merciful and true, the God of truth. No, the God who we would be is the false god, the god of the lie, who is all powerful, who gets his way, who has no accountability to anyone, who is utterly outside any covenant. There we have the lie: whatever falls outside the covenant languishes in the fallen condition of the lie. It can get to be a comfortable condition, the condition of the crowd. And yet, as Mahatma Gandhi once said, even if you are a minority of one, the truth is still the truth. Long before Gandhi, in the nineteenth century Kierkegaard affirmed that the crowd is untruth. The truth is never popular because the truth has a way of robbing us of our comfort zone, our safe space, for to catch a glimpse of the truth is to see that we are forever outside of it. As Tolstoy once said, we are never further from the truth than when we believe we have it in hand: as soon as we seize it, truth slips through our fingers, leaving us with the realization that we never lay claim to the truth, but rather the truth lays claim to us.

We have seen that life is rooted in the bond between word and meaning, which is a bond between one soul and another. The truth abides in just such a bond, in whatever nurtures such a bond. The lie emerges with the tearing of word from meaning, which brings in its wake the tearing of one soul from another, forcing each into an isolation that sucks for the soul. The lie is like a tomb in which we inter ourselves, a tomb in which the soul suffocates in its radical isolation within the lie. The great Hasidic master Rebbe Pinchas of Koretz, a disciple of the Baal Shem Tov, taught that the condition that most profoundly threatens the life of the soul is not meaninglessness but the isolation of the lie that locks us into the terrifying confines of the ego. The lie of the serpent preys on the ego. Locking us into a radical isolation, the lie renders us deaf to the outcry of our fellow human being. In that isolation no one hears you scream, and you hear no scream from the other. It is the isolation of the ninth plague, the plague of darkness, in which "no man could see the face of his brother."

Thus locked into the solipsistic solitude of his own being, the human being collides with his own nothingness and is turned over to the emptiness of what is merely "there," blank and indifferent, echoing nothing but the murmur of silence. This murmur of silence is the murmur of nobody, the murmur of the blank; it says nothing, and we hear nothing but the rumbling void of the lie. The first time Rebbe Pinchas met the Besht, the Master declared to him that we are not alone. We are not alone because our tradition is a living presence in our midst, the presence of truth, through which God himself becomes present. Understood as *mesorah*, which is a cognate of *meser* or "message," our tradition of truth is not behind us—it is before us. How so? Because it places in our care a message and a truth that is infinitely dear. If, says the sage Saadia Gaon, tradition is a mode of revelation, it is a mode of the revelation of truth, which is always revealed and never deduced. It is a revelation of the future. The opposite of the future is not the past—it is the isolation, the amnesia, in which the past is swallowed up. Thus the opposite of the future is the absence of a past. It is the absence of truth.

Just as the lie is rooted in a solipsistic isolation within a fearful, power-hungry ego, so is the truth rooted in a courageous movement into a relation with another and an equally fearsome abrogation of the ego. As the truth takes hold of us, we must release our hold on our handrails. Yes: the truth is scary, while the lie is, at least at first, comforting in its promise of security. It feeds on the longing for assurance, for a guarantee, a longing to be certain of the firm ground under our feet in a world made of a constantly shifting ground. Turning us over to the shifting ground, the truth turns us over to the vulnerability of responsibility to and for the other human being, which is a responsibility to and for God himself. Yes,

God himself is imperiled in the conflict between truth and lie! Truth arises in an embrace of the other human being, and in order to embrace another, we must open our arms and expose ourselves: truth summons our vulnerability, for there is nothing as fragile and vulnerable as truth.

Hillel, you recall, teaches that blessing does not fall upon what can be weighed, measured, counted, and, I would add, observed. Such measures of a strictly material reality are the measures of the lie, the lie steeped in the proposition that the truth is to be found in numbers, and not in the name. And so it came to pass during the Holocaust. When the number takes the place of the name, the unit takes the place of the human being. Recall, for example, the moment in Primo Levi's memoir when a Nazi officer wanted to know how many were on the transport to Auschwitz. He did not ask, "How many people?" or even "How many Jews?" but *Wieviel Stück*—"How many pieces or units?" The discourse of the extermination of the Jews had no room for any discussion of the murder of people; no, it was about processing units. There we have the link between the lie and murder.

When God is dead, the human being is a unit or a piece, but a piece of what? No more than a piece of bone amidst a snarl of bones, so much raw material about to be made into fertilizer, the ashes scattered as pavement over a road leading to a camp, skin used for lamp shades in novelty shops, or hair used for textiles and insulation. Thus the outcome of the age of the Holocaust, the age of transforming names into numbers, the age of the Big Lie. And the star that is Planet Auschwitz, the Star of Ashes, as the survivor and my teacher Yechiel De-Nur calls it, continues to have its sway upon us, like a new sign of the zodiac. The lie leads us to turn to numbers instead of names, as we grope for a lie that would pass itself off as truth, a move that plays into the hands of the murderers for whom the very numbers were a camouflage. We have been taught to speak about the Holocaust and other horrors in the language of big numbers, yet no language distances you from contact with the truth more than such a language. Nothing reduces the person to an object more than a number does, which the Nazis did with totalitarian efficiency: the number is the first weapon drawn in the assault on truth and on the name, transforming the name into a number. And yet how often are we lured into the lie of the number? As Mark Twain once said, there are lies, damned lies, and then there are statistics. And a course in statistics is a requirement in most programs in the social sciences.

It is not for nothing that Satan, the one who preys on the life of the soul, is known as the Lord of Lies. Do not be so naïve as to suppose that Satan is an illusion. He has as much reality as we feed to him by denying his existence. The Evil One feeds on lies because lies are the source of all evil, beginning with the lie of antisemitism, which, at bottom, is the lie that the

God of Abraham is not God. Truth is anathema to the Lord of Lies. Even if you resist the notion that Satan lives among us, know that lies live among us and that they have a way of taking on a life of their own, a life that is antithetical to life. The temptation to buy into the lie lives within us. As I have said, it is the original temptation.

Time for another story, a story about an elderly Cherokee Indian who taught his grandson that there are two hungry wolves inside of each of us, a good wolf and a bad wolf, a wolf steeped in truth and a wolf steeped in lies, and they are engaged in a fight to the death.

"Which one will win, Grandfather?" the little boy asked, wide-eyed.

And his grandfather answered, "The one you feed."

Which one will you feed, my children? Which one?

The lie is the stuff of nihilism, which in our time is rampant. It is the mark of the modern age. The great thinkers of ages past gazed into the abyss of nihilism, shaken by the thought that nothing is true and everything is permitted, and trembled in terror. In our day the intellectuals who peddle their lies wallow in the abyss. Believe me, I know: I live in their world. Nihilism rests upon the lie of science that would pass itself off as the high court of truth, a sheer materialism that reduces the value of the human being to so many chemicals and thereby obliterates the soul. This is what lay behind the Nazis' euthanasia program, when they murdered anyone deemed "an economic burden on the Reich."

I once visited such a killing center in Bernburg, Germany, with Emil Fackenheim, whose uncle was murdered there. At the time I lived in Memphis. As I stood in the gas chamber of that euthanasia center and looked upon the ovens for disposing of the bodies, it struck me: an institution for which Memphis is famous, St. Jude's Hospital—which specializes in hopeless cases—would have been unthinkable in Nazi Germany, in the Reich of the Lie. It was the Reich of Science and Scientists, of Philosophers and Intellectuals, the Reich of the doctors and professors and jurists, who constituted the largest representation in the Nazi Party. Among the war crimes trials were the Doctors' Trial and the Judges' Trial. Think of it! Doctors and judges, the very guardians of truth! Perhaps there should have been a Professors' Trial as well. Or a Philosophers' Trial. How often do we invoke the false god of science or speculative reason to justify our agendas that are otherwise unjustifiable?

Look at how freely we toss about the nihilistic phrase "We make meaning." Does it *matter* what meaning we make? If it matters, then we do not make meaning—meaning, truth, makes us. The truth of the devotion that we behold as we walk through the halls of St. Jude's makes us, as it made one of you, my children. To "make meaning" is to make up lies, even as we are called to the stand to bear witness to the truth. Truth transforms each of us into a witness, as it transformed one of you with the day you spent at St. Jude's.

You remember the story by Dostoevsky I mentioned to you, "The Dream of a Ridiculous Man"? Made into a witness, he declares, "I have seen the truth." What did he see? After all, the truth belongs to the invisible, to what only the heart can see. The truth is not a fact or a dead datum but a living presence that unfolds in a living embrace. No, the truth is not a datum or a *what*. The truth is a *who* or a *you*. We do not know the truth—the truth knows us, lays claim to us, seeks us out, as it sought out the first human being, to ask, "Where are you?" It peers into the heart, through which alone we gaze upon the truth. It takes hold of us, like a hungry and frightened little girl grabbing us by the arm, like a little child who hugs us around the neck and leads us to behold what matters, the way each of you has hugged me around the neck, my children, and opened my eyes to what eludes the eye. Like Dostoevsky's ridiculous man, I, too, have seen the truth in your innocent eyes. The truth is not deduced—it is revealed, as in a dream, from which we awaken to realize it had been there all along, like when Jacob awoke from his dream.

And what did he see when his eyes opened, now opened to the truth? He saw the trace of the Holy One, the Invisible One. He saw what Elie Wiesel has taught: "God is not only truthful, He is Truth itself. Truth is God's seal, just as human beings are in His image." But what does it mean to be God's seal? The seal of God, the seal of the Holy One, is the seal of holiness itself. It is the mark of meaning imprinted on all of creation. The first-century mystic Rabbi Nechuniya ben Hakanah taught that "'living soul' is a name for the 'living God.'" The word translated as "God" in this passage is *Elokim*, which is God as Creator, with the Tetragrammaton, the Holy Name of *yud-hey-vav-hey*, hidden inside. The mystical tradition associates God in the mode of *Elokim*, or Creator, with the created, physical world; according to gematria (a Kabbalistic method of interpretation based on numerical values of Hebrew letters), *Elokim* has the same numerical value as *hateva*, which is "nature" or physical reality. The word *teva* refers to something deeply imprinted into an object; a coin, imprinted with the seal that is part of the coin itself, for example, is a *matbea* (a cognate of *teva*). Just so, nature is deeply imprinted with seal of *Elokim*, and the body is deeply imprinted with the seal of the soul, the seal of truth. Made of the Word of the Holy One, creation bears the seal of holiness: as the seal of God, truth is holiness. And it is all around us. Made of God's utterance, creation—the living soul, heaven and earth and all that is in it—is made of truth, just as it is made of the Divine commanding Voice.

Another story: There was once a man who went through the 613 commandments of Torah and was utterly overwhelmed. How can anyone follow all of these commandments required to be sealed in the covenant with God, sealed in the Book of Life, as we wish each other each year at Rosh Hashanah, the Day of Remembrance and Judgment? Overcome with so many obligations, he went to his rabbi and said, "Rabbi, when I look at all of these commandments from God, I grow desperate. How can I possibly stand before the Heavenly Tribunal? How?! I cannot do it all, I simply cannot!"

To which his teacher replied, "Just do one, my son: speak the truth."

And the man resolved to always speak the truth, nothing more. And once he began to speak the truth, not just with his lips but with his hands, he was led to observe all of the commandments, beginning with the observance of Shabbat. For, according to our tradition, the commandment to remember and observe the Sabbath corresponds to the prohibition against lying. That is how we give utterance to the truth: not just with our mouth but with our hands, with our remembrance and observance, our watching over creation and the Creator, even though we can never take the truth in hand. For the truth is all-encompassing, as the Shabbat is all-encompassing. It wraps itself around us, like the light of God, like a *tallit*, the prayer shawl we don as we plead with God to open our lips and our hands, that we may sing his praise.

The all-encompassing nature of the truth is found in the Hebrew word for truth: *emet*. Made of the first, the middle, and the last letters of the Hebrew alphabet—the letters of which creation itself is made—we realize that creation itself is made of truth. Creation is made of commandment. It is made of Torah, and Torah is made of truth. Day speaks truth unto day, and night unto night. Look up at the night sky, look upon a star and wonder. A capacity for truth is a capacity for wonder, a capacity most rare and most needful. The Hebrew word for "lie" is *sheker*. The Talmud asks, "Why are the letters of *sheker* close together, while the letter of *emet* are far apart? Because falsehood is common, and truth is rare, as rare as it is clear, teeming in the world around us." Do not be blinded by the nonsense and insanity of the world around you, my children. Do not be blinded by the commonplace, by the fads and fashions of a world gone awry. Strive to look past that, even though you cannot see past that. For the lie is so overwhelming that often we cannot see beyond it. And yet the truth abides in the search for truth: the truth is by its nature forever *sought* and never found. Keep on searching, my little ones. Do not despair. For despair is fertile ground for the lie.

The longing for truth is intimately tied to the longing, the wait, and the working for the coming of the Messiah. There is, indeed, something messianic in the wait and the working for his coming, which is a search for truth: redemption rests upon the truth. It is the only antidote to the despair that haunts us. The Talmudic sage Rabban Gamaliel taught that in the generation when the son of David comes, the house of assembly will be a brothel, Galilee will be in ruins, and the inhabitants of Gablan will wander about begging, from city to city, without experiencing pity; the wisdom of the scribes will be in disfavor and God-fearing men despised, the leader of the people will be dog-faced; *truth will be lacking*, and he that departs from evil will be regarded as demented. Rabbi Nehorai taught that in the generation when the son of David comes, young men will insult the old, the aged will stand up before the young, a daughter will rise up against her mother and a daughter-in-law against her mother-in-law, and a son will not be abashed in his father's presence. Sound familiar?

Rabban Gamliel was also known to have said that if the world endures, it is because of three things: justice, truth, and peace. And yet, the Talmud teaches, the three are one: if justice is done, truth is effected, and peace is brought about. But look around you at the repeated cries for justice that only sow discord, as in organizations like Students for Justice in Palestine and the various centers for justice, many of which rest upon a lie, inasmuch as they rely upon inciting hatred and strife. Hatred is inextricably bound to the lie. In many ways, the opposite of the truth is not the lie—it is hatred. Justice is among the most crucial things necessary for peace in a world that is driven by age-old disputes, grudges, hatreds, and vengeance. With the mass slaughter of human beings becoming more and more commonplace, there has been a growing despair over the very possibility of justice in a world where the crime infinitely exceeds any possible punishment—indeed, where crime so often goes unpunished. When tens or hundreds of thousands are slaughtered, there can be no balancing of the scales, either through world courts or through truth and reconciliation commissions. Truth is alien to such commissions, not because they are not well intended, but because truth forever eludes the very structure of a commission.

You, my children, will be asked to support causes for justice. But what, from our Jewish standpoint, do you support in your support of justice, and what does it have to do with truth? The commandment is imposed upon us from on high: "Justice, justice shall you seek": *Tzedek, tzedek tirdof.* It is a commandment to pursue truth. To pursue one is to pursue the other. *Tzedek* is the *justice* that is also *righteousness*: justice, like truth, demands entering into a higher relation. It demands joining the horizontal human-to-human relation with the vertical human-to-divine relation through deeds of loving kindness in an affirmation of the covenant. Justice, like truth, is *tzedakah*, which is charity or giving without expectation of reciprocation: truth lies in this giving. Truth is something offered up to another, in an affirmation of his or her infinite dearness. For truth belongs to the infinite. It is not about getting even *with* the other but an offering *to* the other, as when care is shown toward the widow and the orphan, the beggar and the stranger. To hear the Voice and the outcry of truth is to hear the commandment of the Holy One, who summons from us the justice, the truth, that is also righteousness.

Truth and justice are one. Justice is giving, as we have seen. Truth, therefore, is giving. Truth is life, and we have as much life as we give. We have life, we have truth, as a star has light: it has as much light as it emanates, as it gives. A star that gives out no light is a black hole. Here too, in the wonder of creation, we have the truth of Torah. The light of life shines forth in a question concerning truth and justice, and by now you know very well what that question is. As we have seen, justice and truth begin with the response of *Hineni*, "Here I am for you," to the commandment to love the neighbor and the stranger. This response is an offering of the self to and for the Holy One who commands, and not a contemplation of the essence or attributes of God, which, in any case, are nonexistent. God does not "exist"—he calls, cries out, questions, and acts. Even as we ask whether justice is possible, justice, as commanded by God, is already asking us: Where are you?

To seek truth, like seeking meaning, is to seek a capacity for hearing, not a capacity to believe but a capacity to hear the outcry of our neighbor, of the stranger, for to be deaf to that outcry is to be blind to the truth of the infinite dearness of that human being. If judgment transpires on a bridge, as the Talmud affirms, it is the bridge between ourselves and another, and that bridge is the bridge of truth, which is the bridge of justice, of *tzedek*, the one bond that binds each of us to the other. To assert that word is tied to meaning is to affirm that God is linked to the world. And that link is truth, the seal of the Holy One: truth joins word to meaning by bridging God to a world that is otherwise a wasteland.

Conceived as truth, *tzedek* is a matter not of resolve but of ethical action. It is, as we shall see, a matter of *goodness*. *Tzedek* introduces a vertical dimension to the horizontal relation and thus makes justice essential to our identity, our authenticity, our soul—and to truth. Only where justice is tied to truth does *dwelling* become possible in a world that is otherwise no more than a wilderness in which only the fit survive. Defined by the dimension of height or the holy, dwelling, like truth, is characterized by giving, as when we invite others to our table and offer them a morsel of bread. Here justice is not only *tzedek* but also *tzedakah*, a giving of time, energy, and talent, a giving of bread, without any interest in reciprocity. It is a justice conceived as gratitude, as a gratitude for gratitude itself, a gratitude not for receiving but for giving.

Dwelling in truth, moreover, takes place within community, within *edah*, to use the Hebrew word, which also means "testimony." Testimony to what? Not to a philosophical system or religious creed but to justice as defined by the *mitzvot*, by divine commandments. The truth is spoken only as a witness, as the one responsible. No sooner do I testify, than I realize that I am too late. Although I have given much, I realize through my very utterance of the truth that there is infinitely more that I might have given, like Schindler in the closing scene of *Schindler's List*: "Why did I keep the car? Why did I keep this gold pin? I could have sold them and saved more lives!" The world, then, is the place where justice has forever *yet* to be fulfilled, where truth has forever *yet* to draw its breath. This point may provide some insight into the fact that *olam*, or "world" in Hebrew, also means "eternity." When the world takes on a dimension of truth, we encounter the eternal in time as the eternally meaningful. To have a meaning and mission in life is to be summoned from beyond the world to add what is *better* than the world *to* the world, that is, to add to the world *more* than all there is. That *more*, that trace of the eternal, is truth—and goodness. Where there is truth, there is goodness.

So where are we to seek truth? Neither on the mountain tops nor in the desert, but right here, in the face of this human being who now stands before us, revealing to us what is holy in a plea for help, for a moment of attention, for a moment of our *time*. As all of humanity was gathered into Adam, so is all humanity, all truth, gathered into each human being. That is why the Talmud compares saving a single life to saving the world. That is where the Holy One—the God whose seal is truth, the seal that seals each of us to him and each of us to all—reveals to us the truth. That is where we receive the summons of *tzedakah* that is *tzedek*.

Realizing the bond between truth and justice, I realize that the question is not whether God, world, or humanity will be just but whether *I* shall be just. And that is determined according to a response to two other questions, the questions put to Cain: "Where is your brother?" and "What have you done?" If truth is to be found in the human-to-human relation, then it must be understood as a being-for-the-other that manifests itself in a doing-for-the-other. With regard to humanity, then, truth is an event that transpires between two; it is the event of the unfolding of meaning as one becomes, through the act of giving, a sign of the infinite dearness of the other. Answering "Here *I* am" before another, I expose myself to and for the other. In the realm of humanity, then, truth is not something I enact; rather, it is something I act upon as a response to a summons. Like the Good that chooses me prior to my choosing between good and evil, the truth lays claim to me before I act. That is why truth *matters*. That is why I feel so empty without it. For without knowing the truth, there is no being good.

Goodness

In the Torah the word *tov* or *good* appears for the first time upon the first utterance of God, when he spoke and summoned light into being: "And God saw the light, and it was *good*." This light is, indeed, the light of goodness. When God speaks, God creates. When God creates, he creates goodness. Therefore goodness is not only in the world and of the world, but it is also beyond the world, more than being, better than being. And yet, it permeates creation like the soul of the Holy One himself: the soul of the Holy One is goodness. Like a human being, goodness enters this realm in a breach of being: while creation may *be* good, only a human being can *do* good. Recall the teaching from the Talmud I invoked early on: God's utterance of *Anokhi* should be read as an acronym for *Ana nafshi ketavit vehavit*, or "I shall give my soul to you in writing." Yes: his *soul*. And what do we receive when we receive the soul of the Holy One in writing? The goodness that is his soul. The first utterance of the Holy One resounds in every act of goodness, every act and every word of loving kindness. In the *Pirke Avot* we are taught that creation rests upon three pillars: the study of Torah, the service of prayer, and acts of loving kindness. All three are steeped in the goodness that the Creator called forth, as he gazed into his Torah, in the cry of "Let there be light."

But what *is* this light of goodness that precedes being and yet permeates being? Where does it come from? After all, the luminaries of the heavens were not created until the fourth day. And yet, without the cry of *yehi or*, "There will be light," the luminaries of the heavens would have no light. Their light shines forth from above to create the event horizon of all that transpires in the universe, as the physicists have taught us: the speed of light is the one constant that frames all that transpires in space and time. The light summoned into existence with the first utterance of creation is also a defining constant, but of a different sort. The sages tell us that the light of the first utterance is the light of Torah, a light that does not meet the eye, the light of the Invisible One who is made of that light, which imparts meaning and holiness to all of creation—that is what makes it good. The Good is not what pleases us—it is what sanctifies us and enables us to sanctify creation. Other sages hold that the first light of creation is the light of Divine love, which is the same thing, as that love imparts meaning and holiness and goodness to all of creation. Yes, *love.* It is the light that is hidden in every quark, in every string, of creation, the light of teaching and truth. And God's pronouncement of that light to be good is an utterance of love.

I myself have seen this light, my children, and behold, it is indeed good. It is the light of goodness that graces the green earth beneath our feet, that imparts depth to the blue of the sky, that whispers in the quiet roar of the green sea: God's creation is *good.* I saw the light of goodness emanating from each of you, when I first gazed into your infant eyes. Indeed, I saw all of creation gathered into your eyes. I knew it was the light of the first utterance of creation, because when I looked up and again gazed upon the world, creation itself had been transformed, beaming with the goodness that was shining in your beautiful eyes. The mystery of beauty in our world, in its very existence, is the mystery of goodness. As I have said, I have been blessed to have many teachers, true sages of our time, but in your infant eyes I encountered the most profound teaching of all. The Infinite radiated from the fathomless circle of darkness in the pupil of your eyes, from the wondrous, mysterious smile that spread across your faces, a smile that was your own rejoicing in the goodness of life itself. Peering into your eyes, I knew, if only for a moment, the meaning and the mystery of goodness. I knew more profoundly than ever that I must be good. But have I? Have I been a good man, my children?

Yes, these reflections on goodness now lead me to your eyes, my little ones. I defended my doctoral dissertation on March 1, 1978. On March 4 the first of you was born. For most doctoral students, defending their dissertation would be enough to make it a momentous occasion. But not for me. I gazed into your eyes, looked up, and the transformation took place. In that instant I understood what made all of my pretentious study, all of my self-absorbed writing, the sum of my arrogant erudition meaningful. It was not all my learning (which, indeed, is meager) but the life I held in my trembling hands that imparted to me the scant wisdom that I now bequeath to you. The next time I went into the classroom where I was teaching I looked into the innocent faces of my young students, and I was overwhelmed by the obvious: these are somebody's babies. I must become everything for these children that I would become for my own child, everything that I must continually become for the sake of my children and grandchildren. Writing these words, I now realize the meaning of the bond between father and teacher, between *horeh* and *moreh*, as the Talmud tells us. Both words are cognates of *Torah*, of teaching, fathering, testifying—to goodness.

The goodness that abides in every leaf of every tree, in every shining star, in the song of every creature is not a moral goodness. Transcending the ethical, it makes the ethical possible. It makes the ethical *meaningful*. To be sure, there is no other source or ground of meaning. It is the goodness of the God who is good, who is *the* Good, as we say in our prayers, invoking God as *HaEl HaTov*. Goodness is neither a concept nor a category—no, it is a living presence, the presence of life itself: where there is life, there is goodness. Thus we are forbidden to inflict suffering not only upon our fellow human being but also upon any living creature. If an animal drawing a plow in the field or laboring on the threshing floor wants to stop to eat, we must let it eat. We are forbidden to eat in front of a hungry animal, so that we must feed our animals before we eat. We are even forbidden to take eggs from a nest if the hen can see us, because it would cause her too much suffering. Indeed, this is why we do not mix milk and meat: we are forbidden to cook a kid in its mother's milk, because it would be too cruel: it would not be good. So the refusal to mix milk and meat rests upon kindness, on goodness, which is the essence of kindness, as kindness is the essence of goodness. Kindness is essential to being good, and we must be good to God's beloved ones.

Then there are the laws of *shechita*, the laws of ritual slaughter, which require that the slaughter of an animal be done in a painless manner. If the *shochet*, the slaughterer, as one of my teachers who is a *shochet* taught me, feels the blade of his knife touch the neck bone of the animal, the animal is no longer kosher, because it has caused too much suffering to God's creature. Among no other ancient peoples do we find these laws pertaining to the treatment of animals, not in the Code of Urkagina, the Code of Ur-Nammu, the Laws of Eshnunna, nor even in the famed Code of Hammurabi. For similar reasons, we have commandments that apply to the treatment of plants, trees, and the land, in the laws of *shmita*, which allow the land itself a rest every seven years: *the living earth itself*, the sustainer of our lives, is granted a time of rest. The foundation of these commandments? It is the revelation that all of creation is imbued with goodness. For the act of creation is an act of revelation—the revelation of goodness, the revelation that the light of creation is the light of goodness. It is the light by which the heart sees rightly. It is the light that reveals to us the *innocence* of the animals. Indeed, they were here before us, in all their innocence and goodness.

And so the One who declared the light of creation to be good commands us: "I have set before you this day life and good, and death and evil . . . therefore choose life, that you may live, you and your seed." Choose goodness, that you may live. Choose to live, that you may love and be good. There is no loving in isolation, no being good in being alone. Goodness belongs to a *relation*. And yet, we do not choose the Good. A living presence, a living light, the Good chooses us, lays claim to us. The Good takes hold of us before we have had time to behold anything. That is what makes our choices *matter* and a matter of urgency. The living light of the Good shines upon us from the depths of the child of God who now stands before us, sits in our lap, and hugs us around the neck.

"I asked for wonder," Abraham Joshua Heschel once said. Permeated with goodness, all of creation is a source of wonder most profound. The greatest source of wonder in this world is the goodness in this world, as inexplicable as it is commonplace. Just look at your late grandmother (or great-grandmother), and you will understand. Wonder is as essential to life as air itself, as essential as the simple act of eating, in which we discover one of the greatest wonders of creation: bread. It is not for nothing that in many traditions people pray when they eat. It is not for nothing that the blessing we say is a blessing on bread. The simple act of eating bread opens the empyrean gates to goodness.

I remember when I was a child, I used to love a slice of warm, freshly baked bread with some butter on it. The bread itself was a source of wonder for me: who invented bread, who came up with this delicious morsel? As I grew older, the more I thought about it, the more I learned about it (as your learning increases, my children, so does your wonder), the greater my wonder at the series of transformations that unfold in the act of eating a piece of bread. A stalk of wheat is transformed into dough and the dough into bread. But the stalk of wheat comes from another series of transformations. A seed, some earth, some water, and some light are somehow made into wheat. Think of it: *light* is the *food* that sustains the wheat in the miraculous phenomenon of photosynthesis. Eating the bread, we ingest the light. Yes, *light*, the light that the Creator pronounced to be very good, the light that you can taste in a bite of bread, the light that shines most of all in the offering of bread to another.

Then other transformations transpire. The bread we eat is transformed into blood and muscle and bone, into laughter and tears, into *thoughts* and *words* and *deeds of loving kindness*: into *goodness*. Bread not only tastes good—it tastes like goodness. Goodness: the light of goodness that made the wheat grow, that sleeps in the bread we place in our mouth, that shines in the act of loving kindness born of the bread we eat. That light of goodness, the light of the first utterance of creation, shines most intensely in the bread we snatch from our mouths and offer to another. Only one who eats, who offers another something to eat, can open the gates on high so that goodness may enter this realm. Only one who eats can reveal the truth of the goodness of creation, because only one who eats can take the bread from his own mouth and offer it to another. Goodness lies in this everyday act of flesh-and-blood offering, of giving, of loving. It is not a philosophical abstraction, not a concept or an idea. It is as much about flesh and blood as is the act of eating. It has far more to do with satisfying the hunger of others than with saving their souls. Indeed, beware of one who would save your soul. For they would ascend to the Throne of Divine Judgment to sort out the damned from the saved, and in that ascent of the ego lies evil.

Bread, my children, is the embodiment of goodness, not the bread that we harvest from the earth but the bread that God "brings forth from the earth," *hamotzi lechem min haaretz*, as we say in the blessing at every meal—just as he brings forth the light. It is as though "Let there be light" might mean "Let there be bread." God brings forth the bread so that we may offer it to another, and in that offering we offer up the light that was in the beginning. Bread unoffered is not bread: in the offering lies the goodness, starting with bread but not ending with bread: it includes the offering of a kind word, of our time and energy, of our talent and attention, of our very lives.

According to the fourteenth-century sage Rabbi Israel ibn al-Nakawa, the Jewish leaders of France used to have their coffins made out of the wood of the tables from which they offered bread to the poor. Nor was this practice a mere medieval custom or quirk, for it is written in the Code of Jewish Law that people who offered bread to the poor at their table should be interred in a coffin made out of the planks of that table. As our acts of goodness and loving kindness clothe our souls, so should the table where we fed the hungry clothe our bodies. Taking a testimony of our goodness into the upper realms, we affirm that goodness originates in the upper realms. This is the meaning of the *manna* that sustained the Israelites: it issues from the goodness of heaven, but it is gathered from the goodness of the earth. In the words of the great medieval sage Nachmanides, the manna "was a product of that Higher Light which became tangible by the will of the Creator," who pronounces the light to be good, tangible, as it emanates in the flesh-and-blood relation between two human souls. What is brought forth from the earth is brought forth from above, then taken from the earth as we ascend above.

Here, in the meaning of bread, lies the explanation of why Abraham was chosen for the Covenant with the Creator of heaven and earth. It is not because he was very "spiritual"; no, it is because he was an innkeeper who would go in search of tired and hungry wayfarers in order to bring them to his table and provide them with food and comfort. It was because of his goodness. To be sure, the Torah emphasizes the importance of offering food and drink to another, symbolized most profoundly in the offering of bread and wine, which signify body and soul. Saying the blessing on the bread and the wine each Shabbat, we affirm the holiness and the goodness of creation:

veyekhulu hashamaim ve haaretz . . . , "and He completed the heavens and the earth . . . ." Hence we begin the Kiddush with the act of creation, the act that blessed all of creation with goodness.

When Melkhitzedek, the High Priest of Salem, encountered Abraham on the road, he gave him bread and wine. When Abraham caught sight of the three strangers approaching his tent, he did the same, cutting short his conversation with God—yes, *with God himself*—in order to attend to the physical need of his guests. Like his concern for the strangers of Sodom and Gomorrah, Abraham's concern for the hungry wayfarers lies at the core of his goodness. If the violation of the prohibition against murder is an implicit rejection of God, feeding the hungry is a tacit affirmation of him. For it is an affirmation of God's goodness. The relationship between one human being and another—between one soul and another—is a physical relationship that rests upon goodness, which, in turn, rests upon bread. Once again, we realize that goodness has nothing to do with a "concept of the Good." No, it is about a flesh-and-blood relation embodied in the offering of bread, of our helping hands and words of comfort, to another.

We have a teaching from the Torah: "Man lives not by bread alone but by every word that proceeds from the mouth of God." One of my teachers, Rabbi Adin Steinsaltz, explains that the verse does not suggest that we have a physical aspect and a spiritual aspect, as it is often misunderstood. Rather, he says, it means "man does not live only from the calories provided by bread, but from Divine energy. This is what the Torah calls the '*utterance from the mouth of the Lord*.' It makes the bread 'live' and forms its true essence. In other words, although superficially I am only eating matter, in fact I am ingesting language, because the raw material of bread is the Divine word." And the Divine word is the light of *goodness*. Just so, when we eat bread at a meal, it is incumbent upon us to recite the Blessing after Meals, which opens with the invocation of the goodness of God, a goodness that abides within the bread itself.

Instilled with something that exceeds its material reality, the physical is also metaphysical; the material is also spiritual. Every "item" or "thing," every "tool" or "utensil," is also a "vessel," as these various meanings of the Hebrew word *kli* suggest. A vessel of what? Of the goodness by which all things exist and through which we are commanded to the stewardship of all things: the goodness that creates nature also commands the human being to be good, to choose the Good in the light of having been chosen by the Good. And so Adam was created to labor in the garden of Eden, to attend to the garden and make it flourish. How? Not just by tilling the soil and pruning the trees but, above all, by being *good*.

As goodness belongs to the fabric of being, so does it belong to the fabric of your being: you are *good*, for God has bequeathed unto you his goodness. Remember that. Yes! Remember that: you are good! You are alive because you are good, because you are summoned to do good: as the Creator pronounced the light that gives meaning to creation to be good, so he declared you to be good, for *you* harbor the light of the first utterance of creation. And his pronouncement is a commandment, a *mitzvah*, a connection to the One who alone is good.

Because goodness lies at the core of creation, it is possible for good to arise from what is bad. There was darkness over the face of the deep before the utterance that summoned forth the light was pronounced. Indeed, as we affirm in our prayers, God is the one who *yotzer or uvorei choshekh*, who "forms light and creates darkness." I know that you, my children, look upon the evil that is everywhere, and you wonder: "What good can there possibly be in this?" Indeed, evil so often poses as goodness. Else it would not be so seductive. As Rebbe Nachum of Tchernobil once declared, "I am much more afraid of my good deeds that please me than of my bad deeds that repel me." Why? Because as soon as I hold myself up as being good, I become blind to the good that I have yet to enact, and nothing blinds us more to the responsibility not only to be good but to be *better* than self-righteousness. Because the Good is infinite, my task is infinite. Thus in *Pirke Avot* Rabbi Tarfon teaches that, even though we cannot complete the task, we are nevertheless summoned to engage it. What is the task? To be good.

Psalm 92 opens with the words *tov lehodot*: "it is good to give thanks." Goodness begins with gratitude, a word that we shall explore more thoroughly below. For now, let it be said that there is no goodness without gratitude, gratitude for goodness itself, as the part of creation that makes creation meaningful. Indeed, the Creator's comment on the creation of light is *ki-tov*, because it is good, where goodness lies in the *because*: the *because* is rooted in the Why, and the Why lies in goodness. It lies in what matters, for without goodness nothing matters. Thus God says of the light not just that it is *tov* or "good" but *ki-tov*. Because the soul is made of that light, as the sages teach us, no good deed equals in meaning and importance to that of saving a human life. And yet we never know which good deed might save a life, for the goodness of each deed exceeds our field of vision. Because goodness belongs to the infinite, the goodness of the good deed emanates into the infinite, above and below. As we are taught in the mystical tradition, the movement below stirs the movement above. "Do something good," says one of Elie Wiesel's characters, "and God up there will imitate you; do something evil and suddenly the scale will tip the other way." In which direction does our goodness tip the scale? In the direction of the Messiah.

"What is the Messiah," Wiesel's character continues, "if not man transcending his solitude in order to make his fellow man less solitary? To turn a single human being back toward life is to prevent the destruction of the world," as it is written in the Talmud. To turn a single human being back to life through your act of goodness is to lead him to resolve, "I am going to be good." It is that simple. And that profound. To turn a human being back toward life is to turn the human being back toward the Good, for, as we have seen, to choose life is to choose the Good, and to choose the Good is to choose redemption: to turn back to the Good is to turn to the Messiah, to welcome the Messiah. And it is a turning *back*, a turning toward what has been there all along, closer to us than our shadow. To thus turn back is to become wise.

Wisdom

THERE IS A PRAYER from the Psalms that says, "Teach us to count our days, that we may receive the wisdom of the heart." This counting is an accounting, a kind of *cheshbon nefesh* or "taking stock of our soul." Wisdom comes with this counting and accounting, with this answering for what we do with our days. Wisdom is always the wisdom of the heart, for only the heart can see rightly; what is essential, what belongs to wisdom, is invisible to the eye. The scientists and scholars observe, count, and measure, enamored of quantitative analysis. But there is no wisdom in such analysis. There is not supposed to be. As for philosophy, the purported "love of wisdom," it has become a contempt for wisdom. The teaching by which we receive the wisdom of the heart comes from God, not from observation or statistics, however scientific, nor from philosophical speculation, however analytical. It begins with the turn inward, where we discover that Within and Above are synonyms. The world assesses us from outward appearances, but, says the prophet Samuel, God gazes into the heart, measuring not our knowledge but our wisdom, which is the measure of our days and our deeds. In our deeds lies the measure of our days and our wisdom.

There is a difference between wisdom and knowledge. Knowledge is an accumulation of information, such as you might find in an encyclopedia or on the internet. Indeed, there are those whose knowledge is encyclopedic and who rely on the internet for their information. I have known some whose knowledge is vast, some whose wisdom runs deep, and, among the former, some who are not so wise. Wherein lies wisdom? In the realization—or the revelation—of why we live and why we die, of what there is to love, of what there is to fear and what there is to fear *for*. Our professors are often knowledgeable. Our grandmothers are often wise. Those of you, my children, who have been blessed to have great professors know what I am talking about. And all of you have been blessed to have a wise grandmother, even though some of you never knew her.

The fourth chapter of *Pirke Avot* opens by asking, "Who is wise?" Ben Zoma replies: "One who can learn from every human being." Not just from every wise or knowledgeable human being but from *every* human being, from an infant to an Alzheimer's patient, from the Down Syndrome child at St. Jude's to the resident of the nursing home in advanced stages of dementia. What can we learn from someone who cannot even speak? We can learn something about the image and likeness of the Holy One, who abides in the person and summons us. We can learn more about how to answer such a calling of our name. We can learn our *name*, for only in our response to another can we ever learn our name. Note, too, that wisdom lies not in knowing but in learning. The greatest compliment that one sage could pay to another in the Talmud is to say that he or she is a *talmid chakham*, a "wise student." Being a wise student, of course, entails a capacity for listening.

If you would be wise, my children, learn how to listen, not only to the words that others speak but also to the sounds of the world around you. Creation does not make noise—it *speaks*. For all of creation is made of Torah, so that there is teaching in all things. The prophets were known for their ability to understand the language of the birds. Listen to the wind and the water as well. Listen to the silence of the earth and the skies, the silence of the stars and the silence between the stars. There is more wisdom in that silence than in the pronouncements of the erudite. In order to be wise, we must learn how to remain silent—and listen. "What should be our pursuit in this world?" asked the Talmudic sage Rabbi Isaac. And he answered: "To be silent." And Rabbi Shimon ben Gamliel once declared, "I have found nothing better for a person than silence." These are voices of wisdom.

In the Jewish tradition, learning is a form of praying: each time we learn from another human being, we learn from the Holy One. We pray to him not only with our heart but also with our hands. Wisdom lies in hands that give, in the realization of the infinite in our infinite responsibility, the realization that it grows with each response: wisdom opens up the infinite. But more about responsibility later; it is a life-sustaining word unto itself. For now, know that, because one is wise who can learn from everyone, wisdom arises in the face-to-face relation between one human being and another. The key to wisdom lies in a capacity to behold and to hear—to attend to and respond to—the holiness revealed in the face of this human being who now stands before me. Yes, the face . . . . Everyone who has a face has a tale to tell, and in the tale of every soul there is something to teach us and wisdom to impart to us.

When you are overwhelmed by a sense of meaninglessness and despair, gaze long into the face of another, and you will discover the meaning and sanctity of life that eludes the evidence of the eyes. For nothing about the face that makes it a face is accessible to the eyes. We do not *see* the face—we respond to it with a cry of "Here I am for you!" The face speaks.

It is the origin of the Word that calls us forth from the isolation in which the soul languishes. The Nazis knew this. In their assault on the soul, on the wisdom couched in the millennia-long tradition of Jewish teaching and testimony, they rendered the Jew "ferociously alone" and blind to the face of the other, so that everyone was either an enemy or a rival. Recall one of the most chilling lines in Elie Wiesel's *Night*: "Here there are no fathers, no sons, no friends." And no wisdom. Only where we come face-to-face with an inherent dearness manifest in the face of the other human being do we discover a commanding presence that transcends our knowledge and that lays claim to us: wisdom lies in this implication.

The face makes manifest the origin of the commanding Word, in all its hiddenness, in all its silence. Therefore the face not only speaks, but it transmits a message, a teaching and a testimony—silently. To encounter the face is to encounter Torah, as we affirm in our daily prayers: "By the light of Your Face you have given us the Torah of Life." Because the face transmits the most fundamental commandment of Torah—the prohibition against murder—it is through the face that Torah enters this world *from on high*. Wisdom lies in the revelation of this dimension of height, which finds its highest expression in the embrace of the other human being. Wisdom *is* the dimension of height. Wisdom *is* just such an embrace. Thus the God who created the heavens and the earth through wisdom began with the heavens, with the hidden utterance of "Let there be height." Only one who looks *up* can find wisdom.

So you can see why the face is so crucial to wisdom, why it is the source of wisdom itself: to behold the face is to look *up*. Wisdom is the wisdom of holiness, and the holy is situated in the "face," in the *panim*, a word that suggests a presence both "within" and "before" us, both *bifnim* and *bifnei*. The Hebrew word affirms that to behold the face is to behold just what does not meet the eye, in the vulnerability of the eyes of another. In the time of COVID, the age of the mask, we have at least been privy to the eyes, if not the smile. And yet, the smile is essential to the revelation of the face. Nevertheless, our gaze into the eyes remains a gaze into the inside, into the soul. A cognate of *panim*, *penim*, means "inside" or "interior," and yet it is an interior that *emanates* and *expresses* itself from within the face. The expression of the face is this exposure of the interior without the loss of interiority. It is the highest expression of the soul or the humanity of the other human being. It reveals a *within* that is also an *above*: the height situated within the face and manifest through the face is the height that sanctifies all that there is from beyond all that there is. That is why he is wise who can learn from *anyone*.

The face is not in the world, but rather all the world, all of creation, all of space and time, is gathered into the face of another. Just look into the faces of your children, my children, and you will understand. You will behold the immemorial face of Adam and the eternal face of the Messiah. You will be wise. You will realize that the face is the vessel of meaning apart from any context, for, like wisdom, it is what imparts meaning to every context. Entering this world from beyond this world, the face opens up the absolute, both as what sanctifies and as what commands. Thus whenever we pronounce a blessing upon God, we bless him as the One who sanctifies us through his commandments, sanctifies us with wisdom.

We have a teaching from the Talmud: just prior to its entry into this realm, an angel sanctifies the soul with the wisdom of Torah. I myself have seen it in your infant faces, my children. I have seen it when, upon waking, your beautiful faces beam with joy in life itself: where there is wisdom, there is joy. I have seen it when I have held you and you snuggled into my arms early in the morning, and you looked up at me with that precious smile, beaming with the light of all that is dear, with the light invoked in the first utterance of Creation. It is the wisdom of life, of that level of your precious soul known as *chayah*, which, say the mystics, is the seat of the soul's wisdom.

Our sages teach us that *chayah* transcends the confines of the body; it is what "launches" the soul into the body and, through the body, into this world, through wisdom. Thus *chayah* encompasses and surrounds the body from above and from within. Larger than the body, *chayah* manifests itself in this realm as the *or makif* or "surrounding light," as a person's "halo" or "aura." Those possessed of wisdom shine with this light. I have seen it. I have seen that light surrounding each of you. I go to sleep at night with the memory of that vision, of the light that surrounds you, comforting my soul with wisdom. Yes, wisdom is *comforting*. It allays anxiety and care by revealing to us what there is to care about.

At the level of *chayah* the soul is neither a "thing" nor an "action" but an *efshar* or a "might," in every sense of the word, both as *possibility* and as *potency*. This possibility and potency characterize the entry of the *beyond* into the *within*, of the *might be* into the realm of the *cannot be*. That's it: wisdom opens up possibility where we perceive only the impossible. Whereas the thinking that dominates this world of domination is locked into the categories of cause-and-effect and natural necessity and therefore is blind to possibility, wisdom beholds possibility, as articulated in the prayer to the God who "restores the dead to life." If faith is a mad struggle for possibility, faith is a mad struggle for wisdom. As the great sage Saadia Gaon once said, "What man acquires through wisdom is called 'life.'" And Maimonides once declared, "Wisdom and life are one and the same in Him." Wisdom, like love, like faith, overcomes death in a revelation not only of what there is to live for but also of what there is to die for. The potency that belongs to wisdom robs death of its power.

The father of Moses, Amram, head of the Egyptian Jewish community, determined in the face of Pharaoh's cruel declaration concerning the murder of the male firstborn that the Jews should bear no children into the world. His five-year-old daughter Miriam talked him out of it, understanding that without the Jews in this world, there can be no wisdom of Torah in this world—yes, even before the revelation of Torah in this world. Therein lay her wisdom, the wisdom of a child who had not forgotten the Torah that the angel taught her, a wisdom at which all of us now marvel. A wisdom without which there would be no Jewish people. Indeed, one of you, my firstborn, bears her name. And you live up to it, for all the rest of us.

If the Jews are summoned to be a light unto the nations, it is the light of wisdom that we must radiate. Just as creation is compared to a birth that transpires at every instant, so is the life of the soul such a birth, with *chayah* drawing forth the life that lies in the union with the One who creates through wisdom. This "midwife" is the *chai Yah*, the "life of God," where the image and likeness of God is manifest in the living soul. It is the soul's eternal *yet to be*, the eternal *more* of the soul. If wisdom's orientation is toward the past, toward tradition and sacred history, it is because it is orientated toward the *yet to be* couched in the future. Wisdom tells us that the future is not the opposite of the past; rather, it is the opposite of the absence of a past. No past, no future; no future, no past. No wisdom.

In addition to being the "midwife" of the soul, *chayah* is the "teacher of wisdom," who imparts to the soul the *Ets Chayim* or the "Tree of Life" that is Torah. Trees bear seeds. From the Tree of Life is born the seed that makes possible the flow of *chayah*, the *living* presence of the soul, into the womb of Imma, which is the Supernal Mother. In case this is getting a little too abstract or too esoteric, let me bring it back down to the earth where we live and die: no one is so wise as a mother. No loss, except the loss of a child, God forbid, is as great as the loss of a mother, even though it be in the order of things. Creation is in order when, as horrific as it is, we bury our mother; creation is turned on end when a mother, God forbid, buries her child. Still, the loss of a mother is the loss of the one who first gazed into your eyes and uttered your name with an infinite love and in that utterance drew your infinitely precious soul into this troubled realm. Those of you who are mothers, my children, know this all too well: to be a mother is to receive the seed and the flowering of wisdom. I remember that when I was a callow, calloused, sophomoric college upstart, I would try on the dress of a sophisticated intellectual, decked out in defiance, sewn with the threads of stupidity, and awash in the stink of self-righteous indignation. For each of my logical replies to Thomas Aquinas's five proofs of God, my mother, who could follow none of it (to her credit), finally said, "Don't use your logic on me!" There lay the voice of wisdom.

The potentiality and the potency that I have spoken of lie in the Hebrew word for wisdom itself, in *chokhmah*. As the great sage Moshe Cordovero points out, *chokhmah* is made of the words *koach mah*, which denote the "potentiality of what is," as manifest, for example, in a seed. Potentiality for what? For what is yet to be revealed as what there is to love. Wisdom opens up a future, and the future is made of what there is to love: without wisdom there is no future, no love. In other words, *chokhmah* is the might and the possibility for what *is* to become *more*, the potency and potentiality to *love more*. Opening up the *more* within the *is*, Jewish teaching exceeds the philosophical rumination that merely asks, "What *is x*?" by asking, "What is *better* than *x*?" Jewish thought exceeds the question of essence that is couched in such philosophical inquiries as "What is history?" "What is the good?" "What is metaphysics?" and, most importantly, "What is a human being?" as we shall see in the next chapter. If a human being is *more* than he *is*; if a human being is what she *is not yet*, despite the law of contradiction ($A \neq \sim A$) inherited from the Greeks; if the human being is the "I am that I am *not*" in contrast to the Divine "I Am That I Am"—it is because the human being is a manifestation of a living presence that is beyond being, a manifestation of the *chayah* of the soul. As Rabbi Yechiel Mikhal, the Zlotzover Maggid, has said, only God can say the word *I*. What is the "I am *not*," in the depths and the heights of my soul? It is the face of the Holy One, which, according to our prayers, we must forever seek but, according to Torah, we can never behold. Wisdom lies in that eternal seeking after the Eternal.

Among the senses *chayah* is associated with sight, with a kind of "second sight," an ability to behold what eludes the eye. Similarly, the face of the Holy One is associated with light, with the invisible light brought into being upon the utterance of "Let there be light." With the utterance of "Let there be light" God assumes a face and a Name, as the first letter of the Tetragrammaton takes shape, the letter *yud*, which also parallels the *chayah* of the soul. To be sure, among the ten utterances of Creation, according to Kabbalah, the utterance of "Let there be light" corresponds to the *sefirah* of *Chokhmah*. (I hope you will forgive me, my children, for this extended excursion into mysticism.) As the light of the Divine countenance, this light is the emanation that emanates from the World of Emanation, the *Olam Atzilut*, which is the realm of *chayah*. It is the light of *mind*. Do you see, my children? Or have I lost you? It's okay. You have to first be lost in order to be found.

There is no mind, no wisdom, in isolation; languishing in our isolation, we have only the recurring preoccupation that we cannot get off our mind. Wisdom arises *between* two as something that is always *already* there before it is there. We do not acquire wisdom; wisdom acquires us. That is the silent potential, the *koach mah*, of wisdom. This silence is a defining feature of wisdom: as I have suggested, one who is wise is one who knows how to remain silent, who knows when silence is required, and who knows what to speak when a word is called for. Silence here is the silence that precedes thought, the white fire before it is inscribed with black fire. It is the silence that finds its way into the words and between the words we utter. It is the silence that enables our deeds to speak louder than words. If you would be wise, my children, learn when to be silent and when to speak; learn to speak with your hands, and not with your lips. Learn when to *help*, silently, when to be good *secretly*, like the dew that quietly and ineluctably graces the grass. There is always a secret about wisdom. What is the secret? It is this: wisdom does not proceed from thought; rather, thought proceeds from wisdom.

Where do the thought steeped in wisdom and the wisdom steeped in thought find one of their most fundamental manifestations? In prayer. There is no wisdom without prayer. If you would be wise, my children, cultivate the habit of prayer. Yes: the *habit*. Pray even when you see no point. Especially when you see no point. For it is only by praying that you can ever hope to see the point. The thought that defines wisdom is to be found in prayer, and prayer, as we have seen, is an emanation of the Divine. When we seek to take our thought to the level of prayer, then, listening becomes even more crucial. The *koach mah* that is wisdom, Rabbi Adin Steinsaltz reminds us, is "the capacity to listen, to fully absorb what is given." Here we see that the *koach mah* of wisdom is the "power of the *what*" to be manifest as a *who*: we listen not to some*thing* but to some*one*. Which means: prayer is the transformation of conceptual content into living presence. And wisdom works that transformation.

The person in prayer asks God to help him or her make heard the "silent Voice" or the "Voice of silence" that is "the supernal Voice from which all other voices proceed," the *kol demamah dakah* that was revealed to Elijah in his cave. What is the silent Voice from which all other voices proceed? It is, again, the voice of the *alef* that precedes the *beit* in the first utterance of creation. It is the *alef* that abides silently in every word of wisdom. At every instant God renews the deeds of creation through wisdom, and we participate in that renewal through prayer—manifest as thought, word, and deed, as God's "clothing." Clothed in wisdom, God is made manifest. For, like the invisible man, the Invisible One can be seen only when he is so clothed. You look around yourselves, seeking God, and perhaps he is nowhere to be found. You look again, through eyes filled with the wisdom of what there is to love, and suddenly there he is. He had been there all along. Suddenly, like Ray in *Field of Dreams*, when he gazed lovingly at his wife and child on their front porch, it occurs to you: maybe this *is* heaven. The Talmud teaches that everything is in the hands of God except the awe of heaven. And yet our awe of heaven, our vision of heaven, proceeds from the light of God. It is an awe of the child and a mother sitting on a porch swing.

In Proverbs we are taught that the awe of the Holy One, *yirat HaShem*, is the beginning of wisdom. There is no wisdom without wonder. This wonder, this awe, this Wow!, is the source of wisdom. Wisdom begins with a Wow! But what does it take for this Wow! that is the cry of wisdom to come to bear? It is not about fear. We flee from what we fear, but we seek a nearness to the One who inspires us with awe. Bear this in mind when you read the teachings of, say, the Maharal of Prague, who declares, "Wisdom draws the fear of Heaven in its wake, and if the fear of Heaven does not follow, we can be certain that it is not true wisdom." The fear of heaven is the awe of heaven. It is the Wow! in the face of creation, shining forth from the face of your little ones, as it shines forth from your faces, my children.

The Greeks taught that the voice of wisdom declares, "Know thyself." The Hebrews taught that the Voice of Wisdom commands, "Know God"—with the Hebrew "know" rooted in *daat*, which means to "join together with" or be "at one with." Be at one with wisdom, my children. For that is who you are. Thus my words of wisdom, such as they are, that I now pass on to you. As one of Elie Wiesel's teachers told him, "Take my teaching and undo it." For wisdom can never be captured in words. But by now you understand that. Understanding that, you begin to understand what it means to be human.

Human

The question that decides everything in the life of an individual human being, a community of human beings, and a society of human beings is the question of what it means to be human: where lies the significance, the sanctity, of the human being? How we understand this question determines how we understand everything high and low. From this question issues our sense of meaning and mission, of direction and identity. One of the many remarkable revelations to enter the world through the ancient Israelites is the teaching concerning the holiness of the human being, not according to the accidents of what can be weighed or measured but according to the breath of the Creator, who breathes a "living soul" into every human being. At a time when the value of a human being was understood in tribal and ethnic terms alone, we have the miraculous emergence of the Hebrews' testimony as revealed in the Torah. Indeed, according to that testimony, every human being, body and soul, is made of Torah. Which means: every human being harbors a teaching.

There is no shortage of human disasters in the world, no shortage of the desperate need for humanitarian aid, but where lies the horror in this suffering of humanity? We speak of the importance of human rights, and we are outraged at the violation of human rights, but how is the notion of rights attached to the human being? We cry out for help in the name of humanity, but what is the meaning of humanity? Where lies the holiness of humanity? Where lies the holiness of the human being? Is it merely what some call "speciesism," just a biased interest in one's own "species"? Or does something—*someone*—lay an infinite and absolute claim to us, without which we are not human at all?

My children, by now you know that the Holocaust looms in the background and often in the foreground of all my work, of all my reflections. My teacher and friend, Emil Fackenheim, goes to the core of the Holocaust when he writes that, in its aftermath "philosophers must face a *novum* within a question as old as Socrates: what does it mean to be human?" When, after spending several months in Sachsenhausen, he finally escaped from

Germany on 12 May 1939, he took with him almost nothing except the title of "Rabbi" that his teacher Leo Baeck, one of the most prominent of German Jewish thinkers, had conferred upon him. I spent many unforgettable hours listening to him and learning from him on the balcony of his apartment on Alroi Street in Jerusalem's German Colony. "I used to visit Leo Strauss often," he told me early on. "I was always afraid of disturbing him. But he told me that he did not have so many friends he could talk to and that he enjoyed the opportunity to discuss ideas. So you needn't think you are disturbing me." After my first conversation with him, he was gracious enough to say to me, "I can see that you and I are on the same wavelength." The great medieval scholar Etienne Gilson once said that in all his life he had met only one true philosopher, and that was Henri Bergson. I can say the same of Emil Fackenheim. What he bequeathed to me I now leave to you, my children, as an inheritance. You can read every detail in my book *Emil L. Fackenheim: A Jewish Philosopher's Response to the Holocaust.* It is not an assignment. It is a gift, to take up at your leisure. Once you take it up, cherish it. For in it you will find the meaning of the word *human*.

Fackenheim was a philosopher who was versed not only in philosophy but also in history. He was a true philosopher because he understood the profound connections between philosophy and history: what begins as a philosopher's head-scratching ends up as a way of life and of thinking in the generations that follow—a way of thinking about what constitutes our humanity. Bear this in mind as you peruse the works of the great philosophers. Bear it in mind when you turn on the television and hear the pundits and ideologues of our age. The generations that followed the thinking of a certain line of so-called philosophers followed it all the way to Auschwitz. I think this may be why Yechiel De-Nur once scowled to me: "*Philosophy*! It is a *shabby* word!"

Fackenheim understood that the renewed, post-Holocaust tension in our thinking lies not in the age-old animosity between Athens and Jerusalem but in a new collision between Auschwitz and Jerusalem. Indeed, his *aliyah* to Jerusalem in the early 1980s was a matter not just of relocating to a place where he could live out his remaining years, but of taking up a residence and a presence in the *Makom*, the "Place," from which the Word of God emanates into the world, for the sake of the *human*, contra the radical assault not just on humans but on the very meaning of *human* that took place in Auschwitz. His *aliyah* was a *philosophical* statement and a Jewish ascent made by one of the greatest of the post-Holocaust Jewish philosophers. That is why, when I accompanied him to Germany in 2002, a year before his death, he told me, "I go to Germany not as a former German Jew but as a Jew who resides in Jerusalem. As an Israeli."

And so I sat on his *merpeset* and listened to his philosophical insights, his Jewish insights, among the most profound of which was: "philosophers must face a *novum* within a question as old as Socrates: what does it mean to be human?" For him, to be human meant being a Jew who had taken up residence in the Jewish state, a move that conveyed a teaching and a testimony concerning what it means to be human. Which brings to mind Elie Wiesel's statement that there comes a time in the life of any human being when he or she must assume the Jewish condition in order to remain human—not a condition of the victim but the condition of witness. This is the light that we are summoned to emanate unto the nations, a light that transforms the human being into a witness who attests to the meaning of the word *human*: being human means bearing witness.

Professor Wiesel wrote that in Auschwitz not only man died but also the "idea of man," the very notion of a human being and what it is means to be human. The original title of Primo Levi's famed memoir *Survival in Auschwitz* is *Se questo è un uomo*, putting to us the question that defines the Holocaust and all our lives afterward: What is a human being? What is the basis for the value of the human being? Levi offers one response in the story of his friend Lorenzo, who remained uncorrupted by the anti-world that surrounded him: he remained *good*, through the help that he offered to others. To be human is to *help*. Lorenzo's help, his unremitting *goodness*, says Levi, reminded him, Levi, that he, too, was a man. To err is human? No. To be *good* is human. And so it is written in the *Pirke Avot*: in a land where there are no men you must be a man, which means: you must be *good*, you must *help*, you must *give*. To be human is to *give*, give of your time and your attention, your means and your measure. As a human being, you are what you give: to be human is to be giving. That is the meaning of this extraordinary word, *human*.

So how are we to understand this life-sustaining word? The Nazis had one view, the Jews had another, and the two could not abide in the same universe. From the standpoint of the Nazis, a human being has value first as the result of a natural accident: he or she happens to be born an Aryan, as they defined that racial category. In our own time, with critical race theory (CRT), it means being born into a certain privilege and power, a certain class, as determined by race. Therefore CRT is fundamentally antisemitic, inasmuch as it must fundamentally oppose the Judaic basis of the value of the human being as laid out in the Torah. Further, for the Nazis, an Aryan had even greater value and took on greater substance through a will to power, a view that can also be found among the proponents of CRT, given their insistence upon the importance of political power with regard to the promotion of racial interests. The Aryan is justified by will and power alone. Hence the title of the most renowned of the Nazi propaganda films: *The Triumph of the Will*—not the triumph of truth, justice, or the good, because all of that is determined by the will to power. Here, as in CRT, there is a radical, essential separation between each race and the rest of humanity, especially from the Jew, whom CRT deems white because of a perceived privilege, and with CRT "white," as well as "Jew," is a synonym for evil. Just as the Aryan has no more in common with the Jews than a human has with a cockroach, so with CRT the Jews are so radically other that they lie completely outside the circle of salvation. And you, my children, are adrift in a sea of CRT.

Dostoevsky was haunted by the fear that if power is the only reality, then nothing is true and everything is lawful. And so it came to pass in Nazi Germany, where we find that the view of the human being was inextricably tied to an understanding of law. In Nazi Germany there was no concept of an unjust law. What was lawful was determined by the will of the Volk and the Führer, so that everything done to the Jews was legal. Indeed, when Reinhard Heydrich convened the Wannsee Conference on 20 January 1942 to discuss the logistics of the extermination of the Jewish people, he insisted that everything be done in a legal manner, in accordance with the principles outlined in the Nuremberg Laws of 1935. Pay attention to the fate of the law in the world around you, my children, for how we understand law is tied to how we understand the holiness of the human.

When I was translating *The Complete Black Book of Russian Jewry* from Russian into English, I had a startling realization: what the Nazis did was not unimaginable—it was *everything* imaginable, for the will and the imagination were their only limits. In their assault on God and on the very meaning of a human being, they had eliminated every law, every limiting principle: there was no going too far in their torture and murder of the Jews. And their murder of the Jews entailed the annihilation of the Jewish teaching and tradition concerning the value and meaning of the human being. That is was the Nazis set out to annihilate in the extermination of the Jews. For the word *human* harbors a limiting principle and an ethical demand.

From a Jewish standpoint, a human being is not just valuable or special but is *holy*, because he or she is created in the image and likeness of the Holy One. Therefore the oppression or dehumanization of another human being not only matters—it is *evil*. From a Jewish standpoint, the determination of the identity of a human being on the basis of the contrived category of race is dehumanizing. Fixated on race, class, or gender, we are blind to the human face, from which the holiness of the other human being emanates in a fundamental prohibition against murder and an absolute commandment to *care*. Emanating from the Holy One, each soul is metaphysically connected to every other soul through the Source of all.

And since God begins his creation of humanity with a single human being, each human being is physically connected to the other through Adam, the father of all. Hence in Hebrew a human being is a *ben adam*, a child of Adam. Only from the divine creation of the human being in the image of the Holy One can we ascribe an absolute value and thus assume an infinite responsibility to and for our fellow human being.

Because the identity or the *who* of a human being is rooted in this infinity, a human being is not one creature among the many that inhabit the landscape of being. The human being, rather, is a breach of being, a miraculous appearance in the midst of being of someone who is otherwise than being. There lies the meaning of "holy" or *kadosh*, which is literally "separate from": the holy is not one special item in an inventory of items but is separate from all such "natural" determinations as genus and species. Because the identity or the *who* of a human being is rooted in this responsibility, and contrary to the views of "science," a human being is not an animal. Rather, as we have seen, the animals are among the creatures for whom we, as humans, are responsible, the creatures entrusted to our care.

Beware of so-called animals' rights movements, whose proponents level all species, including the human "species," into a meaningless and valueless sameness. "Species or man of God," Rabbi Joseph Soloveitchik, one of the sages of the last century, poses a decisive either/or, "this is the alternative which the Almighty placed before man." We have arrived at a place in our world, my children, in which there is no third alternative. Recall the question raised in *Pirke Avot*: Who is wise? One who can learn from any other human being. You learn about God, which is the mark of wisdom, only from a child of God, and not from a member of a species, who arises not from the hand of the Creator but from an accident of nature. For only a child of God can teach us about God and about the meaning of being human. And no human being is an accident.

Viewing the human being as a member of a species, modern secular thought views the human condition as a crowded condition, with each human being threatening the space of the other, no more than a number, faceless and nameless, labeled according to the accidents of nature and contingencies of culture, such as race, class, and gender, without any inherent substance or value. Here there are no people. There are black people and white people, rich people and poor people, male people and female people, heterosexual people and homosexual people, but no *people*. If there are no people, there is no humanity, no face—there are only faceless competitors who prey upon one another, trapped in a rat race that goes nowhere and ends in meaningless death. The emergence of a face in the crowd is a transcendence of the crowd: it is the emergence of the *human*, without whom there is no community that may emerge from the crowd. With the emergence of a community, we step before the countenance for the sake of another and thus become a human being. Recall that the Hebrew word for "community," *edah*, also means "testimony." A testimony to what? To the meaning of being human and to the urgency of heeding the cry for help that arises from the face of the other human. The capacity to help is a capacity for being human.

I have related to you the teaching that when we lie in our grave and await our approach unto the Presence of the Holy One, the Angel of Death, the Angel with a Thousand Eyes, comes to us to ask us a single question: What is your name? Asking us our name, the Angel asks, "Are you human?" A fundamental requirement for any understanding of our humanity is a knowledge and understanding of our name—of where our name comes from and how to answer when we are summoned by name to the task inscribed in our name. There, in our name, lies the meaning of our humanity. Each of you, my children, is named for someone who casts a loving gaze upon you from above, who asks you, with love, "What will you make of my name? How will you live up to your name?" As you become more human, you acquire a good name, the most priceless of all treasures.

We do not discover our humanity and our meaning as a human being so much as we return to it, in a kind of *teshuvah*, by returning to a name borne by those who have come before us, to whom we owe our very existence: we come into this world already indebted—or better: already summoned. Through this *already* we are profoundly blessed. Here lies the meaning of *teshuvah*, of the movement of return that we undertake every Yom Kippur, with every *Yizkor* prayer, and, indeed, with the dawning of every day. The confessions of Yom Kippur and of the daily prayers is not a way of saying, "Forgive me, for I am human," but rather an insistence that "I am human, so set me on the right path." How, then, can we tell whether we are living and dying according to the task inscribed in our name as a human being? The Hasidic master Moshe-Leib of Sassov answers: "Ask yourself whether it brings you closer to your fellow human being"—if so, you will realize the meaning of the word *human*.

In the relation to our fellow human being we have life and become human; therefore it is good. What is *lo-tov*, "not good," as it is written in the Torah, is being alone in the isolation of our illusory ego: locked into this solipsistic solitude, the human being has no identity, no name, and—what is the same thing—no love. Alone, the human being is not human, and—dare I say it?—God is not God: at stake in our being human is God's being God. Wherever we have all knowledge, skills, and information, but no humanity, no wisdom, we are not only beggared but also bereaved by our abundance. Upon the utterance of our name God pronounces creation to be not merely "good" but "very good" or "*more* than good," because with the utterance of the name of the soul enters the *humanity* of the soul, of what is *more*, of the meaning of *human*, into this realm. Yes, my children, each of you has your own humanity, your own name, your own help to offer, that no other can bring into this realm. In your humanity lies the "more," the *meod*, in the *tov meod*, the "very good," of God's utterance upon the creation of the human being. For humanity enters this realm only through the human being, only through *you*, my children.

Here is a tale, a tale from the time of the Shoah, to drive home a profound implication of these reflections. The story can be found, with some variations, in several diaries from the Warsaw ghetto. One day a Nazi ventured into the ghetto and was about to take from a Jewish mother her two children. She screamed, cried, and pleaded, "Please, please do not take my children!" To which the Nazi smirked, "I'll tell you what. If you can guess which of my eyes is a glass eye, you may have your children." Without hesitating, the mother answered, "The right eye." To which the Nazi replied, "Why, yes. How could you tell?" And the mother told him, "That one looks more human than the other one." Know, then, my children, that the soul suffers what it inflicts. Treating another as a human being, infinitely precious, our own humanity takes on greater depth. But each time we would dehumanize another, no matter how subtly, we are drained of our own humanity. The Nazis were neither monsters nor beasts; indeed, to deem them beasts is an insult to the animals. They were monstrous and inhumane, but only a human being can become monstrous and inhumane. There are no monsters in the animal kingdom, and there is a reason why "inanimal" is not a word.

Just one more story from the Kingdom of Night, a tale told by another friend, teacher, and survivor of the Holocaust, a man who was an unwilling witness at the Jerusalem trial of Adolf Eichmann: Yechiel De-Nur, the author known as Ka-tzetnik. In the 1970s he went to a clinic in Holland that specialized in treating Holocaust survivors for their nightmares. You see, he had not slept at night for thirty years. While undergoing therapy he had a vision of the day when he was loaded into a truck to be sent to the gas chamber in Birkenau. As he gazed at the sleepy yawn of the SS man who was there to send him to the gas chambers, he wondered: "Does he hate me? He doesn't even know me . . . Do I hate him? I don't even know his name . . . All I know about this German is that on a cold morning he'd certainly prefer snuggling under the covers of his warm bed without having to get up because of some load that has to be delivered to the crematorium."

And a wave of horror washed over him: "He could have been standing here in my place, a naked skeleton being loaded onto the truck, while I, I could have been standing there instead of him!" And he realized: "It's much worse than that he . . . could have been in my place. It's that I—and this is the paralyzing horror—I could have been there in his place!" He realized that here one human being was about to dispatch another to a meaningless murder. He realized that the two of them, dispatcher and dispatched, were both created in the image and likeness of the Holy One! "God did not make Auschwitz. Neither did a devil. It was man. And in making Auschwitz, man made a new image of God." It turns out that the meaning of this life-sustaining word, *human*, is tied to another life-sustaining word: *God*. Indeed, each of these eighteen words that I offer you is inextricably bound to the other. That is how each of them sustains and sanctifies a life with holiness. But where there is holiness, we realize, there is also a seed of horror. The horror? It is this: Not only is each of us, as a human being, responsible for all, but each of is responsible for the *responsibility* of the other.

Responsibility

OUR HUMANITY IS ROOTED in our responsibility. As we infantilize others, relieving them of their responsibility—not due to such tragedies as illness, injury, or other circumstances beyond their control but due to their ethnicity or cultural standing—we dehumanize them and thereby lose our own humanity. Opposite the ruminations of the self-centered, isolated ego, where everything is about *me* and my feelings, we have the Jewish teaching concerning the responsibility of each for all, beginning with *me*. Here my humanity lies not in how deeply I feel but in how profoundly I answer to and for another. In this answering I affirm my answerability, my responsibility, as it exceeds the responsibility of all others. If I am more responsible than all, it does not mean that others bear no responsibility. The principle applies to each and every one of us. But it begins and ends with me.

Thus the confessions we recite in our daily prayer are recited in the plural: *Ashamnu*—"*We* have sinned." This affirmation of *my* responsibility as part of *our* responsibility, is the only antidote to the pandemic of the meaninglessness that sucks forth our humanity. Locked into the isolation of an illusory self, fleeing responsibility as when Adam went into hiding, we languish in mute desperation. Where did he hide? Inside the Tree of Knowledge of Good and Evil, says the Midrash, where he would devise his own good and evil, according to his own knowledge, and free himself of all responsibility, so that he need answer to no one. Thus hidden, he was no longer Adam. To be who I am is to be the one responsible. I come to an understanding of who I am only in the cry of "*Here* I am—for *you*!" This saying of *you*, this *response*, is the key to responsibility.

Increasing the wisdom that adds depth to our humanity, we increase our responsibility. The greater our wisdom, the greater our humanity, and the greater our humanity, the greater our responsibility. Whereas a world inclined toward totalitarianism, woke or otherwise, holds up a final solution and a closing of the ledger, the ethical absolute declares that we are forever in debt and that there is always a summons *yet* to be answered. If the wisdom we receive from what is revealed in the face places us in a relationship with God, it is because the human face opens up the *yet-to-be* settled accounting of responsibility. Responding to the outcry couched in the face of the other, we enter into the time of our life, which is forever future. Indeed, God's identification of himself to Moses as *Ehyeh*, as "I shall be," tells us that God is to be found in the *yet-to-be* of our responsibility, of our movement toward another, offering everyone we meet a kind word or cheerful look or simply saying, "After you." This is why the Talmud commands us to always present a "cheerful countenance" to another. That cheerful countenance can save a life. This is no exaggeration. The question is: shall we be on time for this appointment?

Consider the Hebrew word for "time": *zman*. The Mishnah teaches that when three have sat at the table and eaten bread, they are faced with a duty: *chayavim lezamen*, that is, "they must bench," or *together* say the prayer known as the *Birkat HaMazon*, the "Grace after Meals," literally the "Blessing on What Sustains Us," as these eighteen words sustain us. Therefore when three sit down to share bread, it is incumbent upon them to speak the words of Torah that sustain us. The verb meaning to "say grace after a meal" is *zimen*, a cognate of *zman*, which also means to "invite" or "summon together." Time is an invitation to another. Only one who eats can bear witness to a responsibility to and for another, for only one who eats can snatch the bread from his or her own mouth and offer it to another: the responsibility that lays claim to us is, above all, a responsibility for the *hunger* of another.

Thus the continual assignation that devolves upon each of us, as implied by the word *chayavim* in the phrase *chayavim lezamen*, a word that means to be "obligated" or "compelled," that is, to be responsible, as in Bachya ibn Paquda's *Chovot HaLevavot*, *The Duties of the Heart*, plural because it is the duty to pray and the responsibility to help, again and ever again. What does this responsibility consist of? It is not only to feed the other but to invite the other to pray: the encounter that happens in gathering together to eat harbors a *commandment to pray*. If sharing bread creates a bond with one another, praying together affirms the substance of the bond by affirming the higher relation that sanctifies it. And the higher relation is a relation of responsibility: responsibility is realized in a dimension of height.

Without this responsibility to and for another, we have no yet-to-be and therefore no time, no future, no life. All you have to do in order to get this point, my children, is to take a look at your "schedule," which is a table outlining when you have to be present to another, for another. Perhaps your calendar includes having meals with others, where you might bench the *Birkat HaMazon*. It is that simple and that profound. Languishing in our isolation, we languish in a timelessness void of meaning and of responsibility, empty of any sense of future. For the future lies in this relation to another, in this responsibility that we have forever *yet* to meet. It begins with offering someone something to eat. It is as simple and as profound as that. And how often have you said at the end of a meal, "Won't you have a little more? What, you didn't like the gefilte fish? Have some more kugel." In this simple exchange, in this *more*, there unfolds the miracle and the blessing of an infinite responsibility.

Time devolves where responsibility comes to bear and thus is bared. Inasmuch as our responsibility to our fellow human being is infinite, this responsibility couched in time opens up the eternal. In the face of the other human being, in the hunger of the other human being, the Eternal One is made manifest in the manifestation of our eternal and infinite responsibility: he is manifest as one who is hungry, as one who is thirsty. Recall the story of Mother Teresa. What does it mean? Just this: when we step before the face of another, we come before the face of Another, the One who continually speaks the commandment that comes to us through the face of the other human being *here and now*. If responsibility is always something we have *yet* to meet, it is because it is always *here and now*, in a present that demands our presence.

Time lived lies precisely in this responsibility, which is revealed as a commandment, as a *mitzvah*. As we have seen, the root of *mitzvah* is *tzavta*, which means "connection," and that connection consists of responsibility. Time, says Nachmanides, is made of the Divine question put to the first human being on the first day of his life, which was the sixth day of creation: "Where are you?" Hence the sixth day, not the first day of Creation, is the day when time and responsibility were created. That is why Rosh Hashanah is the anniversary not of the first day of creation but of the sixth day.

Judaism measures time from Rosh Hashanah, the "New Year." It is the Day of Judgment, when the Book of Life is opened, and we stand before the Celestial Tribunal to proclaim our responsibility to and for our fellow human beings, which is where we express our responsibility to and for the Holy One: on that day, his fate, too, is placed in our hands, as he cries out to us, "Return, O Israel, and I shall return!" As he takes us by the hand, we take him by the hand and into our arms to cherish him and protect him, even as we pray for his protection. Nikos Kazantzakis once said that perhaps God is not so almighty after all, that he is as helpless as an infant, like you, my infant grandchildren. And, Kazantzakis said, if we do not love God and nurture him and take care of him, he will die. And so the Book of Life contains the life of God, the God who *is* life. The death for which we are responsible is not only the death of our fellow human being—it is the death of God himself! The covenantal responsibility that delivers us from the horror of meaninglessness is a responsibility for God himself, as we bear in mind his outcry in the *Sifre*: "When you are My witnesses, I am God, but when you are not My witnesses, I am not God." Yes! Our responsibility extends that far! We are responsible not only for human suffering but also for the Divine suffering, as the Divine suffering stems from the human suffering we inflict.

Absurd, this notion that God can suffer? That we might be the saviors of God? Nevertheless! Only the suffering of God can make human suffering *matter*. If the claim that God can suffer in the collisions with evil is an absurdity—if the teaching that we might be the saviors of God is an absurdity, as when Isaiah declares, "In all their suffering, He suffers"—then the God of Abraham and the prophets is an absurdity. And if that is the case, then the Divine prohibition against murder is an absurdity. Then none of us is responsible for anyone but ourselves, if that, as we choose or choose not to choose, curled up in the false haven of the Tree of Knowledge. If God's suffering is an absurdity, it is an absurdity that we desperately need.

Here, in the infinite suffering of the Infinite One, lies the infinite in the infinite responsibility that lies at the core of our humanity. To "hear, O Israel, *HaShem* our God, *HaShem* is one" is to hear the outcry, the pain and the suffering, the loneliness and despair, that pours forth from God through the lips of our fellow human being. In that cry lies the cry of our suffering God, the God who suffers because he loves and because he, yes *he*, feels responsible for us. I am reminded of a story about the great Hasidic master Rebbe Barukh of Medzebozh. His grandson Yehiel, a little one like you, my grandchildren, went to him one day crying because he was playing hide-and-seek with his friends, and when he hid, no one looked for him. His grandfather answered: "God too is unhappy; He is hiding and man is not looking for him. Do you understand, Yechiel? God is hiding and man is not even searching for Him . . . !" So you know how God feels, too.

God's responsibility as the God of the Covenant is our responsibility. And if we are to love, then in our love we take on a responsibility for all suffering, both human and Divine. This is where the suffering soul prays for the sake of God's suffering, for the God who, in his loneliness, alone as no other is alone, suffers both through our transgression and through the suffering by which this transgression might be expiated. I have noted that the real problem confronting us is not suffering but meaningless suffering. This responsibility that guides us in our search for redemption is what delivers us from meaningless suffering. For redemption is redemption from meaningless suffering. Redemption is the realization of meaning. And our responsibility for the suffering of another is a responsibility for meaning.

The Talmud tells us that God suffers with the human being, with the child of God, much more than that person himself feels it. Those of you who are parents, my children, know what it is to suffer in the suffering of your children, God forbid. Whereas Rabbi Yose heard a Divine Voice like the "cooing of a dove," we know from Jeremiah 25:30 that "God roars, howling over His city," over *Yerushalayim*, the city whose name is one of His Divine Names: just as there are seventy names of God and seventy names of Torah, so are there seventy names of Jerusalem. His Holy City is His *Shekhinah*, the body of Israel. How does God roar? Through the cry of his people, through the screams of "Mama" that reverberate throughout the camps and ghettos and shatter the souls of the Jews, through screams that threaten to undermine the very fabric of creation. Rabbi Kalonymos Kalmish Shapira, Rebbe of the Warsaw Ghetto, writes in horror, writes *through* his horror: "It is a marvel how the world exists after so much screaming." Each of us, in all honesty, knows how those screams reach into our soul and implicate us. That is why we cannot bear to even read about those screams. Hence the responsibility of each for all is a responsibility for creation itself, a responsibility for every scream.

The aspect of the soul that would be there for the sake of another belongs to another, provokes a responsibility, often against my will, as when I receive a summons: "Someone is asking for you, *by name*," as when we are called to the Torah by name. There lies the meaning of chosenness: to be chosen is to be chosen for a responsibility that precedes all of my other choices and therefore makes all my other choices *matter*. It is an answerability that insists upon an answer *now*. Thus to have meaning is to be answerable, and to be answerable is to be chosen, so that the other who lays claim to me from within and from beyond—the one whose presence emanates from the human face—is God, who through the Jewish people proclaims that every human being is chosen for one responsibility *more*. Invoking this "more," God commands me to love him *bekol-meodekha*, "with all your 'more,'" precisely by loving the neighbor and the stranger. The *more* with which I love is a messianic more. Thus we have the Jewish teaching that in addition to a trace of the soul of Adam, every soul harbors a spark of the soul of the Messiah, the Anointed One of the house of David. Thus every soul harbors a messianic responsibility.

From a Jewish standpoint, Messianism is not an abstraction concerning the "end times," but a matter of concrete urgency here and now, a matter of my responsibility: if the Messiah has not arrived, then I must turn not to God but to my own responsibility. *My* next act of loving kindness, *my* next *mitzvah*, just might be enough to put us over the top: salvation is *at every moment* possible. I do not await the coming of the Messiah—I *expect* it, *anticipate* it, *work* for it, even *insist* upon it. Even as I cry out to God, "How long, O Lord, how long?!" so he cries out to me, "How long, Avraham David ben Avraham, how long?!" Each of us is blessed with a commandment to act, in an affirmation of a messianic responsibility, as though each of us were the Messiah. Messianism lies in my responsibility to bear the suffering of all. So what about the literal meaning of the Messiah, the scion of David, whose coming we pray for three times a day? It is all too literal, more literal than we wish to think: *I* am the one who must take upon myself the messianic task and testimony—literally. *I* am the one who must attend to the care of the widow, the orphan, and the stranger—literally. *I* am the one whose bears responsibility for creation and humanity—literally.

In my infinite responsibility for God and the other human being, time and eternity merge in a surpassing of the horizons of my birth and death. That, my children, is why I take up this ethical will. Whether or not I shall be alive when you read it remains to be seen and really does not matter. Indeed, I am sure that my grandchildren among you will not read it until after I am gone. So be it. I give all thanks to God for allowing me the hour of offering you these words. May these words also be inherited by my grandchildren's grandchildren and their grandchildren. And yet, I shall be with you, watching over you, responsible for you over the generations. I shall be there in your prayers when you lie down and when you rise up and in the Kaddish you will say for me. I am reminded of a teaching from the greatest Jewish philosopher of the last century, Emmanuel Levinas: "To be *for* a time that would be without me, *for* a time after my time, over and beyond the celebrated 'being for death,' is not an ordinary thought which is extrapolating from my own duration; it is the passage to the time of the other. Should what makes such a passage possible be called *eternity*?" Eternity? Yes. This living for a time beyond my time is called responsibility, perhaps a synonym for eternity. Like the soul, it extends into the immemorial past and into the fathomless future.

This "being for a time after my time" is precisely what it means to live and ultimately die for the sake of another, by living out my responsibility to and for another unto the end, creating angels through my thoughts, words, and deeds, who will go into the world and into the upper worlds and to their work, now and forever. In this living responsibility we have the very project of redemption, where the redemption that I must bring about for humanity is a redemption of the Holy One himself. If "the salvation of God is identical with the salvation of Israel," as it is written in the Midrash, it is because the messianic presence of the Holy One in this realm rests upon Israel's responsibility for the task of humanity's redemption for which every Jew is chosen. The messianic responsibility does not lie with people of Israel alone: the Talmud teaches that each soul who enters this world must accomplish the task for which it was created in order to open the way for "the son of

David." Once each soul has met that task for which he or she was created, the Messiah will become manifest.

And so with the measure of the messianic time we return to the measure of time itself, the measure of our days, which is the measure of our responsibility. Remember that on the sixth day God declares creation to be not just "good" but *tov meod*, that is, "*very* good" or "good and *more*." This "more" is embodied in the human being who is *more* than being because each human being has one responsibility *more* than all others. Through human responsibility to and for the other human being *time* enters being, and with it meaning enters being. It is not good for the human being to be alone, because it is not good for the human being to be without meaning, without this responsibility. In order for a human being to be who he *is*, he must become *better* than he is. That is to say, he must *change*. For no other creature is change or becoming better such an issue. The animals are what they are, fulfilled in what they are, and therein find their perfection. The beginning of the "year" or the *shanah* is the beginning of the "change" or *shinui* that introduces time into creation through human relation rooted in human responsibility: responsibility is transforming. That is why it is humanizing.

Only in relation to the other human being, who transcends the coordinates of space and time, do we *have* time, for only in the relation to the other person does the eternal come to bear. Having time, I have life, that is to say, I live. Living out my time, I draw nigh unto the other, which is a movement into the future, a movement of response and responsibility. Hence the more I answer, the more I am responsible; the more I approach the neighbor with whom I am entrusted, like a child turned over to my care, the further away I am. This debt which increases in the measure that it is paid is the infinity enfolded within the finite flesh-and-blood human being who now stands before me. Here lies eternity, without which we have no time: there is no time divorced from eternity. To assert that I have no time is to assert that I have no life, no responsibility to and for another, that I have only the horrific isolation of my own pitiful being.

As I draw nigh unto another, I realize that I had always been called and that I am eternally too late. In this "too-late" time and the other merge in the one task *more* that I must *yet* perform for the sake of the other. What is the ultimate task that I face in the face-to-face relation with the other? It is dying for the other. Or better: it is choosing my own death over the death of the other. That is where the infinite in my infinite responsibility shows itself. Most of the time this dying for the sake of another does not mean throwing myself on a hand grenade. No, it means something even more difficult: it means devoting my life to another, to others, day by day, even unto death.

From the standpoint of Jewish teaching, the death that concerns me is the death of the other person, so that time lies not in the realization that I shall die, that no one gets out alive, but is precisely a being *against* the death of the other person. We have all wondered what the great philosophers have wondered: "Why is there something instead of nothing?" That there is something—that there is all of *this*—is, to be sure, a source of wonder. It reminds me of a remark I once heard from an astronomer, who said that every night he gazes upon the heavens and contemplates whether or not we are alone in the universe. "Either way," he said, "the prospect is mind boggling." And so it is. But the question that haunts us in our humanity and responsibility is not "Why does all of this exist" but "Do I live by killing? Does my life come at the expense of someone else's life?" Like Private Ryan, whose life was purchased at the expense of other lives. One of the most powerful moments in cinema comes at the end of *Saving Private Ryan*, when, after his tale has unfolded on the screen, he stands up in the midst of the military cemetery in Normandy and asks his wife, his voice shaking with desperation: "Have I been a good man?" All of us, my children, are Private Ryan. Like Private Ryan, we are responsible for the dead, the living, and those yet unborn. If we have no ethical responsibility to the dead, then we have no ethical responsibility to the living or to the yet unborn.

In Judaism, too, the question of whether our lives come at the cost of other lives comes to bear. We see this in the Talmudic teaching that, even if it means our own death, we must refuse to murder another person. Refusing to commit murder even at the cost of our own lives is a *Kiddush HaShem*, a "Sanctification of the Name," through the affirmation of an absolute responsibility that I have *to* the other *before* God. Refusing to murder the other human being even if it means my own death situates the other in a dimension of height, above me, more dear than I. Only where the other is revealed in this aspect of height do we have the revelation of the Holy One as the Most High. So we see on a deeper level—on a *higher* level—what it means to say that I have one responsibility *more* than the other. We see on a deeper level what it means to say time is made of this "more," because the responsibility to be met for the sake of the other human being is one responsibility *more*, to be met *once more*, forever *yet* to be accomplished. The famed French philosopher Albert Camus once declared that there is only one serious philosophical problem, and that is suicide. To which Rabbi Abraham Joshua Heschel answered, "No, the one serious philosophical problem confronting us is martyrdom." The one serious philosophical problem confronting us is the question of our responsibility.

Not surprisingly, this teaching that I bequeath to you can be found in the Hebrew word for "responsibility": *acharayut*, whose root *acher* means "other." This Hebrew word confirms what I have tried to convey, namely that the responsibility that lays claim to me comes not from within myself, not from what I think or how I feel, but it descends upon me from on high, as revealed in the face of the other human being. Because only *I* can meet *this* responsibility, my responsibility is what defines who I am. Which means: I am the "not-I"—the "other," the *acher* in my *acharayut*. That is why when I fail in my *acharayut*, I become *acher* to myself, "other" than who I am, hence absent from my fellow human being. Absent from my fellow human being, I have no time, a point underscored by the verb *achar*, meaning to "be late," to "tarry," or to "lag behind," and by the noun *acharit*, which means "end" or "future." The other human being *is* my end, *is* my future—*is* my meaning. Hence only through the responsibility that defines me do I generate a presence before the other, where I have time because I am on time—for the *relationship* that decides who I am.

Relationship

No human being can live for too many years without feeling alone. It is one of the earliest signs of a despair that creeps into our soul, of what Søren Kierkegaard called "the sickness unto death." Despair is, indeed, a sickness of the soul, a sickness that befalls every soul at one time or another. A sickness *unto* death, it is a sickness that we cannot die away from, as it devours us from within and leaves us no exit. In despair we are desperate to be other than who we are, deaf and blind to the truth that who we are can be realized only within a relationship, and never in the isolation of our illusory self. If you are old enough to read this, my children, I know you have endured the pain of such a feeling. It makes my heart ache for you. My hope, my prayer, is that these words might help you to feel a little less alone in times when you feel utterly alone—or even worse, God forbid, abandoned.

More than a longing for company, loneliness is a longing to share when it seems there is no one to share *with*, no one to be *with*. It is a solitude in which you hear no one and no one can hear you, not even your outcry. It is not necessarily that no one else is around: it is, rather, that no one can understand, no one can connect, or no one cares. In such an anguished hour words fail, and so you take to writing poetry, just as you may write poetry when you are filled with a love that surpasses words. Wherever relationship comes to bear, in its absence or in its presence, words fail. They fail because the relationship is *prior to* words: the words do not issue from the relationship, but rather the relationship gives rise to words. In the beginning is the relation, as Martin Buber says. And so I offer you these eighteen words precisely because words fail. Above all, they fail to be understood, even as I seek to help you understand these eighteen words as best I can, knowing that there is always more to said, an inexhaustible depth to be fathomed.

Professor Wiesel once said of the prophet Elijah, "When he is alone, he is the loneliest creature on earth; when surrounded by crowds, he is even lonelier." It is one thing to be able to sit alone in the solitude of your room or on a beach or in a forest, where you gather your thoughts and your strength, where you might take stock of your soul. Someone once said to me that an hour in the forest is worth six weeks on a psychiatrist's couch. But then there is the crowd, which is the opposite of a community: to be alone in the midst of the madding crowd is quite another matter. The loneliness in the midst of a crowd lies in the anonymity and namelessness that define the crowd: crammed together shoulder to shoulder, we are miles apart from each other.

Think of how much you love hearing your beloved say your name, of how pleased you are when someone remembers your name. Relationship inheres in a memory and a name. You can see why something as mundane as the lyrics to the theme song of the television sitcom *Cheers* might have such a powerful appeal:

> Sometimes you want to go
> Where everybody knows your name
> And they're always glad you came
> You want to be where you can see
> Our troubles are all the same
> You want to be where everybody knows your name

You want to be where you feel less lonely. You want to be where you are *recognized*, greeted by name, like Norm. You might be thinking: "You quote the great sages of our tradition, and now you bring in a TV jingle?" Well, yes. Everything around us has its Torah, its depth dimension, its secret side, and there is a reason for the popular appeal of these lines. The reason lies in the soul's longing for *relationship*, without which it suffocates. So we take a break and smile at the opening lines of the *Cheers* theme song, ready to laugh at Sam, as he goes through one frustrated conquest after another. In his desire to possess another, he is bereft and beggared, like Phil in *Groundhog Day*: not until Phil was oriented toward another for the sake of another, rather than for himself, could he find a kind of redemption from meaninglessness through relationship and a return to time: if time is the dimension of meaning, it is the dimension of relationship.

Loneliness is, in some ways, fundamental to the human condition. "In the beginning," Professor Wiesel has said, "man is alone. Alone as God is alone. As he opens his eyes he does not ask: Who am I? He asks: Who are you?" And yet elsewhere Wiesel writes, "When he opened his eyes, Adam did not ask God: Who are *you*? He asked: Who am *I*?" A contradiction? No. For the soul that comes to life in the midst of a relationship, there is no *I* without the *You*. Just as this is true of the human being, so is it true of the Creator: when he says you, he reveals himself as I, as *Anokhi*, which is the first word of revelation uttered at Mount Sinai, the utterance that, according to the *Mekilta de-Rabbi Ishmael*, corresponds to "In the beginning . . ." God's utterance of "I" at the time of the revelation signifies his pronouncement of you at the time of the Creation. It is a cry of "I" that means "I am lonely for you."

This question—whether "Who are you?" or "Who am I?"—is steeped in a desire not for another but to be there *for the sake of* another. So we realize something more about the meaning of God's pronouncement that "it is not good for the man to be alone": it is not good for God to be alone. Just as God is there for the sake of the human being, so is the human being there for the sake of God. Each needs the other in order to overcome the horrific solitude and intensity of self that each one endures. Herman Melville once noted that when sailors on a ship bathe at sea, they stay very close to the ship, even if they are expert swimmers, because they cannot stand the intense concentration of self in the midst of such a heartless immensity, in the midst of a pitiless infinity. So it is with God and man. Yes, even with God. As we have seen, when God cries out to Adam, "*Ayeka!?* Where are you!? How could you!?" he is crying out in the pain of the loneliness he suffers over Adam's fall from their relationship. You recall in the opening pages of this ethical will my remark that God created humanity because he loves tales, for tales are the stuff of relationship. Tales alone overcome the isolation of loneliness. As relationship rests upon the ineffable, so do tales give voice to the ineffable.

Therefore the *Sifre*, an ancient commentary on the book of Deuteronomy, tells us that if we would know the One who spoke and brought heaven and earth into being, then we must know the *Aggadah*, the tales of Torah and tradition. Why? Because God's utterance of the Torah from which everything is created is the utterance of a tale. The ancient Kabbalistic text known as the *Sefer Yetzirah* teaches that God created heaven and earth with three things: *sefer*, *sefar*, and *sipur*, that is, with a book, an accounting, and storytelling. "In the beginning there was the word," Elie Wiesel states it. "The word was the tale of man; and man is the tale of God." So the word that sustains creation is a tale told by both God and man, the tale that establishes a *relationship*. Both man and God are made of the tale, of the *Aggadah*, that is Torah. Buried in the silence of Sinai is *Aggadah*—the Talmud, Midrash, and Kabbalah that form the Oral Torah and that incorporate the tales of the sacred Jewish tradition. One of the remarkable aspects of the Torah, in fact, is that it includes the tale of the Torah itself, as related in the book of Deuteronomy. Why does Moses relate this tale? Because it is essential to our relationship with God and with one another, the relationship that sustains the life of the soul.

Exchanging tales—*relating* tales—is how we enter into the relationship that enables us to break free from the horrific isolation of our being.

Think about it. When you first meet someone and you are trying to get to know each other better, what do you do? You relate your stories. You tell the tales that belong to the substance of who and how you became who you are and who you aspire to become. That is how you create a relationship, both to the other human being and to God. For each time you relate your tale to another, a Third party is present, listening, witnessing, as you bear your witness through your storytelling. Yes: to tell a tale is to bear witness. That is why relating tales has redemptive power, as we see from a Hasidic tale about storytelling.

As the story is told, when the Baal Shem Tov was confronted with a calamity threatening the Jewish community, he knew just what to do. He would slip off into the forest to a special place, where he would light a fire in a particular manner and say a prayer that he kept for just such emergencies. Having completed this ritual, the miracle of deliverance was accomplished, and the community was saved.

A generation later, the task of petitioning the Holy One for the miracle of deliverance fell to the Baal Shem's disciple, Rabbi Dov Ber, the Maggid of Mezeritch. Like the Baal Shem before him, the Maggid would go off to a certain place in the forest, where he would cry out, "Oh, Lord, King of the Universe, hear me! Though I know the place in the forest, I do not know how to light the fire. Nevertheless my teacher taught me the prayer. And this must be sufficient!" And so it was: the miracle of deliverance was accomplished, and the community of Israel was saved.

After the great Maggid had gone to join his fathers and mothers, Rabbi Moshe-Leib of Sassov was entrusted with the task of intercession. Whenever catastrophe threatened the Jews, he would seek out the very same place in the forest where his masters before him had uttered their prayers. "Oh, Lord, King of the Universe, hear me!" he would cry out. "I cannot kindle the fire of the Baal Shem, and I never learned the prayer that he and the Great Maggid offered up to You. But, as You can see, I do know the secret place in the forest. And this must be sufficient." And so it was.

Finally the responsibility for seeking deliverance fell to Rabbi Yisrael of Rizhin. And yet, even as the winds of destruction were about to sweep over the community, Rabbi Yisrael stood in his study as though paralyzed, his head buried in his hands. In his despair he did not cry out but spoke hardly above a whisper, saying, "Oh, Lord, King of the Universe, have mercy! The secret of the Baal Shem's ritual of fire and his prayer for salvation are long forgotten. Here I stand before You, unable even to find the place in the forest. All I can do is tell the story. And this must be sufficient." And so it was: having told the tale of the fire and the prayer and the place in the forest, Rabbi Yisrael found the salvation he sought for the sake of the community. Having related the tale, he sustained the relationship that lies at the core of redemption.

In the Zohar it is written that there are three levels of speech: speaking (*ledaber*), saying (*l'emor*), and relating (*lehagid*). We can speak truths or lies; we can speak languages. And we can say anything that comes to mind, sometimes regretting what we happen to say. Speaking and saying, then, come from the surface, not from the depth of the soul. But relating comes from the depths of our being, in the effort to enter into a relationship with another. Relating a tale is a calling of deep unto deep, of soul unto soul, of soul unto God. To transmit a tale is to transmit a portion of one's soul. The soul in me is the tale in me. When God breathes a living soul into Adam, he breathes into him the tale that constitutes his soul, the tale of Torah, a tale that I have sought out in each of you when you were babies, a tale you related in your babbling before you had time to forget the tale that the angels had taught you, the tale of God himself. Thus tales are transmitted not mouth to ear but mouth to mouth. To receive a tale is to become part of the tale, which happens when we transmit the tale in turn: to receive a tale is to become a storyteller by virtue of our relationship to another. Created in the image and likeness of the Holy One, the human being not only *speaks*—he or she *relates* tales, seeking out a relationship with another human being, another human soul.

Those of you who have children and who were children, my little ones, know how much children love stories. Having babbled to you their own tale of Torah, they long to hear stories in turn. There is another song that comes to mind, one that you may recall from when you were little:

> Tell me a story,
> Tell me a story before I go to bed,
> You said you would if I'd be good,
> And I've been good, you said you would,
> So tell me a story before I go to bed.

I can hear you singing it even now. The memory brings a tear to my eye. You sang the song, and I tried to come up with a story, often the story of one of our pets whom you loved, like Sologdin the cat or Daisy the dog. Remember?

There is depth here, too, in these simple moments.

Judaism in general and Hasidism in particular rest upon the human relationship that transcends the isolation of the soul. "A Hasid alone is not a true Hasid," Wiesel teaches us. "Solitude and Hasidism are incompatible." Thus, he adds, "Hasidism tore down the walls that exist between

God and man, creation and creature, thought and deed, past and present, reality and soul: the secret lay in oneness," in the oneness of a relationship, in which inheres the oneness of God. Solitude is not a solution, and there is a solution to solitude. In our tradition everything turns on relationship. Creation is a movement into relationship. The pervasive commandments to love—to love God, neighbor, and above all the stranger—is the commandment to live within a relationship, else we have no life. God could not endure being alone, and so he created. There is no God apart from relationship, where the relationship with God finds its expression in the relationship with our fellow human being, *ben adam leMakom* and *ben adam lechevero*. Relationship is central.

The Holy One enters this realm through the between-space of human-to-human relation. For only through that between-space can understanding and insight open up. Hence the Talmud's insistence on friendship as the one thing most essential to human life. No one understands you like your friend understands you. Like my friend Luis. I can tell him anything, and he can tell me anything, without fear of being judged and with the assurance that each of us will understand the other. That is what relationship is about: not only loving each other but *understanding* each other.

Know, then that the Hebrew word for "understanding," *binah*, has the same root as the word *bein*, which means "between," so that meaning or understanding transpires in a relationship *between* two—not just between above and below but also between human and human, beginning with the relationship between mother and child. No one loves you like your mama loves you. You know this, my children. Even if, at times, your mother makes you crazy. I have spoken about the soul's longing to be understood. God, too, longs to be understood, as an infant longs to be understood. Those of you who are mothers know exactly what I am talking about. You understand me. You, too, will make your babies crazy, precisely because there is no one closer to them than you are. As those babies babble, all of the sages would be at a loss as to what they are saying, but you, their mama, understand.

Once again, we see that all of creation, including the creation of every babbling baby's soul that enters this realm, rests upon a relationship. Where meaning in life is concerned, we indeed seek understanding, yes, but we long for more than understanding—we long for the depth and dearness of a relationship to another: we long to love. Here we discover the purpose of our lives: it is to transcend the terrifying silence of isolation through the "Here I am for you" of a loving relationship: only by drawing another out of his or her isolation am I delivered from my own isolation, which is the isolation of a tomb. The purpose of our lives, in other words, is to transform the bread we eat into love by offering bread to another.

And if our responsibility to and for another is a messianic responsibility, as I explained in the previous chapter, in our relationship to another lies the key to redemption. Every encounter quickens the steps of the Redeemer, for in every encounter, in every relationship, we draw meaning into what is otherwise a meaningless and empty wasteland. Only through this transcendence of loneliness, only through a relationship to another, do we come to a realization of what there is to love and of what must be done, of why we live and why we die—and what is at stake.

I have explained that the movement of creation is a movement into a relationship. As God moves into this covenantal relationship he is himself transformed, the Infinite One delivered from his infinite isolation. The Kabbalists tell us that in this move God, as it were, becomes God, *Elokim*, the word used to refer to God as the Creator. They read *bara Elokim*, "created God," as the nameless *Ein Sof*, the Infinite One, undertaking a movement from which God, *Elokim*, would emerge. In this word for "God," *Elokim*, we have the secret of relationship. The Zohar elaborates:

> When the most Mysterious wished to reveal Himself, He first produced a single point which was transmuted into a thought, and in this He executed innumerable designs, and engraved innumerable engravings. He further engraved with the sacred and mystic lamp a mystic and most holy design, which was a wondrous edifice issuing from the midst of thought. This is called *Mi*, or "Who," and was the beginning of the edifice, existent and non-existent, deep buried, unknowable by name. It was only called *Mi*. It desired to become manifest and to be called by name. It therefore clothed itself in a refulgent and precious garment and created *Eleh*, or "These," and *Eleh* acquired a name. The letters of the two words intermingled, forming the complete name *E-l-o-k-i-m*.

While the teaching that *God created* is a first principle of Torah and Judaism, God is neither a First Principle nor a First Cause—God is a *Who*, and not a *What*.

There is no entering into a covenantal relationship with a principle or a cause. No one ever cried out, "Father!" to the Aristotelean First Principle, nor did Abraham enter into a dispute over the righteous of Sodom and Gomorrah to try to move the Unmoved Mover. Because creation entails a movement into a covenantal relationship, Judaism is concerned not with *what caused* the world but with *who created* it, from beyond being, and how we are to view our relationship to the Creator. The prayerful phrase "Who is like You," which Moses prayed upon crossing the sea, is not just a rhetorical question—it is an affirmation: precisely the *Who* is what resembles God, and each time we enter into a relationship with a *who*, we entered into a relationship with God, with *Elokim*. Without the emergence of this *who* of a relationship, there is no saying *you* to another. Here lies the reason behind Martin Buber's declaration that in every human you we encounter the Eternal You.

Here we would do well to recall another teaching from the Zohar: instead of reading *Bereshit bara Elokim et ha-* . . . as "In the beginning God created the . . . ," the Zohar reads it as "In the beginning God created the *alef, tav, hey* of *atah*: You." The Zohar explains: "The word *et* consists of the letters *alef* and *tav*, which include between them all the letters, as being the first and last of the alphabet. Afterwards *hey* was added, so that all the letters should be attached to *hey*, and this gave the name *atah* (You)." Only a *who*—only one who bears a name and not an essence or a number, only a unique one—can say *you* and be addressed as *you*, in an affirmation of the relationship that decides the meaning of our lives.

Where there is no *who* there is no *why*: relationship is the medium of meaning. Hence the stark reality with which Primo Levi collided in the camp: *Hier ist kein warum*—"Here there is no Why." There is no Why because there is no Who, no relationship in this anti-world where everyone was ferociously alone, where everyone around you was either an enemy or a rival, where everything in the anti-world was *hostile* to every human relationship. That is how the Nazis set out to murder souls before murdering bodies. In the act of creation, then, the Creator is revealed not as an authoritarian power that would be as god but as one who, opposite the anti-creation that was the anti-world, says, "you," with care, concern, and kindness. From beyond being he summons heaven and earth into being, giving renewed meaning to his cry of "Where are *you*?" The very presence of a *Who* in the midst of being, the *Who* that constitutes a relationship, is a transcendence of being.

This entry of more than all into the midst of all transpires every day, every hour, in every relationship, every friendship. It is to be found in this writing of my ethical will, as I now urge you: be a friend. Seek out a friend. Make just one person less lonely, just for a moment, and you will be less lonely. So will God. Relate to your friend the tale of your life and, even more importantly, listen carefully and responsively to his or her tale. Relationship lies in the face and in the eyes, caring and attentive. It lies in the offering of a smile, in the giving hand that reaches out. That is what all of this esoteric, Kabbalistic reflection amounts to: the simple gesture of one hand reaching out to another, as God's hand reaches out to Adam in Michelangelo's famous painting. The force, the living presence, behind that reach that is the substance of every relationship, high and low? It is love.

Love

All of us have loved. Loving another belongs to our humanity. We have been in love, we love our family, we love our friends, we love our parents, and we love our children. We have known the fiery flame and the slow burn of love. It takes hold of us, like a living presence arising from beyond us, sometimes in spite of us. But who among us can say what this enigmatic word means? We say the words "I love you," we long to say those words, and we long to hear them said, no matter where they come from. There is perhaps no word in the language more widely used, abused, and misunderstood than the word *love*. And yet without this word, we are without meaning, mission, and life.

There is romantic love, brotherly love, and parental love. There is love for food, for leisure, and even love for life. Christians often note the four Greek words for "love" that appear in their Scriptures: *eros*, *storge*, *philia*, and *agape*, referring to romantic love, family love, brotherly love, and Divine love respectively. From a Jewish perspective, God's love runs throughout all of this, throughout every manifestation of true love, which is a willingness to die for another, gladly and with gratitude. As we have seen, God creates through wisdom, and where there is Divine wisdom there is Divine love. If creation is a movement into a relationship, it is a movement of love or *chesed* in Hebrew, and *chesed* emanates from *chokhmah* or wisdom. Nothing can stir us to action like love. It stirred the Holy One to act, to create, in all his wisdom, through his wisdom. Where there is wisdom, there is love: a wise person is a loving person.

In the Psalms it is written that God creates all things through wisdom. Created through wisdom, all of creation is permeated with love, is teeming with love, a love offered, received, and summoned. To that offering and that summons belongs the true meaning and miracle of love. Yes, a *miracle*: there is no miracle apart from the miracle and the manifestation of love. Like faith, love does not arise from the miracle but the miracle from love. Every time your mother or father, you grandmother or grandfather, comes to visit you, it is a miracle—not because they do not want to but because they are driven to be with you. For love has taken hold of them and guided them, lovingly, like a living presence that has entered them from beyond them.

We are awash in love in certain miraculous moments in our lives, like when we hold an infant in our arms, when we are overwhelmed with a love for God's creation, in a merging of love and awe. In those moments we know the meaning of *love*. We gaze into those eyes, bask in the radiance of that smile, and we are inundated with wonder at the love that abounds all around us. Those eyes and that smile are the eyes of creation that tell us, miraculously, that we are loved. I have seen your love for me in your eyes, my children, and I am in utter awe: How can anyone love *me* like this? How can *I* merit such love? Can it be real? But then love does not come through any such calculation, like a business transaction. That is what makes it so miraculous. For many of us, the most difficult truth to grasp is that we are *loved*. Loved how? By whom? Why? How can this little one I hold in my arms love *me*? How can anyone love *me*? How can God love *me*? And yet . . .

Love is never deserved or merited. Beyond weight and measure, beyond any balancing of the scales, it is beyond any calculation of what can be deserved. Indeed, merit does not enter into the equation, because there is no equation: nothing is equal to love because love is the infinite contained within the finite, and the infinite comes in small packages. Do you understand, my children? Love binds one soul to another in an overlapping of souls, from time immemorial, from the depths of the eternal, surpassing the contingencies of time. It shines in the *or pnimi* and in the *or makif*, in the light that lies within the soul and in the surrounding light that exceeds the soul and yet belongs to the soul. This is why we are commanded to love with all our soul: as the soul is made of love, so we love with all our soul.

Love is the breath breathed into the soul to bring it to life. Love is not a feeling. Feelings we have within us, but love is a living presence that abides *between* two. All sorts of feelings swirl about within us, like the weather, but they are strung like pearls along the string and stirring of love. Feelings ranging from joy and delight to anger and frustration can issue from love. There are times when, at our wits' end, we shout to someone we love, "I hate you" (God forbid), a shout of emotion uttered in the moment that would erupt only to someone we love. And immediately we regret our careless, hurtful words. For words can hurt only someone we love and who loves us, and words uttered can never be taken back. They are out there, with all the evil angels our words create. Therefore love demands a caring vigilance over our words. Yes, love, the greatest of all blessings—because it *is* the greatest of all blessings—can also result in the greatest of regrets.

Even though two people who love each other may be separated by vast tracts of space and time, love lives between them and collapses those distances, for the living presence of love transcends space and time, even centuries. There is no love in isolation, outside of a relationship: self-love is a deadly illusion because it blinds us to the face of the other. Do not buy into the fashionable lie, my children, that if you do not love yourself, you cannot love others. Love lives only in the relationship. That relationship can arise between souls who knew each other long ago, perhaps in a previous life, or between souls destined to meet again, here and now. Yes, love is *destined.* Love summons us to our destiny, which is always by design.

Destiny is the opposite of fate, as opposite as meaning is to emptiness or as redemption is to doom. Whereas fate strikes us dumb, destiny or *yiud* demands a "testimony," an *edah.* Destiny lies in being chosen for the sake of another, chosen to love another, in the light of which we must now make a choice. It is the *yiud* that belongs to *yaad*, which is "mission," "purpose," or "aim." Without love we have no purpose. To love is to have a purpose for which we are chosen and to which we attest. You all know this, my children. But sometimes we have to articulate what we know, so that we may truly know it.

Do not confuse self-respect with self-esteem or self-love. Self-respect arises through respect for others, whose respect, in turn, we strive to earn. What, indeed, can it possibly mean to love yourself? Do you say to yourself, "I love you"? To whom do you offer thanks? Whom do you hug? To whom do you offer a kind word or a piece of bread? Do you offer up your life for yourself? Do you extend your hand to the mirror, like Narcissus gazing into the pool, where, in the end, he starved to death, beggared by his abundance? As in the case of Narcissus transfixed by the image in the pool, there is no You of an I-You relation here. There is no relation. There is no love. There is only the illusion, always empty and often deadly.

Where there is life, there is love—again, not as a feeling but as a giving, a giving to another, even unto death, whether we feel like it or not—especially when we do not feel like it. That is why love is commanded. The Hebrew word for "love" is *ahavah*; its root *hav* means to "give." The commandment to love our neighbor is "*Veahavta lereakha k'mokha*—You shall love your neighbor as yourself." According to the Baal Shem Tov, this commandment—this giving relationship—is the basis of the entire Torah. If we examine the Hebrew word *k'mokha*, "as yourself," as well as the *le-* in *lereakha*, "your neighbor," a better translation would be: "You shall show love *toward* your neighbor, for that loving relation, that giving relation, *is* who you are." The soul "has" only as much life, only as much love, as it *gives*: life and love are not diminished but rather grow in the giving. Life and love are one.

The commandment is followed by the phrase *Ani HaShem*, "I am the Lord," indicating that the human love and the higher love are of a piece.

With the collapse of the human relation comes the collapse of the higher relation. How to show God our love for him? By giving a piece of bread to another, for in the hunger of the other aches the hunger of God, as we have seen. Yes, God, too, hungers, hungers for a relationship: a suffering God is a hungry God. Without the relation of love for another human being we have no relation to or love for God. And God goes hungry.

Hence the Nazis' determination that the human being would be ferociously alone, without father or son, friend or brother, mother or sister, and thus rendered inhuman. Only within a loving human relation, says Sforno, can the purpose of our being created in the image and likeness of the Holy One be realized: to live in that image is to live in a loving relation to another, for the sake of another. Ultimately, it is to make our dying part of our living, by dying for the sake of another. In the relation to our fellow human being we have life; therefore it is good. What is *lo-tov*, "not good," is being alone in the isolation of our illusory ego: alone, the human being has no identity, no name, and—what is the same thing—no love to offer.

While the commandment to love our neighbor may be the basis of the entire Torah, the commandment most frequently repeated in the Torah—thirty-six times—is the commandment to love and care for the stranger. The late Rabbi Jonathan Sacks, one of the great sages of recent times, writes, "We encounter God in the face of the stranger. That is, I believe, the Hebrew Bible's single greatest and most counterintuitive contribution to ethics. The human other is a trace of the Divine Other." Because the Divine Other is the most radically Other, no Other is stranger than God. To approach the living God, to come before the living God, to fall into the hands of the living God, is to have our every preconception about God, everything we had presumed to know about him, undone. God is strange because God's love for us surpasses all that is familiar to us, all thought, all reason, all rumination.

Because God is most radically the stranger, he is most radically encountered in the stranger. That is why the commandment to see to the care of the stranger is Judaism's single greatest and most counterintuitive contribution to ethics, for in this ethical relation we have the meaning of a loving relation: to be ethical is to love, and to love is to be ethical. Ethics has nothing to do with categorical imperatives or philosophical deductions and everything to do with loving, especially when loving comes hardest. The commandment is repeated so frequently because it is the first commandment we are prone to forget. I do not have to be reminded so often to love my neighbor, the one who is like me, who shares my outlook on the world. He is my buddy. He is a regular at my table. His political and religious views are the same as mine. We watch the games together, and together we enjoy a beer now and then. But the stranger? The one who does not look like me or think like me, who speaks with a weird accent that I have trouble understanding, the one whom I regard as a nonbeliever and politically backward if not barbarous? I need to be repeatedly reminded to love him or her.

Our eyes reveal to us only the What, and not the Who, of the other person, only an object to be appropriated, possessed, or oppressed, as in Caesar's "I came, I saw, I conquered." It happens every time we resort to the label, the stereotype, or the fixed formula into which we file the other person, the category of an It, so that we all too easily slip into the delusion of knowing the other, of knowing "their kind." In this way we dismiss the stranger as one of "them," as we seek to hide and protect ourselves from "them." It happens every time we look someone over or size someone up, every time we assess someone on the basis of his or her resume or make a note of the markers of color, religion, culture, politics, and ethnicity, or race, class, and gender, making a note of which pronoun the other might go by.

Fixated on *What* this person is, according to these accidents, we become blind and deaf to *Who* this person is, blind to the hunger and deaf to the outcry of the *Who*—blind and deaf to the meaning and value of the other human being, blind and deaf to what there is to love. On that day we shall surely die, for on that day we shall surely search for justifications for murdering the stranger: the soul suffers what it inflicts, as we turn even our brother into a stranger, as Cain did with his own brother. Emptied of our capacity to love, we often find ourselves viewing the stranger with suspicion, taking him or her to be a threat to us. When this attitude forms the basis of a worldview, as Primo Levi understood, it ultimately leads to Auschwitz.

The commanded love and care for the stranger, including the nonbeliever, is a testimony to the first utterance at Mount Sinai: "I am God," the assertion repeated in the utterance of the commandment to love. If the formula for the philosopher is "I think, therefore I am," for the one fixated on the creed it is "I believe, therefore I am"; for the woke crowd it is "I feel, therefore I am." In each case the accent is on the illusory *I*. In each instance the stranger poses a threat, either to my freedom or to my salvation, either to my solipsistic self or to my "safe space." But where there is love there is no safe space—there is only the open arms of vulnerability. Love is scary.

For the Jew, the only threat that the stranger poses to my safety or my "salvation" (if that term even applies) lies in my failure to treat the stranger with loving kindness. The effort to convert the stranger or to save his soul or to make him submit to my ideology so that I may feel safe or avoid having my feelings hurt is a deadly attempt to grasp what no power can lay claim to. The essential dimension that escapes my grasp? It is the dimension of the holy. Where there is no loving relation, there is no relation to the holy.

According to one of our holy books, the *Tosefta*, God begins with one and not two, so that "in this world the righteous could not say, 'Our children are righteous, and yours are evil.'" No one can say to another, "My side of the family is better than your side of the family," because there is only one side of the family, so that each of us is spiritually, physically, and therefore ethically tied to the other—spiritually through the Creator, physically through Adam, and ethically through the commandment to love. As we have seen, the Hebrew term for "human being" is *ben adam*, literally a "child of Adam." Just as each beam of light that radiates from a star is connected, through the star, to every other beam of light, so is each soul connected to every other soul through God, from whom every soul emanates. And each body is connected, through Adam, to every other body, which is itself an aspect of the soul: the body does not have a soul, but rather the soul has a body. Therefore loving another is about attending to the needs and the suffering of his or her body, and not about saving his or her soul.

According to the Torah, the Creator chose Abraham to enter into a Covenant not for the sake of his own household, but so that through the Covenant of Abraham "all the families of the earth shall be blessed"; thus, says *HaShem* through the prophet Isaiah, "[I] set thee for a covenant of the people, as a light unto the nations." As Abraham is associated with *chesed* or "loving kindness," that light unto the nations is made of love. You, my children, are summoned to be such a light: treat everyone you meet with loving kindness, as our Father Abraham did. We have seen that the Jews are chosen to say to the world that every human being is chosen, every human life has meaning and value, regardless of this creed or that, and each of us is infinitely responsible to and for the other.

Recall the two cherubs that rested on top of the Ark of the Covenant; recall that the Voice of God emanated not from inside the ark but from the space between the two cherubs. The Talmud tells us that as long as the Jewish people live according to the Torah, the two cherubs on top of the ark that contains the Torah face one another in a loving embrace, and only then can the Voice of the Holy One be heard: love is what makes his Voice heard. But when the Jewish people turn away from the Torah and do harm to themselves and others, beginning with the stranger, the two cherubs turn away from one another, so that the Voice of the Holy One falls silent, turning us over to the horror and the silence of a devastating indifference. The Zohar teaches that the cherubs atop the ark had the faces of children. When we love another, we love the child within the other. Rabbi Nachman of Breslov notes that, through the cherubs with the faces of children, an angel brings blessing into the world, beginning with the children, as it is written in the Torah:

"May the angel who redeems me from all evil bless the children." Again, to love another is to love the child within the other.

"The stranger who dwells among you," the Torah teaches, "shall be as one of your own, and you shall love him as yourself. For you were strangers in the land of Egypt: I am *HaShem* your God." That is, you shall love him *k'mokha*, "as yourself," an echo of the commandment to love your neighbor, your fellow Jew, *k'mokha*, which, again, means "that is what you are like." In other words, "you shall love the stranger, for the love you show toward the stranger *is* who you are": that loving is the *who* that you are in the depths of your being. Loving the non-Jew, including the nonbeliever, has *the same urgency* as loving our fellow Jew, and both are necessary to our love for God. Oriented toward a love of God and Torah, then, Jewish teaching is oriented toward the other human being, who, even though he is a stranger, *is no alien other*. So, my children, when new neighbors, or strangers, move in next door, bring them a piece of cake.

Love for another, whether neighbor or stranger, precludes judgment of another. Let God be the judge of who is righteous and who is not, my children, of who has a place in the World to Come and who does not. That is beyond our reckoning: anyone who would presume to determine who is redeemed and who is damned is one who succumbs to the idolatrous worship of the illusory ego. What is not beyond our reckoning is the need, the hunger, the suffering of the stranger. If we determine that our fellow human being has no place with God due to his or her unbelief, we can have no relation with that person, nor can we have any place with God, with *HaMakom*, with "the Place." Contrary to traditions that declare theirs is the only path to God, the Talmud teaches that the non-Jew, too, has a place in the World to Come—indeed, even more readily than the Jew, since the Jew has a much greater responsibility to fulfill. The stranger has a place in the World to Come because he or she has a place *in this world*: since God's purpose in creation is to create a dwelling place, a *Makom*, for himself, it is to create a dwelling place for one another, Jew and non-Jew alike, in this physical realm—*especially* for the stranger, because the "strangeness" of the stranger is precisely his or her "homelessness," being without a place. His homelessness is God's homelessness. As God can be hungry, so can God be homeless. The stranger is strange to us because the world is strange to him or her. We must make it otherwise. Through love.

Maintaining that the gates to God's kingdom "are at all times open" to the stranger, as it is written in the Midrash, Judaism does not paint itself into the theological corner of declaring that the path to God leads only through Judaism. Recall the teaching that the Torah has seventy faces or facets, like a diamond, corresponding to the seventy nations: they, too, have their perspective on Torah. The stranger, too, has a Torah to teach us through our love for the stranger. Love is required for learning. And for teaching: you cannot teach those whom you do not love. I say this as a teacher.

To exclude the stranger from the World to Come is to exclude the stranger from this world; if he has no place with God, *according to his deeds and his righteousness*, then he can have no place with his fellow human being. And neither can we. If we say to the stranger, "Only through this path can you come to God," then we can have no human-to-human relation with him or her; such a stance reduces the stranger to a commodity, to an It, which, alas, is our inclination. Judaism, therefore, *commands* a loving and giving human-to-human relation with the stranger, however counterintuitive it may be. "Beloved are the strangers," says the Midrash, "for Scripture in every instance compares them to Israel." Beloved by whom? Beloved by God, as taught in another Midrash: "I have loved you," we read in words of the prophet Malachi, refers to the stranger. According to Jewish teaching, each time a Jew encounters a stranger, he or she encounters one of God's beloved, one of God's children, encounters God the Father himself. Because the Jews cry out "Father!" to God, they cry out "Brother!" to the stranger, with love.

Before anyone was chosen to be a Jew or a non-Jew, we have the tale of Cain and Abel. In that story, you remember, God puts to Cain two questions: "Where is your brother?" and "What have you done?" To answer one question is to answer the other: we answer to where our brother is—Israelite or *ger*—through what we have *done*, concretely, and not through what we *believe*. The point in responding to the questions put to Cain is not to enter the kingdom of heaven but to transform *this* kingdom into a dwelling place for God, that is, into a heaven, by making it a place where the stranger can dwell. Each time we harm the stranger simply because he or she is a stranger, we damage all of creation. Creation is made of love *for the stranger*. As God is strange to us, so are we strange to God, and yet he loves us with an infinite love.

If time happens where responsibility happens, time unfolds where love unfolds: time made of responsibility is time made of love. Love enriches time. Love is the vessel of time. Nothing makes us so intensely conscious of the passing of each hour as love does. All of you, my children, know this already. Inasmuch as our responsibility for the stranger demands a love for the stranger, it is infinite, so that here, through our love for the other, time opens up the eternal. The face of the stranger is a manifestation of the Eternal One, who is hungry and destitute, crying out as the beggar cried out to Mother Teresa, "I am thirsty." Calling upon us to answer, the stranger presents us with a task, the task of loving.

Thus, as we open up to the stranger, the face of the stranger opens up a meaning and a mission, a path toward a horizon that we eternally have *yet* to reach. That meaning and mission are steeped in love: meaning is made of love, as once again, we see in Dostoevsky's "Dream of a Ridiculous Man." Understanding at last the meaning of life, he was filled with love for all life. Time is the presence of this love for the stranger in the realm of space, which is the presence of the Holy One, here and hereafter. Time does not consist of the wait for the reward in the afterlife, which leads to a disregard for, if not an oppression of, the stranger. If you would know the meaning of the word *love*, look, again, to Mother Teresa. She hardly marked time or waited around. She understood that when we step before the face of the stranger, we come before the face of the Ultimate Stranger, the One who from time immemorial has spoken the commandment that comes to us through the face of the stranger *here and now*. Love always happens in the present tense.

We have seen that the holiest space on earth, according to Judaism, is not Mount Sinai or the Temple Mount, nor even the Holy of Holies within the Temple. No, it is space *between* the *cheruvim*, the two angels, atop the ark, a space that is even higher than the space within the ark, where the Torah lies hidden. From that between space the Voice of God emanates as the Voice of Divine love, without which there is no human love. Just so, the face of the stranger summons us, and we respond precisely by showing our face, despite all our apprehensions and suspicions. That is why the Voice from Sinai is not behind us—it is before us, contemporary with us, resounding from the face of this strange human being who approaches me here now, not just commanding but beseeching my love. Only in the response to this summons—to this commandment to love—from the face and by moving toward the face do I assume a face and thereby become who I am. My identity lies not in my genealogy or in my roots, for we all have the same roots, in Adam. It lies in my love for another.

"Who am I?" you ask yourselves. The answer: I am the one singled out to love this human being who now stands before me—not to love "mankind," for there is no such thing. Ivan Karamazov told his brother Alyosha that he loves mankind; it's just that he cannot stand the sight of his next-door neighbor. That is where he fails to understand what love is and what life is, where any meaning that might be found in life eludes him. There is no loving "mankind," which is an empty abstraction: you cannot embrace "mankind." But you can offer a kind word, a giving hand, and a loving embrace to this flesh-and-blood human being who now reaches out to you. Commanded to love the stranger, you must be grateful for the demand: gratitude is made of that *commanded* love. There is no being grateful without being commanded.

Gratitude

My opening words to you, my children, for this reflection on gratitude are: thank you. Thank you for the wisdom you impart to me, for the wisdom that I attempt to lay down in these pages. What little wisdom I have to offer was revealed to me through your infant eyes, so that I am indebted to you for everything I have to give you, and I thank you. Without you I would have no wisdom, no understanding, no love, no life to impart. Without you, I would have no ethical will to write, no inheritance to leave to you, no affirming flame to light my way and yours through the night that seems to be descending upon us.

In this world, in our time, we are surrounded by the darkness of negation and despair. You can see it everywhere you look, from television ads to news headlines, from social media to so-called social justice, from critical race theory to the Boycott, Divest, Sanctions movement. And yet there are, in truth, points of light that quietly illuminate the darkness, as the righteous exchange their insights and do their deeds, shining with a light that the darkness cannot comprehend. Let those lights ignite your soul with the affirming flame of thanksgiving. You have seen by now that gratitude is a theme that runs throughout these reflections. More that striving to be "happy," strive to be grateful. Be mindful of the *Dayenu* that we sing each year at the Passover Seder. Hum it throughout your day: Had You only done this little bit for us, "*Dayenu!* It would have been enough," and yet you have blessed us with so much more, with far more than we could possibly merit. Our cup runneth over. I had a friend who, as she lay dying of cancer, whispered, "We have so much to be grateful for." Her last words.

The one thing that the Hasidic master Rebbe Barukh of Medzebozh feared most was that he might somehow, God forbid, lose his gratitude: "How can I live without gratitude?" he would ask. Elie Wiesel once described our teacher Moses as "gratitude personified": God chose Moses to receive the revelation of Torah for his humility and his love for the Jewish people, yes, but above all for his gratitude. When the Torah was revealed at Mount Sinai, it is written, "the house of Jacob and the children of Israel" were gathered at the mountain to receive the revelation. The house of Jacob refers to the women, and the children of Israel are the men. Why are the women mentioned first? Because, according to tradition, they knew the meaning of gratitude. The letter *beit* that begins the Torah, says the Zohar, is the womb from which the Torah and all of heaven and earth are born. And to give birth is to give thanks: wherever there is life, there is thanksgiving. Thus, without the gratitude embodied by the mothers and daughters of Israel, the children of Israel had no hope of receiving the Torah. As gratitude is the substance of Torah, so is it the key to receiving the Torah.

Like Moses and the women gathered at Mount Sinai, another Hasidic master knew the meaning of gratitude: it was Moshe-Leib of Sassov, a great *Tzaddik* who lived in dire poverty and who often went hungry. What was his reaction to his plight? Professor Wiesel tells us: "You see, Moshe-Leib, he said to himself, hunger is more important than food. Think of all the over-fed, over nourished princes and leaders who can eat and eat and eat until the end of their lives—are they happy? No, they are not. They are not happy because they are not hungry. But you are, Moshe-Leib. As hungry as a lion—so what are you complaining about? Thank God for your hunger! Louder Moshe-Leib! You have a strong voice, shout! Tell God how *grateful* you are—and not only how hungry you are." Yes: shout! Why? Because gratitude must be shouted and sung out loud, or it will not be at all, sometimes with a note of defiance and especially when things do not go our way. Gratitude does not rest upon having things go our way. It is not offered in exchange for having received something. It is, rather, the sustaining substance of life itself. The true hunger that threatens us is the hunger of a thankless soul; to be sure, a thankless soul is a dead soul, drained of its lifeblood by bitterness and indignation. If the Jews are a stiff-necked people, it is not because they stubbornly resist the commandments or stubbornly insist on explanations. It is because they stubbornly insist on gratitude.

Life is not about seeking happiness. Indeed, lives are squandered in the search for a happiness that never comes, so that in the end we do not live but merely hope to live. The most powerful bulwark against despair, my children, is not happiness, which has a way of slipping through our fingers, but gratitude; it is the essence, the *who*, of your identity as a Jew. For the Hebrew word for "Jew," *Yehudi*, means "one who is grateful." If Jews are chosen to be a light unto the nations, it is the light of gratitude, *in spite of everything*. This *in spite of* unlocks the gate to the gratitude that defines who we are, not only as Jews but as human beings. To be human is most fundamentally to be grateful; what is human in the human being arises in a cry of gratitude. According to the Midrash, Adam, the first human being, composed the 92nd Psalm, the *Mizmor shir leyom ha-Shabbat*,

"A Psalm. A Song for the Sabbath day." It is a song of joy and gratitude: the first human song was one of gratitude.

Gratitude for what, exactly, you ask? Where are we to look to discover what we might be grateful for? Listen to a Hasidic tale from the School of Pshishke about a certain Jew of Cracow named Eizik, son of Yekel.

Eizik and his family were poverty-stricken, with nothing in their meager home but a stove and a few sticks of furniture. He lived in a constant state of longing and despair. One night, as he lay on his bed of straw, Eizik had a dream about a great treasure buried under a bridge in Prague. At first he dismissed it as just a foolish fantasy, but the dream kept returning to him night after night; finally he took the dream to be some sort of sign from above. So he packed a knapsack and set out for Prague. Wandering through the city, he came upon the bridge that he had seen in his dream. He started digging in the spot he had dreamed of, when a police officer happened upon him, arrested him, and hauled him off to the police station. The policeman interrogated him, demanding to know what he, a foreign Jew, was doing in Prague and why he was digging under that bridge. "Surely you must be a Jewish spy!" the officer accused him. Too frightened to make up a lie, Eizik told the truth: he had a dream about a treasure buried under the bridge, and he came to Prague to find the treasure.

The policeman laughed and said, "That is just like you stupid Jews! I had a dream too, about a treasure hidden under a stove in a hovel in Cracow, where there lived a Jew called Eizik, son of Yekel. You don't see me running off to Cracow, do you?"

Indignant at the stupidity of the Jew, the policeman sent Eizik on his way, whereupon he hurried home to Cracow, looked beneath his stove, and found the treasure.

What does it mean? Simply this: In all the world there is only one place where a great treasure is hidden, and that place is the spot where you are standing. How to behold the treasure? Through eyes filled with gratitude before you have seen what there is to be grateful for. Gratitude is an optics. It enables us to see the invisible, to behold the treasure lying at our feet, sitting in our lap, and hugging us around the neck. It opens our eyes to the heaven in our midst, to the wonder all around us, to the truth of the prayer of thanksgiving that we say three times a day, thanking God "for Your miracles that are with us every day, and for Your wonders and Your favors that are with us at all times, evening, morning and afternoon." Thanking God for opening our eyes to life and love, to mission and meaning. As Rebbe Barukh said, what would we be without gratitude? We would be utterly bereft of life and meaning, of purpose and direction, left to languish in horror, hanging by our heels over the abyss of nihilism and nothingness.

Whenever you have asked me how I am doing, you have heard me answer, "*Barukh HaShem!* Thank God!" Although the phrase *Barukh HaShem* literally means "Blessed be God," it translates as "Thank God." *Barukh*, "blessed," is a blessing of gratitude. To be grateful is to be blessed and to offer a blessing in turn, a blessing on gratitude, which is a gratitude for gratitude itself. Both conferred and received, blessing is rejoicing: gratitude is always steeped in joy. Therefore blessing and gratitude arise between two: it is the meaning and substance of relationship, both between human and God and between human and human. Each time we perform a commandment we say a *brakhah*; that is, we give thanks, not for what we receive but for being commanded, connected, chosen, and summoned. As God's wonders are forever present, evening, morning, and afternoon, so God is forever present: what matters, for God and man, is to be present, and there is no being present without being grateful.

Gratitude is steeped in prayer, as prayer is steeped in gratitude. If a human being is a cry of gratitude, it is prayer that makes it so. We have seen that prayer, *tefillah*, is not supplication—it is confrontation and reckoning, witnessing and wrestling. It is a wrestling with ourselves, wrestling a word of thanksgiving from the depths of our souls. The first word that begins the morning prayer service is *Hodu*, which is the root of *todah*, "thank you." To pray is to give thanks, and to give thanks is to pray: in every "thank you" the Eternal You abides. Beginning our morning prayers with *Hodu l'HaShem*—"thanks and praise be to the Name"—we begin our prayers with a declaration of what it means to be a Jew: to be a Jew, as we have seen, is to give thanks. Inasmuch as prayer is about memory, it is about the memory of what we have to be thankful for. Where there is no gratitude, there is no memory, and where there is no memory, there is no gratitude (more about memory below). Praying with gratitude is the only way to retain our memory of who we are. Shaken from our amnesia, we utter a cry of gratitude. When Jacob awoke from his dream and cried out, "God was here all along, and I did not know it!" it was a cry of gratitude. Without gratitude, we can come to no such realization. Gratitude is just such an awakening. That is why, when we awaken each morning, we say, "Thank you." It means "I am awake."

One of the most common ways of referring to God is by the phrase *HaKadosh Barukh Hu*, which means "the Holy One, Blessed be He." The verb *berakh*, from which we have the word *barukh*, means not only to "bless" but also to "thank," hence the translation of *barukh HaShem* as "thank God." As the Holy One, God is the Giving One, for holiness manifests itself in giving; hence the Holy One is the One to whom our thanks are due. It is a gratitude for every breath we take, regardless of circumstance, a gratitude for the opportunity to give thanks for all we *give*, as holiness enters our lives through our every act of giving. Nothing is more essential to attaining a nearness to God than thanksgiving. Here we discover once again that, in a very profound sense, life's meaning lies in giving thanks. The You in the *Modeh ani lefanekha* that we utter each morning reverberates in every offering of thanks. For this is the You whose first utterance at Mount Sinai was *Anokhi*. The You in "thank You," then, is the Holy One, whose nearness we seek each time we give thanks or utter a blessing.

The Hebrew phrase for "gratitude" is *hakarat todah*, literally "consciousness of giving thanks"—not just giving thanks but *consciousness* of giving thanks. It is a consciousness without which we have neither conscience nor conscientiousness. To be conscious is to be awake, attentive, and responsive, so that without this consciousness of giving thanks, we remain unconscious, somnambulists who merely sleepwalk through life, deaf and blind to the suffering of the humanity that surrounds us and to the blessing bestowed upon us. Losing our consciousness of giving thanks, we lose our care for another and slip into a solipsistic, egocentric cave of indifference, where the soul suffocates in anger and resentment. Gratitude opens our eyes and ears and hearts to the suffering of others—not a gratitude for the suffering, God forbid, but a gratitude for the truth that it *matters* and that *we* are commanded to do something about it. Gratitude is gratitude for this responsibility and for being summoned into the vulnerable openness that defines our responsibility. Here gratitude become a gratitude not for safety and security but for that vulnerability, for that responsibility.

And yet we flee from gratitude as we flee from responsibility, as we flee from *consciousness* and sink into the mire of unconsciousness, rushing from drug to drug, from diversion to diversion. Why? Because gratitude implicates us. Knowing that we are blessed with more that we can ever merit, we remain forever in arrears, no matter how much we give. If gratitude is a gratitude for what we have, it is a gratitude for what we have to *give*. But we do not want to know about our indebtedness, and we find ingenious ways of not knowing. Thus the refrain from the citizens of Nazi Germany, who could smell the stench of the camps in their very midst: "We did not know." Wallowing in our longing for self-righteousness, we descend into unconsciousness. Just look at the multibillion-dollar industry of intoxication, anesthetization, inebriation, and other forms of a counterfeit suicide. Slipping into this sleep, we imbibe a slice of death. To choose life, as the Torah commands us, is to choose to be grateful, again, without waiting to see what there is to be grateful for. It turns out that the question of what there is to be grateful for is not a question at all, because the gratitude that defines who we are is not offered in exchange for anything. Gratitude is not gratitude for any sort of benefit or profit. It is not about profit—it is about goodness: one cannot be good without being grateful, and to show our gratitude is to be good. Like Private Ryan. You remember him.

Remember what I told you about Psalm 92: composed by Adam, it was the first song to rise up from a human being. Following its opening line we have the words *tov lehodot*: "it is good to give thanks." Giving thanks *is* goodness, and goodness lies in giving thanks. I repeat: you cannot be good without gratitude, and you cannot be grateful without being good. Because the desire to be good lies at the core of our humanity, it can become a source of confusion. In our own time the confusion lies in the deception that to be good is to be a victim. But gratitude is alien to victimhood. Being grateful, in fact, entails a certain obliviousness to being a victim. Just as inebriation is a multibillion-dollar business, so is the victim industry, the drive to blame our every misfortune on someone else, in a flight from responsibility. Born in the mire of meaninglessness, the "Why me?" of victimhood eclipses the "Here I am!" of gratitude, from the halls of academia to the streets of our cities, where the ungrateful often turn violent. Can anyone whose life is steeped in gratitude engage in looting, burning, or otherwise harming others? No. Gratitude is the opposite of vengeance, which always arises from feeling cheated. No one who is grateful feels cheated.

Here it is worth looking at the *Modeh Ani* more closely. When upon waking we utter the words *Modeh ani lefanekha*, "I give thanks before You," for returning my soul to this realm, we give thanks for allowing us not to enjoy another day of living but to rejoice in being chosen for another mission, without which we have no meaning, no soul, no identity. Note well: the first words we utter each morning are not words of Torah but words of thanksgiving, for the words of thanksgiving transcend even the words of Torah, which, indeed, are themselves words of thanksgiving. We are taught that all of the Torah written as a single word, from the *beit* of the first word to the *lamed* of the last word, is one of the Names of God. If the words of Torah are words of thanksgiving, then God's name means *Modeh ani*, "I thank you." Yes, God, too, is grateful, grateful for every act of kindness we show toward another. Note, too, that in the Hebrew, contrary to the usual subject-verb word order, the *Modeh* or "thanks" precedes the *ani* or "I": the gratitude is expressed first because without the gratitude there is no I. Who am I? I am the one who is grateful.

The *Modeh Ani* ends with *rabbah emunatekha*, "great is Your faith [in me]." *Emunah*, "faith" or "trust," then, is an issue not only for us but for God as well. It means that no matter how much I have failed until now, I am grateful that God has enough faith and confidence in me to assign me yet another task for the sake of his creation, blessing me with yet another opportunity to be who I am as a Jew and a human being. And so we begin our day by saying, "Thank you." The longest portion of the central prayer of the liturgy, the *Amidah*, is the prayer that begins, *Modim anakhnu lakh* . . . , "We give thanks to You . . ." The *lakh* is feminine, perhaps because, as we have seen, the women gathered at Mount Sinai knew the meaning of gratitude. This prayer of gratitude is addressed not to God the Father but to God the Mother, the Supernal Mother, who in the beginning, says the Zohar, gave birth to heaven and earth. We give thanks to the Supernal Mother because there is no one so grateful as a mother, as the two of you who are mothers know very well. Not just the women but the *mothers* gathered at Mount Sinai knew the meaning of gratitude most profoundly. To be sure, Leah named her fourth son Judah, a name that means "thank you."

The Talmud tells us that blessing comes to a home only through a woman, above all through a mother. It is she who ushers in the Sabbath with the lighting of the Sabbath candles, which illuminate the home with the holiness of gratitude. The gratitude of a mother is what transforms a home into a dwelling place: there is no home, no dwelling in the world, without gratitude. Void of gratitude, we are adrift in the wilderness of exile, no matter how "nice" the fortress we have struggled to fashion into a home, which, in the end, is no more than a tomb. The ultimate dwelling place is the *Beit HaMikdash*, the "Home of the Holy One," atop the Temple Mount. In the Temple there shined the *Ner Tamid*, the Eternal Flame or the Flame of the Eternal One. That is why in the synagogue we hang a *Ner Tamid* over the holy ark, in which the Torah scrolls abide in silence but not in darkness. That Eternal Flame, that Flame of the Eternal One, is the affirming flame of gratitude. The Messianic Age that will bring about the restoration of the *Beit HaMikdash* will bring about the restoration of gratitude in the world: the Age of the Messiah is the Age of Gratitude. Which means: gratitude is redemptive. There is no redemption without gratitude.

Therefore, it is essential to wait and work for the coming of the Messiah not with impatience and frustration but with anticipation and gratitude—gratitude not only for the advent of the Messiah but for the wait itself. Steeped in gratitude, the wait for the Messiah is itself messianic. In the Midrash Rabbi Yochanan famously teaches in the name of Rabbi Menachem the Galilean that in the messianic age all prayers will cease except the prayers of thanksgiving. These prayers of thanksgiving are neither for what has befallen us, God forbid, nor for our deliverance from suffering. Rather, they are an expression of a gratitude for having been commanded and thus entrusted with the mission of hastening the coming of the Messiah, no matter how impossible the mission may seem. It is a gratitude for the meaning of the Messiah and for the strife of the spirit and the hunger of the heart that the *achakeh*, the wait and the anticipation, entail. Whenever we have managed to endure a trial and see it through, according to a Hasidic teaching, we must give thanks to God for three things: for bringing the trial to an end, for giving us the strength to endure it, and for the trial itself. So it is with waiting and working for the coming of the Messiah.

The Hasidic master Menachem Mendl of Kotzk taught that the heart is God's favorite dwelling place, for it is the dwelling place of Torah. The Hebrew word for "heart" is *lev*, made of the *lamed-beit*, that comprise the last and the first letters of Torah—the last and the first because the end of the Torah leads into the beginning, like a circle. And so on *Simchat Torah*, "Rejoicing in the Torah," when we celebrate the completion of the annual cycle of reading the Torah, we read directly from the last word into the first word of the Torah, from the *lamed* into the *beit*. This reading is accompanied by singing, dancing, and rejoicing, as we take all of the Torah scrolls from the ark and dance though the synagogue and into the street. If in the time of the Messiah all prayers will cease except the prayers of thanksgiving, this, I think, is what those prayers will look like. For the advent of the Messiah will bring the advent of gratitude, when the truth of the Torah will be written within every heart. God will find his rightful dwelling place within our hearts, and he will smile with our every utterance of "thank you."

Simchat Torah, the day of Rejoicing in the Torah, is a day of thanksgiving for the Torah. It falls soon after Rosh Hashanah, which is also known as *Yom HaZikaron*, the Day of Remembrance. On *Simchat Torah* we remember at last what we are summoned to remember on the Day of Remembrance. We remember that we are grateful, that deep down we have always been grateful, and that the gratitude in our heart opens up the Torah in our heart. Without gratitude we have no memory, for without gratitude the first things we forget are the most important things. And the most fragile.

Memory

THE MEMORY THAT CONCERNS us here, my children, is not the failing memory treated with Prevagen. Nor is it nostalgia or reminiscence, recollection or recall. It is not about our ability to call up dates or places, names or faces. It has more to do with memorializing than with memorizing. It resides not in the recesses of our mind but in the depths of our soul, in the between space of the embrace that reminds us of why we live and die, of what to hold dear. This ethical will is about what I would have you remember, my children, and what I must instill in my own memory: I offer it to you so that I myself shall not forget. This reflection on memory is about what sustains life and conquers death; it is a way of being against death. Memory, indeed, is a matter of life and death. Where there is life, there is memory, and only where there is memory, is there life.

"What would man be without his capacity to remember?" asks Elie Wiesel. "Memory is a passion no less powerful or pervasive than love. What does it mean to remember? It is to live in more than one world, to prevent the past from fading and to call upon the future to illuminate it. It is to revive fragments of existence, to rescue lost beings, to cast hard light on faces and events, to drive back the sands that cover the surface of things, to combat oblivion and to reject death." Yes, a passion, something that burns, and yet does not consume. A soul on fire is aflame with memory. No less powerful than love, memory is steeped in love; it is memory of what we love, whom we love, and why we love. If words create and destroy worlds, memory traverses their boundaries. The wings by which the soul takes flight are made of memory. Memory is memory not of the past but of the future, a mindfulness of the future, which, as we have seen, is the dimension of meaning and holiness. Without memory we have no future because without memory we have no past, no tradition, no teaching for the future. Memory is oriented toward the death that lurks in the next hour: it is a rejection of that death—not the death that threatens me but the death that stalks the other human being. Able to see more than he can see, I can see what is coming up behind him, and that makes my responsibility greater than his.

Memory arises from within a relationship in which my fear of death is a fear for the other person, and not my own death.

Memory is testimony. It is memory not only of what has come to pass but of what makes it meaningful. That is what makes memory and remembrance a form of testimony: the question of why it matters, what it means, and how it implicates us. When memory speaks, the truth speaks and calls us to the stand, where we must take a stand. If the Hebrew word for "testimony," *edah*, also means community, memory unfolds only within the midst of a community. Without the testimony that is memory, we have no community, and without community, we lose our memory. Community requires two things: a higher relation that forms a center around which the community revolves, and a human relation expressive of the higher relation. Therefore memory is the memory of the Most High.

Memory is teaching, both for the one who remembers and for the one who receives the memory; it is a teaching that transforms each into a witness. Thus transformed, the witness transforms others through the teaching and testimony she offers to others. Because it is transforming, memory can be undermining. In the ancient world forgetfulness was a gift sent by the gods. In Greek mythology Lethe, whose name means "oblivion," was the daughter of Eris or "strife," so that forgetfulness born of strife was viewed as a kind of blessing. I have known a few Holocaust survivors who contracted Alzheimer's disease and who, in the last weeks or months of their lives, God help them, believed they were back in the camp: that was the memory that had taken hold of their afflicted souls. For them there was no oblivion to be had from their strife. But that memory laid claim to them because, due to the insidious disease, they had lost all other memory. It was the fragmented memory of a devastated soul.

In our tradition nothing is more important than memory. The wounds we have suffered in the past are healed not by forgetting them but by remembering why they matter and what we must do in response to them. Three times a year we say the *Yizkor* prayers, the prayers of remembrance that transform remembrance itself into a prayer. In the words of the Hasidic master Rabbi Nachman of Breslov, prayer "has the power to improve the memory and banish forgetfulness" and "is a *segulah* for developing a good memory." Praying the *Yizkor*, we remember those who have lived before us, to whom we owe our very lives. We remember the martyrs of the Talmud and of the Middle Ages, the victims of the massacres and the pogroms, and the holy ones of the Holocaust. When we visit those who lie in their graves, we ask them to remember us, as we place a stone on top of the site for the sake of memory, in an effort to build up what might otherwise be buried by the sands of time. Without memory we have no tie to our origins, no tie, therefore, to our identity. Memory binds us to Abraham, Isaac, and Jacob, as well as to the God of Abraham, Isaac, and Jacob. Memory is our sole link to Torah and tradition. As soon as we lose our memory, we lose our way and fall prey to the poison of fashion and fad. We fall prey to evil. For when we lose our memory, we lose all memory of the Good.

On the High Holy Days not only do we pray to remember and remember to pray, but we also plead with God that he, too, might remember, as when the Israelites were exiled in Egypt, "and God heard their groaning, and God remembered His Covenant, remembered Abraham, Isaac, and Jacob." We implore him to remember, so that we may remember, for he alone can restore our memory: without God, we have no memory but only contrived fabrications, what the postmodernists call "narratives," which are nothing but lies devised for the promotion of power. As the prophet Joel declares, God insists that we remember the Covenant, else the sun will lose its shining, and we will forget our very names. What do we beg God to remember? His immemorial movement into his Covenant with the Jewish people. Without this immemorial summons to a covenantal relation, there would be no memory on the part of God: it is the immemorial Covenant that stirs God to remember and to hear our cry, to remember our names and his own Name.

The immemorial, my children, is the Good that chooses us prior to all time to make our choices meaningful and thus situate us in time. The immemorial is antecedent to all memory, to all time, to all meaning. It is situated not in what happened long ago but in what is precedes every "long ago." Coming "before" all memory, it goes beyond all memory: memory is mystical. Imbued with the immemorial, memory *is* the mystical. Always already, the immemorial is the eternity of the eternal, which makes memory eternal: without our memory of the immemorial there is no goodness, no love, no meaning, no commandment, no God, no humanity. The space in which we live and the time of our lives are infused with the immemorial: our lives entail living out the life of Adam, whose tale transpires not in time but in the immemorial. It is a trace that leaves its mark on our face, which, tradition teaches, is also the face of Adam. That is why *panim*, the word for "face," is plural: each of us has two faces, our own unique face and the face of Adam, who was instilled with eternal life when God breathed into him a living soul. Life "eternal" and immemorial is life *noad*, or "destined." Eternal life is not endless life; it is meaningful life. There, in the memory of the immemorial, lies the meaning of the Covenant with the Eternal. Without the revelation of the Covenant there would be no revelation of the immemorial to consummate the liberation from Egypt. There would be no liberation from Egypt. There would be no children of Israel.

And so God, *Elokim*, the Creator of heaven and earth, who in the immemorial act of creation entered into a Covenant with his creation and with humanity, hears and remembers as though awakened from some sort of sleep. And yet, we are taught, he is the One who neither sleeps nor slumbers. Note well, my children: not only does he hear, he hears and *remembers*, as though he might have forgotten. As the Covenant imparts the faculty of hearing, so it imparts the faculty of remembrance both to God and to humanity: in the commandment to hear, *Shema!*, we have the commandment to remember, *Zakhor!* Can God forget? Can you imagine the God of Abraham an amnesiac? Perhaps. He forgets when we forget. Or better: he remembers what we forget. For, as it is written, he did not lose his ability to hear the cries of the Jews of Egypt. If God could forget, the Nazis need not have undertaken their war against memory, as Elie Wiesel and Primo Levi each described the Holocaust. The truth is, we plead with God to remember in order to show him that we ourselves remember. Yes: God's amnesia stems from our amnesia. Still, it takes the human outcry to awaken God from his forgetfulness—not our prayers but our outcry, our groaning, our screams, when we have run out of words and prayers. There are times when prayers become screams, as we beg him to remember, so that we may remember.

The Ten Commandments or the Ten Utterances of God appear twice in the Torah, first in Exodus and again in Deuteronomy. In the book of Exodus we are commanded to remember the Sabbath, while the commandment in Deuteronomy is to observe the Sabbath, where "remember" is *zakhor* and "observe" is *shamor*. "Why two words?" the sages ask. "Which word did God actually utter?" And they answer: *Zachor veshamor bedibur echad*—"Remember and observe were given in one word," for God can speak two words in a single word. And both words, be it noted, pertain to the Sabbath, the only day of the week that, in Hebrew, has a name; the other days are called "first day, "second day," and so on. Memory, my children, begins with the memory of the Sabbath. *Shabbat* is one of the Names of God, and we must remember and observe that name. *Shamor* means more than "observe"; it means "watch over," "take attentive care of," "protect." Memory is just such a watching over this Name of God, lest we forget our own names and, with the forgetting of our names, forget those for whom we are named: each of us is a *bat* or *ben*, the "daughter" or "son" of someone, as inscribed in our name. That is why the fifth commandment, the commandment to honor our mother and father, is in the category of commandments pertaining to our relation to God. To forget our name is to forget the meaning and mission of our lives, thus not only losing but betraying the inheritance bequeathed to us by our mothers and fathers.

Apart from the Covenant, God has no Name; only when he enters into the Covenant with his witnesses does he become God and take on his Name, and only then do we remember our names. In the covenantal movement of Creation, the sages teach us, God becomes *HaShem*, "the Name," by assuming the ineffable four-letter Name of *yud-hey-vav-hey*. The memory of this Name is inscribed in our own names. Each of you, my children, is named in memory of one who went before you, one who calls you to a devotion to the Name. Forgetting our name, we fail to answer when we are called; forgetting our name, we lose our way. Remembering his Covenant, God remembers his own Name and comes to the aid of the Israelites. In his *zakhor*, his "remembering," lies a *shamor*, a "watching over," through a loving care for his children and their names; as we have seen, the two words come in a single utterance. For God and for humanity, to remember means to watch over and to care for, else remembrance loses its meaning. In his prayer to God for the people of Israel in exile, the prophet Habakkuk pleads with God to remember "compassion," *rachem*. Does the *Av HaRachamim*, the "Father of Compassion," have to be reminded to remember compassion? Perhaps. But what we realize here is that the memory of the Covenant is a memory of the need for compassion, without which there is no Covenant. Once again, as God must remember, so we must remember, especially if it means reminding God of his own Name: *Av HaRachamim*.

The Hebrew word for "memory," *zikaron*, also means "a source of speech." Here we are reminded that, according to our tradition, the *Shekhinah*, the Divine Presence, is the source of speech, where speech lies in speaking the truth. Hence the link between memory and testimony, as testimony is testimony to the truth. When we lose our memory, we lose our speech, struck dumb by the despair that is our exile, which is the exile of the *Shekhinah*, the exile of speech. This is known in the mystical tradition as the "exile of the word," the *galut hadibur*, which in turn is the exile of truth. Wherever we take up our testimony to what there is to hold dear, memory speaks. It speaks the truth.

Memory, however, can be very painful. It is not for nothing that the Greeks understood Lethe to be the daughter of Eris. When it is fragmented and broken, memory can lead to despair. And yet, among the things we remember is that we *must not* despair; *because* we remember even the pain we would forget, we must not despair. We must remember the importance of gratitude, which is the one antidote to despair. Memory is the expression of our longing for God, even if, at times, we rail against God, not because we have forgotten but precisely because we have remembered and therefore cry out for God to remember. In that outcry rooted in memory, God attains his victory over us: God will not be rejected. Memory makes it impossible to reject God. As one of Elie Wiesel's characters once asserted, "You think you're cursing Him, but your curse is praise; you think you're fighting Him, but all you do is open yourself to Him; you think you're crying out your hatred and rebellion, but all you're doing is telling Him how much you need His support and forgiveness." And, above all, his memory. Why? Because only memory—our memory of God and his memory of us—can lead us back to God. There lies the meaning of redemption.

The Baal Shem Tov teaches that, as exile is tied to oblivion, so is memory bound to redemption. Exile does not lead to a loss of memory, but rather a loss of memory leads to exile. Therefore in our exile, memory becomes a matter of even greater urgency. If memory is memory of the future, it is memory of a messianic time, a time of redemption entrusted to our care, my children, yours and mine, for the sake of all humanity. If our memory lies in our hearts and souls, God's memory resides in the Jewish people, and, says the Zohar, the Jewish people are the *Shekhinah*, the source of speech and remembrance. Memory resides in the Holy Tongue, for in the language of a people lies its memory. Prayer is essential to memory because the language of prayer, which is the Holy Tongue, is the vessel of memory. That is why for a Jew, for each of you, my children, who bears a four-thousand-year-old memory, not only does despair arise from a loss of memory, but it is blasphemy: with the loss of memory comes the loss of God. Despair drives God out of this world, regardless of our reasons to despair. If, as I have said, gratitude is the antidote to despair, memory is memory of what there is to be grateful for. If, as I have said, truth is the antidote to despair, memory is memory of the truth of the sanctity of the other human being. If, as I have said, the word is the antidote to despair, that word is *memory*. Despair is a wallowing in the emptiness of the ego; memory is a movement into a relation to another, the movement that alone can show us the way out of exile.

The horror and insanity of exile seethe in a state of *behalah*, which is "fright," "panic," or "confusion," all of which suck forth the memory from our soul. Ridden with this horror and insanity that undermine memory, we live in a chronic state of flight, desperate to escape we know not what, and, as long as we have lost our memory, we cannot escape it any more than we can run from our own shadow. In exile we are forever in a hurry, plunging headlong into oblivion in an effort to "get it over with." Having lost our memory, we squander our lives pursuing a dream that is nothing more than a delirium. Like Alice and the Red Queen, we frantically run in place, just to stay in the same place, in this bustle that gets us nowhere, living the life of a ghostly *other*, bereft of memory. In our hustling and bustling, in our oblivion, we have forgotten the way, estranged from ourselves, so that in the end we look into the mirage of the mirror only to find a stranger gazing back at us. Exile is the desolation of this aimless wandering that is a plunging headlong, this impatience that is a paralysis, this hurry that is a hunger.

There is a story about a town in a land far away, where the people were stricken with a strange and terrible disease, whose only symptom was the loss of memory. The town's elders were baffled and soon grew afraid, as more and more people could not remember their way home, the names of their children, or even their own names. They forgot the names of objects and of animals, until the town's council members decided to take action before it was too late. They set about making signs, labels, and name tags to identify people and things, to remind the citizens of who they are, where they live, and what this thing or that was called. Before they themselves should forget what was most essential, they made a very large sign and placed it in the town square to remind the townspeople of what must never be forgotten. The sign said: "God Exists."

As Jews, we surround ourselves with such signs and reminders, lest we forget; among them are *mezzuzahs* on our doorposts, fringes on our garments, and coverings on our heads. Blessing us with these commandments to surround ourselves with these reminders, with these things that stir our memory, God understands how forgetful we are. He knows that among the first things we forget are the truths that are most fundamental and most fragile. They remind us that he is there, our watchful Father and our wise King. Reminding us in these ways of his presence, he reminds us of our responsibility to and for one another. These reminders are like signposts that show us the way out of exile and into the dwelling that is redemption. Thus memory is tied to redemption, as the Baal Shem has said. Without these reminders, we lose all sense of the meaning of redemption, wherein lies the task for which we are created.

The Brothers Karamazov ends with a scene between the young and wise Alyosha and a group of boys who had just buried one of their friends, Ilyusha. The boys had mistreated little Ilyusha and had injured him when they were throwing stones at him. His injury led to his death, which devastated the boys. After the funeral Alyosha gathered the boys together and told them to remember this day, to remember the child whom they had wronged, and to remember how much they had longed to repent for the harm they did to him. "One day, when you have grown up," he said to them, "you may fall into despair and lose your way. You may forget what there is to love. On that day remember the little one we just buried. Remember not only the wrong you did to him but how deeply you wanted to undo it and how you promised yourself to be good. That memory can help you find your way back to life. You see, boys, a single memory can bring you salvation." Yes, a single memory, the memory of a moment of rejoicing in the promise to be good. "We are unhappy," Dostoevsky once put it, "because we have forgotten that we are happy . . ." We despair because we have forgotten the words and the realization of Ray Kinsella in *Field of Dreams*: "Maybe this *is* heaven!" Remember?

Memory is bound to redemption because memory makes possible *teshuvah*, the movement not just of repentance but of return: *teshuvah* rests upon a memory of the way back. *Teshuvah* also means "response": it is the response of "Here I am for you." With this "Here I am," we remember where we are, and in this way we find our way when we have lost our way: memory is memory of the way home when we have lost our way. *Teshuvah* comes to bear not when we are sinking in the quicksand of indignation or vexation over our own lot but when we awaken to the harm we have done to others, which is almost always harm we have done to those whom we love most. The most painful of our memories is not the memory of our own suffering but the memory of the suffering we have caused our loved ones. Indeed, those who love us are most vulnerable to us. And the suffering we inflict upon them is a suffering we inflict upon God, for it is a damage that we do to our own soul. That is why God suffers: because we have harmed not only others but also ourselves. That is why God cried out to the first man *Ayeka!?*—"How could you!?": "How could you have done this to yourself!? How could you have done this to me, the One who loves you infinitely!?"

In the painfulness of such memories lies our redemption, our return to the path that leads us home, and, as I have said, goodness lies in the direction home. How often have you had the dream in which you cannot get home? You are away from home, trying to find your car or recall the directions to the airport. Or you are in the city or neighborhood where you live, and everything is at once familiar and strange. It is like the dream of a failed responsibility, as when, in the dream, you have enrolled in a class or, in my case, were assigned to teach a class for which you never showed up. (Or am I the only one who has had such dreams?) Such dreams are akin to a nightmare, the nightmare of exile and oblivion, a nightmare in which memory never comes. At times you even know it is a dream, and yet you cannot awaken from it. I often wonder whether such nightmares are related to the nightmares I have about the Holocaust, about being inside a sealed train or in a camp. You know, my children, that I have dedicated much of my life to this remembrance and that, therefore, I cannot speak of memory without speaking of that memory, a memory that haunts the generations ever after.

The memory of the Shoah bequeathed to us has become part of our consciousness as Jews and as human beings. If we are to bear this memory, as we are summoned to do, then we must bear in mind what is at stake. The Holocaust memoir is a search for the God who is essential to the life of the soul, a struggle to find our way back, a *teshuvah*. The terrible cry of "Where is God now?" that rises up from the depths of Elie Wiesel's *Night* resounds from the margins of every page of all the memoirs. "If they had the courage to write them," Wiesel once said, "we must find the courage to read them." Just as recording these memories was an act of courage, so is reading them an act of courage: memory demands such courage. "Remember it before it comes and observe it after it has gone," as it is written in the *Mekilta de-Rabbi Ishmael*: once again, we have the *zakhor veshamor* of memory. If the Holocaust memoir is against silence, it is against the silence of God and the silence of humanity, when the world fell silent, deaf to the outcries of the Jewish people, to the screams of the Jewish children.

Through the memory of God's silence, that silence takes on a voice heard in the memory's act of response. God speaks despite himself. He speaks because the Jew who remembers will not allow him to be silent, will not allow him to forget. Nor will the Jew allow the world to forget, which is one reason for the world's persistent hatred of the Jews: that hatred is rooted in a desire for the oblivion that obliterates responsibility. The Holocaust memoir is the soul's memory of itself and its struggle to recover itself through memory. Similarly, it is the soul's memory of God and God's memory of himself in a struggle to recover himself. Thus the general point I have made about memory and the future applies most dramatically to the Holocaust memoir: here memory moves from a perception of the past toward a recovery of the future, which is a recovery of time, through a relation to the other. The essence of memory in the Holocaust memoir lies in the fact that, even though it is a memory of the void, it is not uttered in a void. Rather, it comes as a response from one soul to another in the aftermath of history's most radical assault on the soul.

Soul

The soul is made of a disturbance within its depths: it is the deep that calls unto deep, the stirring of the word that longs for a reply. What does that depth consist of? Responding to this question is crucial to the quest for the soul's healing. And in the Jewish tradition we find a response most profound. Before we can answer this question, however, there are other questions that must be answered. And in order to wrestle with those questions, we must sound the depths of the soul. Only in this way can we return from the world of lies, in which we have lost our way, and move into the interior of who we are, even if we find that return terrifying. As it is written in the Talmud, "even if there is the terror 'within,' the 'sword' will destroy more without." Within the soul lies the terror of exile that is upon us. And within the soul lies the remedy to that exile. In these reflections on the soul we shall confront the terror together, my children, and seek the remedy.

According to Hasidic teaching, there are three forms of exile: the exile of the *Shekhinah*, the exile of the soul, and the exile of the body. All three are interrelated, with each one instilled with the other, the *Shekhinah*, the soul, and the body. Wherever the soul does not dwell in a relation to the *Shekhinah*, living according to the teachings of Torah, both are in exile. And when these two are divorced from one another, the yet-to-be-sanctified physical body is divorced from both. The exile of the body, in other words, is not just a geographical exile from one's homeland: it is the exile of the body from the spiritual essence that is its Divine origin: there are two dimensions of exile, the vertical and the horizontal. The rising number of refugees and homeless people in our world is not merely a social or political problem. It is a symptom of a much deeper problem, the problem of a spiritual crisis within us: what is around us also lies within us.

Our spiritual crisis is, among other things, the outcome of our thinking God out of the picture and thinking ourselves into an illusory, egocentric autonomy, where, in the end, power is the only reality and weakness the only sin. Born of the deadly Tree of Knowledge, this thinking entails knowing, and knowing entails grasping or possessing. Thus we fall into the deadly confusion between *having* and *being*, into the illusion that the more we *have* the more we *are*. The exile of the soul is the exile of the One in whose image and likeness the soul is created. And yet the very reality of the Holy One is manifest in our longing for holiness. Which means: even in "exile," even in *galut*, there is "revelation," *galui*. Or perhaps better: *only* in exile is there revelation. For only in exile is revelation needful. Only a soul that has lost its way can make the movement of return, of *teshuvah*, that opens up its depths. And where there is *teshuvah* there is revelation. In order to receive the revelation we must acquire a capacity for hearing the Voice that speaks not only from beyond the soul but from within the soul. As it is written: "It is very nigh unto thee to do it." It is very nigh unto thee to do it because the Voice is speaking to you from within you. Listen carefully, and you will hear the call of your soul.

Arising through the Divine Word, every detail of creation has a Voice, what the Zohar calls "the supernal Voice from which all other voices proceed." Which means: every detail of creation addresses us and has meaning. No detail, however small, is insignificant, and our every move is laden with profound implications for the life of the soul. Hence there is no separating the soul from the body, the spiritual from the physical, the religious from the secular: *everything* is spiritual, *everything* affects the soul. The infinity of the Holy One lies in his concern for every detail, every iota, of creation, no matter how minute. Hence every blade of grass is assigned an angel. For every blade of grass teems with the Divine utterance of the soul of God, from which every soul emanates upon the Divine utterance of "Let there be light." Every soul is summoned to draw this Light into creation and thus sustain creation—and with it the soul—through the observance of *mitzvot*. The *mitzvah* is a portal through which the Holy One enters the world; without the *mitzvah*, God cannot enter the world. When God cannot enter the world, evil flourishes. And the candle of the soul dims to darkness.

The soul is not an object or entity: it is a *speech act* of the Holy One. It is, as it were, God's prayer to and for a creation that in turn sings his praise. What we make of our souls lies in whether we join our speech to that Divine speech by transforming our thoughts, words, and deeds into modes of prayer through the performance of *mitzvot*. What is the Divine speech that is the substance of the soul? It is Torah. And the Torah is made of fire: as the soul is made of Torah, the soul is made of fire. Indeed, the soul is more like a flame or a flow than like an entity or an object. Thus the great medieval sage and mystic Solomon ibn Gabirol wrote a poem—or a prayer—on the soul, saying:

Thou hast imparted to it the spirit of wisdom
And called it the Soul.
And of flames of intellectual fire hast Thou wrought its form,
And like a burning fire hast Thou wafted it
And sent it to the body to serve and guard it,
And it is as fire in the midst thereof yet doth not consume it,
For it is from the fire of the soul that the body hath been created,
And goeth from Nothingness to Being,
"Because the Lord descended on him in fire."

Note well: "It is from the fire of the soul that the body hath been created." This weaving together of body and soul can be seen in every electrical impulse that charges every nerve and that guides our every movement, from the beating of the heart to the movement of the hand.

Just as the Torah is made of black fire on white fire, so does the soul, says the Zohar, originate "in fire, being an emanation from the Divine Throne." Therefore, it is written in the Midrash, when the angel tried to frighten Jacob as they wrestled at Peniel by making fire shoot up from the ground, Jacob cried, "Do you think you can frighten me with fire? Why, I am made of that stuff!" Even prior to the revelation of Torah at Mount Sinai, Jacob knew that his soul was made of Torah. Levi-Yitzchak of Berditchev taught that every Jewish soul corresponds to a letter of Torah. When the soul burns with the fire of Torah, the Light of God emanates into the world through that soul. There is no other means for the light of Torah to find its way into this realm. For only the soul, in its manifestation as body, can perform the *mitzvot* through which the Divine light shines. Two verses in the Book of Proverbs underscore this point: "The commandment [*mitzvah*] is the candle [*ner*] and the Torah the light," and, "The soul of the human being is the candle of *HaShem*." The light of Torah enters into the world wherever two souls enter into a loving relationship, as we have seen. Our love for the other human being is the meaning of our life, from which the soul draws its breath, the light that we are commanded to emanate into the world upon the Divine utterance of "Let there be light."

The soul transforms darkness into light by transforming isolation into relation. If the darkness of Egypt was such that "no man could see his brother," the light of the soul reveals the face of our neighbor. The darkness of Egypt is the darkness of an outlook that cannot determine any fundamental connection between one soul and another. Such an outlook can understand love only as an elevated feeling inside of us, and not as a living presence between us. Understanding the soul precisely in terms of an external relation, and not as an internal isolation, Judaism knows nothing of the solitude of being that characterizes modern thought. The soul emanates from God and, through God, is tied to every other soul. The soul *is* that linkage.

Realizing that the substance of the soul lies in a relation to the *other* human being, we realize once again, on a deeper level, that the self is a self-deception. The deception inheres in the ego's preoccupation with *my* feelings, *my* space, *my* status, *my* material being, and above all *my* spiritual being, as if anything that belongs to the essence of my soul could belong to *me*, *me*, and more *me*. Lost in the deception of the *me*, we take "spirituality" or "religious experience" to be something that meets *my* needs and makes *me* feel good. And so we scurry from cult to cult, from fad to fad, seeking a new rush. Foundering in the egocentric illusion, a life lived with *me* at the center is a life lived in the lie of the dative case, forever trembling over the questions of what will happen "to me" and what is in it "for me."

And so we come to a realization: *the soul is just the opposite of the self.* Therefore a *bitul heyesh*, or the "obliteration of self," is the one doorway to truth. And the truth that instills the soul with life enters the soul when the soul enters into a relation with another: the soul is the other within me. Which means: I am not who I thought I was, and whoever I am lies in my responsibility to and for my neighbor. Because that responsibility is forever *yet to be* fulfilled, I am forever *yet to be* who I am: I am that I am not. The soul stirs when, contrary to all self-interest and self-fulfillment, I risk myself for the sake of another, despite my repeated assertions, like Humphrey Bogart in *Casablanca*, that "I stick my neck out for nobody." It stirs when another will eclipses my will, which is the Will of Another. If the Infinite One manifests himself in the disturbance of his witness, it is a disturbance through which the Infinite One makes an infinite claim upon the witness. Precisely this unending assignation, this infinite responsibility, constitutes the infinite dearness of the soul.

To receive the light of Torah is to radiate its light: the soul does not simply live, my children, it *shines*. In Hebrew a verb meaning to "give out light" or to "shine" is *halal*. Its cognates include *hilel*, meaning to "praise" or "glorify," and the noun *hilah*, which is a "crown of light," a "halo," or "glory." I have seen that halo surround each of you. Remember what I have already tried to teach you: the soul that lives by emitting the light of glory is a soul that illuminates its Creator through praise. Greeting our fellow human being, we praise God, and our halo grows just a bit brighter. Recalling another word for "praise," *hodayah*, we find that the soul lives by the thanks it offers, for *hodayah* also means "thanksgiving." A human being is one who beams with gratitude. Gratitude for what? By now you know: for the mission entrusted to our care. That is the light that the Jews emanate unto the nations: it is a revelation to all that each is chosen to rejoice and give thanks, as all are made of the Divine light. If the soul is the candle of God, it shines with a halo of gratitude, offered to God in the greeting offered to another, who is my brother.

When God asks Cain, as he asks each of us, "Where is your brother?" he asks, "Where is your soul?" When he asks Cain, "What have you done?" he asks him, "What have you made of your soul?" To be sure, in his very name, *Kayin*, one discovers the ruin of his soul. For words related to his name include *kanah*, which is to "acquire" or to "possess," and *kinah*, the word for "envy." Obsessed with a longing to possess—believing the more he *has*, the more he *is*—Cain is seized with envy. He feels but one thing: cheated. The more he clambers to possess, therefore, the deeper he sinks into despair. Squandering his days in envy and despair, Cain lives in a state of *kinah* or "lamentation," until he ruins his soul altogether by taking the life of his brother and casts himself into utter isolation. Just before he took his brother's life, it is written in the Aramaic translation of Rabbi Yonatan, Cain declared to Abel, "There is no judge and no judgment!" Thus in the act of murder he usurped the God who forbids murder and slipped into the darkness of the isolation of the ego. Just as the creation of light teaches us something about the relation that constitutes the life of the soul, so does the first murder teach us something about the isolation that destroys the soul. It is an isolation that leads to murder. In our own time it has reached a scale never before imagined.

As I was once walking home from synagogue with some friends, a little boy of five asked me, "Where is my soul?" I paused, thought a bit, and asked him, "Where do you think it is?" He, too, paused, reflected, and answered, "I think it is everywhere." Here, from the mouth of this babe, we have a confirmation of the wisdom of the Talmud: whoever murders a single soul, it is as if he had destroyed the whole world. For the entry and the exit of every soul into and from creation transforms the face of all of creation. Each soul permeates all of creation, and all of creation pervades every soul. That is why the news of every tragedy cuts us to the quick. Israel is compared to a lamb, it is written in the *Pirke de Rabbi Eliezer*, because when a lamb is injured in a single limb, its whole body feels the pain.

So once again I received a teaching of wisdom from a little one whom the world had not yet corrupted. His wisdom can be found in the wisdom of the greatest of the sages: The *Orchot Tzaddikim* teaches that the soul is "greater and broader than heaven and earth, knowing its extent and height, the ways of the sun and the constellations and all of their satellites—all is encompassed by the soul." The soul is an emanation of what is more than all there is into the midst of all there is. Larger than the body, as I have taught you, it is made of the *or makif* and the *or pnimi*, the "surrounding light" and the "inner light." Like a neon light that has an intense ray of light within it and light radiating from it, the soul radiates an aura that exceeds the boundaries of the body and that transcends space and time. Thus when a mother passes away, God forbid, her children can simultaneously sense her presence and her passing into other realms, even though they live in different parts of the country. As it transcends space, the soul can also transcend time, lingering throughout time in the same place, as it does at a gravesite or in a "haunted" house. A trip to the cemetery to visit a loved one is not something that soothes our psychological wounds; no, what takes place alongside the grave is a genuine encounter.

To say that the soul is made of an inner light and surrounding light is not to turn it over to some empty abstraction. To my knowledge, only in Judaism do we find the notion of a physical dimension of the metaphysical soul, what is called *nefesh*. This concrete understanding of the soul is part of the teaching that the soul has five levels or dimensions, where each level requires the other in order for any to exist. The highest, most transcendent level of the soul as it emanates from the Creator needs its lowest, most material aspect in order to be what it is, just as much as the lowest needs the highest in order to have meaning. Indeed, each of these five dimensions of the soul needs all the others in order for the soul to be a soul and the body to be a body. Unless our thinking allows such a move, the physical body has no sanctity, and the metaphysical soul has no meaning.

The Greeks taught that the soul has three levels: appetite, emotion, and reason, with reason as the only true aspect of the soul, since appetite and emotion threaten the life of the soul. Not to be confused with the Greek model, Jewish tradition identifies three "lower" levels of the soul as *nefesh* or "soul," *ruach* or "spirit," and *neshamah* or "living soul." *Nefesh*, however, is no more reducible to appetite than *ruach* is to emotion, although they do have these associations. The soul's purpose in this world is not to suppress its physical aspect but rather to elevate it. As for emotion, it is to be channeled, so that through the passion of joy and loving embrace the soul may draw more holiness from the upper worlds into this world.

From the Jewish mystical tradition we inherit a beautiful and profound teaching concerning the five levels of the soul. They are: *yechidah*, *chayah*, *neshamah*, *ruach*, and *nefesh*. If, as we have seen, memory can transcend the boundaries of different worlds, it is because the soul transcends those boundaries, with each level corresponding to a world. Therefore each level of the soul has a memory of its own, extending back into time immemorial and into the future, as the upper levels of the soul, *yechidah* and *chayah*, lie beyond the confines of space and time. Only where all five levels are at work do we have the possibility of the human-to-divine and human-to-human relations that constitute the soul and impart meaning to this realm from beyond this realm.

The uppermost level of *yechidah* is where the soul is joined with God, as a beam of light is joined with a star. Within the word *yechidah* is the word *yachid*, which designates a "singularity." In this world a singularity is what cannot be described or accommodated by the laws of nature, and so it is with the soul: going beyond the confines of strictly rational thought, we have this singularity that transcends both thought and being, like a black hole that confounds the astrophysicists. That is why in every thought something more than thought manifests itself. In a sense, *yechidah* is not exactly part of the soul but is above it, just as a black hole is not part of space and time but beyond them, where none of the laws of space and time apply. And yet, the soul has no reality in this world without singularity. As the fountainhead of the soul, *chayah* is both above it and part of it. And so we see that the soul is not in the body, but rather the body is in the soul; the body is but a moment in the life of the soul, not just instilled with but also surrounded by the light of the soul: the body cannot contain the soul. The soul is a flow or emanation of holiness from on high into this physical realm. More than life, what is transmitted in that flow through the understanding couched in the *neshamah* is an understanding of the *sanctity* of life.

I have already spoken of the next dimension of the soul, the *neshamah*, a cognate of *neshimah*, which means "breath": it is the breath of the word that God breathes into the first human being, a breath breathed into no other being. That is what makes the human being a breach of being. Associated with thought or the word, the *neshamah* belongs to the realm of *sechel*, which translates as "intellect," "reason," "intelligence," "wisdom," and "insight." The understanding manifest through the *neshamah* lies in the wisdom that is a revelation of the sanctity of life. The sanctity of life is something that is manifest in time, which belongs to the dimension of *ruach*. In a sense, *ruach is* time. It is the *life* time of the soul. For time is the invisible presence that is manifest in spatial movement. *Ruach*, then, is the "spirit" that moves us, body and soul. *Ruach* channels the life above into the life below; it is the intermediary between *neshamah* and *nefesh*. In its association with the body, *ruach* is tied to the *lev* or "heart." Thus the Torah engraved in the soul is engraved in the heart. But unless Torah, like the soul, has a physical aspect, we can have no part of Torah.

Nefesh, as I have said, is the physical aspect of the soul, a manifestation of the Divine Presence wherever that Presence is intense enough to animate the inanimate. It is written in the Torah, for example, that the *nefesh* is in the blood, so that there is no essential distinction between body and soul. Our purpose, again, is not to suppress the appetites of the body but rather to elevate them and thus impart a certain dignity to our physical being. This union of *nefesh* with our physical being can be seen in its association with the "liver" or *kaved* in Hebrew, whose cognate *koved* means "weight" or "gravity." *Nefesh* is what imparts to life its gravity. It provides life with ballast, thus enabling us to keep our feet on the ground, lest we forget the plight of our neighbor in some mystical flight of ecstasy. At the level of *nefesh* life grows heavy, but heavy with meaning.

In the Jewish tradition, particularly in the Hasidic tradition, one place where the soul and its weight, the *nefesh* and its *koved*, come together most powerfully is in the "dance" or *machol*. Moshe Leib of Sassov once declared, "When someone asks the impossible of me, I know what I must do: I must dance!" At the level of *nefesh* the soul *is* the dancing body. In the dance the spiritual descends and the physical ascends to arrive at new levels of insight and realization. Thus Rabbi Barukh, the son of the Great Maggid of Mezeritch, once exclaimed to Rebbe Aryeh Leib ben Boruch, the Shpole Zeide: "What you achieve by dancing, others do not attain by praying." Becoming a "dancer," a *mecholel*, we concretely affirm the holiness of God. An alternative meaning of *mecholel* is "doer," one who makes things happen in this physical realm: as the *nefesh* starts to dance, it makes things happen in the physical realm. The *machol* elevates not only the physical realm but also the *nefesh* that is engaged in the dance. I have urged you to write poetry, my children. I now urge you to dance, dance with all of your body, all of your *nefesh*, all of your soul.

The Talmud teaches that of the 613 commandments that make up the Torah, 248 correspond to the 248 bones of the body, and 365 to the 365 sinews of the body. Commenting on the 613 commandments that comprise the Torah, the body, and all of creation, the great sage Rabbi Yaakov Culi writes, "Like man, the earth is also divided into 248 parts, with a head, eyes, mouth, and other limbs. It also has 365 arteries. Every time a person observes a commandment, he sustains one of his limbs, as well as part of the world." Therefore not only the human body but also all of creation rests upon the condition of the soul manifest as body, that is, as *nefesh*. Our concern with the body is not merely a personal concern; no, it is a matter that concerns all of reality, both physical and metaphysical. Because *nefesh* is created from beyond all there is, it does not evolve from some primordial ooze. The human being is *already* holy: he or she does not "evolve" into holiness.

Therefore our responsibility to and for the physical well being of our neighbor is *already* absolute. The flesh-and-blood human being who now summons me by name has a name and is not just another specimen from an evolved "species." Reducing the human being to so much biological material, evolution empties the soul of life by emptying the soul of meaning; guided by the principle of the survival of the fittest, evolution's sole directive is to survive at the expense of the neighbor. Evolution is a lie that undermines the life of the soul.

Because *nefesh* is a fusing of body and soul, Job could cry out, "From my flesh shall I behold Godliness." Indeed, if we cannot behold Godliness from the flesh and in the flesh, we cannot see it at all. Too often the result of this blindness is the spilling of the blood. And the *nefesh* in the blood that soaks the earth cries out, "Thou shalt not murder!"—not only from on high but from the depths of the earth itself, as when the blood of Abel cried out to God, so that the very ground burns beneath our feet. Through the flesh-and-blood body we behold the fire of the soul, and in the fire of the soul the fire of Torah, from which the body is made. The body is like a wick that burns with the fire of the soul, both part of and distinct from its flame.

Inasmuch as animation indicates movement and movement occurs in space, the movement of the body is an emergence of the soul *in space*. And yet, the more life it has, the less space it takes up. Rather than taking up space, the soul opens up space, in such a way as to allow space for another soul to dwell in the world—that is what constitutes *nefesh* as the physical dimension, as the spatial dimension, of the soul: its capacity for opening up a space where another soul may dwell. To open up space for another is to welcome that person into the space of our open arms. The most basic way of opening up space for another is to make room at our table and offer that person something to eat.

"Take care of your own soul," said the Koretzer Rebbe, "and another man's body, but not your own body and another man's soul." How do we meet our spiritual need? By attending to the physical need of our fellow human being. The Chofetz Chaim taught that the act of kindness shown in the care for another person's body sanctifies our own body, our own *nefesh*. This physical care, and not some form of conversion, is what it means to "save a soul." To violate the laws of Sabbath observance for the sake of *pikuach nefesh* means saving a physical life, not saving a soul in any redemptive sense. More than saving life, we are commanded to nourish life, which begins with feeding the hungry. As *nefesh* emanating from above, the human being is not what he eats—he is what he offers another to eat, in a sacrifice of his own physical space, comfort, and complacency.

More than in prayer and meditation, the life of the soul lies in the caress of another, where one flesh-and-blood soul enters into a physical contact with another flesh-and-blood soul. Only in the aspect of *nefesh* can the soul be *felt*, in a hug or a handshake, in a kiss or a caress—above all in the caress, for what is sought in the caress can never be seized. A cognate of the Hebrew word for "caress," *letifah*, is the adjective *latif*, which means "kind." And kindness requires a concrete, flesh-and-blood relation to another person; there is no being kind to oneself, no kindness in the abstract. The caress of kindness is what makes a home a *dwelling* place, and not just a shelter or a place to stay.

Here we discover the movement out of the exile of the soul: it is as simple as inviting someone to our table or extending a comforting hand in a pat on the shoulder or in a loving caress. To dwell is to caress—physically—whether as husband or wife, as father or mother, as friend or neighbor. The caress searches, not in order to *have* but in order to *give*. Recall that the two words at the very center of the Torah are *darosh darash*, which translates as to "search diligently" but which literally means to "search and search again," through the caress and the kindness that sustain the soul. Indeed, only through physical human contact, says Sforno, can the purpose of our being created in the image and likeness of the Holy One be realized. Hence the horrific punishment of Cain, which, he said, was more than he could bear: he was marked so that no human would lay a hand on him.

What has been said about the act of loving kindness that characterizes the life of the soul becomes even clearer when we consider certain Hebrew expressions that contain the word *panim*, the word for "face." *Hisbir panim*, for example, means to "welcome" or "be kind to," and *hasbarat panim* means "friendly treatment," "welcoming face," or "a smile of greeting." These expressions are from the verb *siber*, which means to "interpret" or "explain"; the corresponding noun is *hasbarah*, meaning "interpretation" or "explanation." The implication? To welcome another with a smile of greeting is to correctly understand what the face signifies: in the face is manifest the soul of flesh and blood in the other. Hence the Talmudic teaching that we must always present a face full of joy to our fellow human being.

More than the physical dimension of the soul, *nefesh* is the face of the soul. Here lies what is human in the human, which opens up another insight into why the Hebrew word *panim* is plural: it is because the face both exposes and veils the depth dimension of the *inner* being of the soul that is nonetheless *distinct* from being. It opens up the *in*finite that is with*in* the finite. It is a *within* that is also an *above*: the height manifest from within the face is the height that "ordains being," as the great philosopher Emmanuel Levinas puts it. Thus sanctifying being, the face of the soul as *nefesh* imparts meaning to a concrete, flesh-and-blood reality that is otherwise meaningless. And being can be "ordained" only by what is otherwise than being. Because the soul is the radiance of the face, the face has meaning *without context*. That is what makes its meaning absolute. The soul *is* the absolute that makes everything matter, prior to all "context." Emptied of the holy, which is beyond all there is, we are turned over to the nothingness of all there is and drained of all that can be deemed *life*.

Life

My children, by now you may have a sense of what, exactly, is sustained by these eighteen words that sustain a *life.*

Still, of these eighteen words that we here explore, the word *life* is perhaps the most widely abused. It turns up in the names of board games, self-help titles, and songs in the key of life. We find it in clichés such as *c'est la vie*, life is what happens while you're making other plans, life is short, life sucks, life is a dream, life is what you make it, and where there is life there is hope. We invoke life with every *l'chaim* and every birthday wish for a long life. We speak of the good life, a dog's life, and the time of our life; of life insurance, lifestyles, and life sentences; of signs of life, lust for life, and even sanctity of life. But what does this word mean?

Socrates is famous for having said that an unexamined life is not worth living, but what does it mean to examine my life, and why does that make it worth living? What do I examine when I examine my life? Is it my bank account? How many toys I have? My health? My accomplishments? My moral character? The Nazis had a notion of *Lebensunwertes Leben*, that is, "life unworthy of life." As for how Socrates understood it, he once said that in our learning we must put aside all other studies and focus on one thing: the ability to distinguish the life that is good from the life that is bad. Fair enough. But in what does the life that is good consist? Is it the same as the good life? The Socratic implication is that life lies in goodness, and there is wisdom in that implication.

As always, if we turn to the Torah, to the Tree of Life, we begin to have a better sense of the depth and meaning of the word *life*. In the Torah God calls out to us, "Behold, I have set before you this day life and good, and death and evil. . . . So choose life, in order that you may endure, you and your seed." Already, however, we run into a difficulty: what does it mean to choose life? Who, indeed, chooses life? It would seem that life chooses us. None of us chooses to be born. In fact, our tradition teaches us that every soul, except the soul of a *tzaddik*, enters this world against his or her will. And the Good? As we have seen, we do not choose the Good; rather, the Good chooses us before we have had time to lift up our eyes and make a choice. That is why our every choice *matters*: it is because the Good has *already* chosen us. And here we have the key: having been chosen by the God who is Life, we have been chosen by the Good. In the light of that chosenness, we must now choose life, choose the One who has already chosen us.

Because the Good has already chosen us, God summons us to choose life, where "choose life" is *uvaharta bachayim*, which can be translated as "choose by means of life": live a life of choosing, of decision and decisiveness in the light of this having been chosen, so that you and your children may live. Life is not a random accident. Nor is it a gift, exactly. Rather, it is an assignment or a calling, a calling to choose life. Life arises in the choosing of life, through life, a choosing that lies in the assertion of "*Hineni!* Here I am for you." To choose life, then, is to choose to answer the call of another *for the sake of another life*, and not for my own sake, not so that I may feel good about myself, but so that I may *give* more of myself.

So what are we to say about the fact that none of us chooses to be born into this life? The Talmud relates a famous dispute between the House of Shammai and the House of Hillel. The House of Shammai maintained that it would have been better for us never to have been born. The House of Hillel insisted that it is better that we have been born. After thirty months of discussion, the issue came to a vote. And lo and behold, this time the House of Shammai prevailed: yes, it would have been better for us not to have been born. But, the sages ruled, we *have* been born into this life, so that, in the end, the question is not a question. Having been born, we must search the hidden recesses of our heart and our soul, we must scrutinize our every action, seeking out its meaning and its impact. In other words, our actions must confer a meaning upon our lives and the lives of others: we must choose life, in the light of the Good and the meaning that have already chosen us and called us forth by name. We must choose life, so that others may live, beginning with our children and grandchildren.

Just as we do not give birth to ourselves, so we do not name ourselves. Others have borne our names before us. Often we are named in their memory, so that in being named after others, we bear not only their memory but also a portion of their soul. Therefore through our names we are *already* entrusted with the task of remembrance and vigilance: to bear a name is to be commanded to choose life. When God breathes into us the *nishmat chayim*, the "breath of life," he breathes into us our "soul" or *neshamah*; at the center of *neshamah* are the letters *shin-mem*, which spell the word *shem* or "name." To have a life is to be summoned by name to the task for which we are created, every day, every hour, every moment. To choose life is to answer to our name when we are called by name. To choose life is to give and to love, as per the *hav* or "give" at the root of *ahavah*, which is "love."

This choosing is not a matter of making up our mind but of reaching out our hand, offering help and healing to another. To choose life is to choose this healing, for we are healed only by the healing we offer to the other human being. And to God himself: God commands us to choose life so that we and our children may live and he may be healed. For each time one of his children is harmed, says the Talmud, God cries out, "O woe, my head! O woe, My arms!" Remember the story of Mother Teresa? When asked, "What has God said to you?" she answered: "I am thirsty." There, in her life, we have an understanding of the word *life*.

By now we can see that choosing life does not mean choosing to stay alive at all costs; choosing life and choosing to survive can be two different things. "Life and Death are brethren, dwelling together, inseparable," says the sage Bachya ibn Paquda, "holding fast to the two ends of a tottering bridge over which all the world's creatures pass. Life is at its entrance; Death is at its exit. Life builds, Death breaks up. Life sows, Death reaps. Life unites, Death divides. Life strings together, Death scatters what has been strung together." While the Torah enjoins us to choose life, making this choice does not mean that we no longer pass away from this earth. Rather, it means that in choosing life we understand death to be part of the process of sanctifying life, the testimonial outcome of a life steeped in Torah, prayer, and deeds of loving kindness. These are the things we choose when we choose life. Death is not eliminated; rather, like life, it is situated within the contexts of the sacred. Understood in terms of the sacred, death is the culmination, not the negation, of life. It is not opposed to life as darkness is opposed to light; it is a task that confronts us in the course of life. Murder is evil; in itself death is not. Standing by while people die is evil; in itself dying is not.

To live as a human being is to die as a human being. And to die as a human being is to affirm even in death that life is very good, speaking the Name of the Holy One in a declaration of "*Shema Yisrael!*" as we cross over to the other side. There is an important teaching from the Midrash in this connection. On each of the first five days of the creation (except the second day) God pronounced his labor to be good; but on the sixth day he declared it to be *tov meod*, that is, "very good." The word *meod* means "more"; its cognate, the verb *himid*, means to "increase." What could possibly be *more* than the good? Is the good not good enough? How can it be increased? The good that belongs to creation is increased with the creation of the human being; the human being is *more* than being. What is the sign of his life being *more*? It is his death, which, conceived as a task, becomes his infinite offering for the sake of the infinitely dear. Therefore, the Talmudic sage

Rabbi Meir maintains that the *meod* in *tov meod* signifies death, a category belonging to human life alone. To choose life is to choose not only the Good but the *tov meod*, the Good and *more*, that distinguishes the human from the animal. Choosing the *tov meod* means understanding that the basis of our relation to another human being—underlying the commandment to love our neighbor—is our fear for his death.

It bears repeating: choosing life over death does not mean choosing to stay alive at all costs. On the contrary, it means choosing "martyrdom" or "Sanctification of the Name," *Kiddush HaShem*, and thus attesting to a good that is higher than our own survival. Indeed, the task of life is to sanctify the Name from which every life derives its sanctity. And we engage that task precisely by doing good. For the Name is the Name of the Good. A *kiddush HaShem* is a *kiddush HaTov*, a sanctification of the One who is the Good. Left with nothing but ourselves to live for, we have nothing left to die for; with nothing to die for, we have nothing to live for. There lies the death that truly threatens us, the death that invades us even as we live and breathe. When we choose the life that is *very* good, death is situated within the contexts of the Good as an ultimate sanctification of life. Thus taking death to be part of life, we begin the mourner's *Kaddish*, the prayer for the dead, with a magnification and sanctification of the Holy Name, in which all life has it origin. And we end by declaring, "Amen."

Choosing life, then, means choosing to sustain the lives of others, and not our own lives. For we have no life apart from the life of another. Why do we say *Kaddish*, what is known in Hebrew as the "orphan's prayer"? (One day you will be orphans, my children, but that is as it should be. When we bury our parents, creation is in order—not when, God forbid, we bury our children, when creation is turned on end.) Saying the *Kaddish* assists the soul of the one who has passed in his or her ascent through the upper realms, where their lives continue. It is not that the departed ones go to a "better place." No. I am reminded of a scene from the movie *Hud*, when the grandfather dies, and a preacher tries to console his bereaved grandson Lonnie by saying, "He has gone to a better place." To which Lonnie replies, "I don't think so. Not unless dirt is better than air." From the standpoint of Judaism, *this* is a better place. The *Kaddish* is an affirmation of our abiding relationship with the departed, body and soul. And let me add this: *if we have no relationship with the dead, we have no relationship with the living.*

Just as there are times when we are summoned to martyrdom, so are there times when choosing life means choosing to live, not for our own sake, but, again, for the sake of others, even those who are as yet unborn. Rabbi Yitzhak Nissenbaum of Warsaw, for example, declared to the Jews that in those days of destruction known as the Shoah, *Kiddush Hashem* meant doing everything possible to survive as Jews, as witnesses. And so, when Pelegia Lewinska stood in Auschwitz, she says she "felt under orders to live." But whose orders? It was the Voice of the Holy One and of the generations to come afterward, who commanded her to choose life so that she might bear witness to this radical assault on all that instills life with holiness. For her, to choose life was to move into a testimonial relation with the dead, the living, and the as-yet unborn.

We have no life of our own; we have only the summons to live in such a way that other lives are elevated: like doing good, *chayim*, "life," is an event that transpires between two. It is not what happens while you are making other plans, a catchy but empty phrase, in its misguided supposition that life is what happens to *me*, what frustrates *me*, inasmuch as my plans are plans I make for *me*. We have no life apart from our bond with other lives. That is why *chayim* is plural: where there is life, there is life between two. When we do good, we "do life," "make life," and "create life," which brings to mind the Hebrew expression *asah chayim*; literally meaning to "make life," the phrase translates as to "rejoice in life." If this rejoicing is an act of creating or generating life through the Good, then the Good is precisely something we *live* through joy. Yes, *joy*, not because of but in spite of the projects and aspiration of my ego. Therefore it is possible to rejoice in what some deem a hard life, a life of need. For even when we are in need we have something to give to another—a song, a smile, or the touch of our hand.

Choosing life means choosing the Torah that is the Tree of Life, which, as our martyrs demonstrate, can result in our death. For without the Torah we are turned over to the horror of a living death that is empty of all meaning, all sanctity. The Torah teaches us to love and trust in God, to hearken to his voice and to cleave unto him, even unto death; for God *is* our life and the measure of the days of our lives, though he may slay me, "I shall argue my ways before Him," as Job did, not for my own sake but for the sake of the afflicted and the oppressed, for the sake of God himself. There are times when choosing life means raising the cry of "Why!?" as Job did. It happens that in such an outcry we grow even closer to the God who is Life. For the cry of "Why?" is a cry of life.

My teacher Rabbi Adin Steinsaltz once said, "When we say, 'He is our life,' the intention here is not that He is the giver of life, but that He Himself is our life. When I search for the I in the body, I find the I of the soul; when I search for the I of the soul, I find the I of the Divine." Life, Abraham Joshua Heschel states, is "a transcendental loan; I have neither initiated nor conceived its worth and meaning." Therefore I am accountable for it before the Infinite One as something of infinite value that has been entrusted to me. God is our life because when he breathes life into us, he breathes into us his own life. There is no distinction between God and life: where there is no life, there is no God, if one may speak such words. When he commands us to choose life, he commands us to choose him, who has already chosen us for a life through which he has life: the living God is the *lived* God. Only by thus choosing life, by choosing Torah, can we come into contact with the God who is Life and who dwells within us and between us.

To live a life, my children, is to live God and Torah, to bring God and Torah to life through the *mitzvot*, beginning with the *mitzvah* to choose life. To choose life, to choose God, is to choose the *mitzvah* as a *tzavta*, as a "connection" to the Creator of life who is indispensable to all life. According to the mystics, the word *mitzvah* (*mem-tzadi-vav-hey*) contains the four-letter Holy Name (*yud-heh-vav-heh*), so that the Holy One is *in* the *mitzvah*. While the last two letters of the Name, *vav-hey*, are apparent in the last two letters of *mitzvah*, the first two letters of the Name are hidden in the letters *mem-tzadi* of *mitzvah*. When transformed according to the *At-bash* method of interpretation, where the order of the letters of the alphabet are reversed, so that *alef* corresponds to *tav*, *beit* to *shin*, and so on, the *mem-tzadi* becomes *yud-heh*, the first two letters of the Name. The commandments of Torah form a portal through which the Holy Name enters the world, hidden in the *mitzvah*: God is present as the Hidden One, as life is present in what forever eludes the eye. It is not reducible to brain waves, heartbeats, or blood pressure. To live the *mitzvah*, to live God, is to live meaning. It turns out that life does not *have* meaning—life *is* meaning.

Here you can also see why the meaninglessness glorified by nihilism in all of its mutations represents choosing death and evil and ultimately murder. Religion is often blamed for mass murder, and it cannot be denied that many have been murdered in the name of a false god. But if we measure this death and evil through body count alone—as accumulated, for example, by Hitler, Stalin, Mao, Pol Pot, and other ideologues—there is no comparison in the scope of what has been termed "murder by government" perpetrated by godless regimes. Once God has been taken out of the picture, so has every limiting principle that might curb the scope of murder. Recall a point I made earlier: what the Nazis did was not unimaginable but everything imaginable, as the imagination and will were the only limits to their actions. And so it has come to pass, as God has been ideologically cast into exile. What is the mark of death by which we may recognize this evil? It is the silencing of the word in a tearing of word from meaning.

Where a word is summoned, life is summoned; where a word is silenced, death speaks. Auschwitz is, above all, silence, the silence not of death but of the absence of death; for where there is no life, there is no death. Getting rid of God, the Nazis get rid of every relation to the other human being that is essential to life; getting rid of the other, they get rid of death. Only others lie in cemeteries. But during the Holocaust even those who lay in their graves were under attack. Eliminating the "others"—the Jews—was the Nazis' aim, and this they did, in part, by unearthing Jewish cemeteries. Usurping God, the ultimate Other, the Nazis are literally grave robbers: they rob the Jews of their graves and thus unbury the dead. Not only did the Nazis undertake the task of desecrating the dead and removing death from Jewish life, but they forced Jewish hands to engage in the task of destroying the graves where they once said the *Kaddish* over their mothers and fathers and, God forbid, their children.

The silence that is Auschwitz echoes in the silence of the death that nihilism and its cancel culture would impose on the word that is life; it is the silence of nothingness and meaninglessness. It is the rumbling silence of what is merely "there," which renders us deaf to the silent eloquence of God, who, says the Talmud, is "announced by a deep silence," in the *kol demamah dakah*, the "thin Voice of silence," revealed to the prophet Elijah. The most powerful moments of our lives, moments when we are most profoundly bound to one another, are moments of silence. In that silence we can hear the sound of life. Think of the silent gaze of joy in the eyes of your little ones when they look up and smile at you, rejoicing in nothing more than life itself: look into those eyes, and you will begin to fathom the meaning of the word *life*. This is the silence that is life, the eloquent silence between two who love one another with a love that exceeds all utterance.

The imposed silence that defines the nihilism surrounding us, which renders us deaf to the word and the silence of God and the outcry of the other human being, obliterates the silence that is life and turns it over to the silence of a blank. This is the "silence" that in Hebrew is *shtikah*, a cognate of the word *shituk*, which means "paralysis." Thus paralyzed, we are rendered deaf even to the deep silence that announces the presence of God in the eyes of our little ones. Death comes in the silencing of that silence. Life lies in the silence between two. Not in the electrocardiogram that measures the beating of a heart but in the silent offering of a heart, which is without measure. We are commanded to love God *bekol-levaveka*, "with all your heart," with every beat of your heart; it is a love that eludes the electrocardiogram.

In the *Shema* that commands us to love God *bekol-levaveka* the word for "heart" has two *beits*. Some say the two *beits* require us to love God with both the evil and the good inclinations of the heart, and, as ever, there is wisdom in that teaching from our tradition. But I say it also means to love God *and* the other human being. It means refusing the silence that threatens our life each time we grow deaf to the cry of God that resounds in the cry of the other. To hear one is to hear the other: life lies in this hearing, in this *shema*, in this overcoming of the silence of the cosmos that terrified Pascal. That silence, more than any physical threat, threatens our lives. Hence the Hebrew verb *nadam*, which is to "be silenced" or "rendered mute," also means to "be destroyed." Each time we turn another over to this silence, we are ourselves rendered mute and thereby lose our lives. When God enjoins us to choose life over death, he calls upon us to choose the word over silence—or a word that transmits silence—by offering a word in response to his word—and to his silence.

Which word are we to choose when we choose life? Recall here what I related to you early in these meditations, about the time when one of you was very small, and you asked me, "What does *Adonai* mean?" I replied that it is a Hebrew word we use to refer to God. And, a bit puzzled, you answered, "I thought every Hebrew word refers to God." And so it does. What word are we to choose when we choose life? What word harbors the mystery and meaning of life? It is the word of the Holy Tongue. The *Sifre* teaches that when a child begins to speak, his father should teach him Torah *and the holy tongue*; if his father fails to teach his child the holy tongue, it says, "it is as though he had buried the little one." So in this ethical will I have offered you some words from the Holy Tongue, that you may find life in them. Why is it as though the father had buried his child? Because the word of the Holy Tongue is the word that sustains life; it is the word of truth, of *emet*, in which inheres the essence of life. Spelled *alef-mem-tav*—the first, middle, and last letters of the alphabet—*emet* contains all the letters of all the words that sustain a life. The first letter, *alef*, as we have seen, signifies the Name of the Holy One. If we lose the *alef* of *emet*—if we lose the Holy One in the wholeness of the Holy Tongue—we are left with *met*, which is "death."

Since we are talking about the word *life*, let me say a few words about the ones who gave you life: your mothers. Whatever life you have begins with your reverence for your mother, which, as we learn from the fifth commandment to honor your father and mother, is a reverence for the God who is Life. It takes three, says the Talmud, to create a life: a father, a mother, and God. And yet, your mother, not your father, confers upon you the blessing and the summons to your identity as a Jew and as a human being. A Jewish mother, and not a Jewish father, makes a Jew a Jew. To have an origin—to have a mother—is to be already marked for a mission: origin implies destiny, when that origin is seen as a *mother* and not as some primeval ooze. Situated at the origin of human sanctity, a mother represents not the primeval but the immemorial. Once again, the lie of evolution is exposed. Life does not evolve—it is created, borne from the womb of the Supernal Mother, whose face gazes upon you through the loving face of your mother. Evolution unfolds through time. Life unfolds through the eternal.

Signifying an eternal, immemorial past, the mother who gives you life reveals an open-ended future and therefore the mystery of the *yet to be*. Life lies not in what is but in what is yet to be, as in the act of giving birth. Nothing is more laden with potential and possibility than birth: life is *possibility*. Hence the prophet's messianic pronouncement: "Behold, a young woman will conceive and give birth." To have meaning—to have the very possibility of life, in other words—is to have a *mother*, without whom there is no home or dwelling place, which is the guiding star on the compass of life. Thus we see more clearly than ever that, through her tie to the *beit* at the origin of Torah, the mother is both the foundation of Torah and the center of the home. A dwelling place is not a place where we are holed up, looking out for ourselves. It is a place where our mothers set a table for others, to sustain the lives of others, beginning with their children.

The mystery of value and meaning unfolds wherever we make room for another—that is the meaning of dwelling: we do not usurp the place of another but set a place for another at our table. A mother is precisely the one who does not usurp the place of another. Rather, miraculously, with God's help, she creates room for another life within herself, in the very depths of her physical being. There is no giving more profoundly holy than giving birth and thereby giving life. Like the God who is Life, a mother is *other*-oriented. Maternal love, then, embodies the radical opposite of material interest, which is the Nazis' interest in *Lebensraum*, or "living space," a term that designated the usurping of the place and the space of another. Hence wherever the Nazis extended their *Lebensraum*, death and evil followed in its wake. And among their first targets were not only Jewish children but also Jewish mothers.

Defining the mother as the vessel of life is the "womb" that is *rechem*; it is a cognate of *racham*, which means to "love" or to "have compassion" as only a mother can love and have compassion. That love and compassion are the vessel of life. Joined with *rachamim* —that is, "compassion" or "love"—the father becomes the Holy One, as in the expression *Av HaRachamim*, "the Father of love and compassion" or "the loving and compassionate Father"—the Father who is also Mother, the God who is Life. Without God the Mother we have no access, no relation, to God the Father. The Oneness of God is a singularity that entails the Oneness of the Supernal Mother and the Heavenly Father; when these two origins are *uniquely* One, the purpose of life becomes clear: to create a home.

We see more clearly now what it means to say that through the mother we have the Torah: bearing life into the world, she bears Torah into the world. Again, it cannot be repeated too often: the Torah is the *Ets Chayim*, the "Tree of Life," that sustains all life. Thus the Talmud compares the Torah to a woman, the source of life. Thus in the Zohar it is written: "First came *Ehyeh* (I shall be), the dark womb of all. Then *Asher Ehyeh* (That I Am), indicating the readiness of the Mother to beget all." The "I shall be" posits the yet-to-be that is the horizon of meaning. The "That I am" or "What I am" is the manifestation of meaning along that horizon: begetting all, begetting life, the mother begets meaning. Begetting all, the Zohar says further, the Supernal Mother begets all of humanity: "The [Supernal] Mother said: 'Let us make man in our image.'" Bearing in mind the association between the mother and the House of Jacob, we recall a Midrash: "The Holy One, blessed be He, said to His world: 'O My world, My world! Shall I tell thee who created thee, who formed thee? Jacob has created thee, Jacob has formed thee.'" For the House of Jacob signifies the mother of creation. From the womb of the mother's compassion, from the *rechem* within the *rachamim*, human life itself begins to stir. Thus the mother links us to the Creator, to the absolute origin of all things.

Only a mother can beget a mother: only the vessel of life can give birth to the vessel of life. Thanks to the mother, the world itself is sustained and all of creation becomes a dwelling place; thanks to the mother, creation has meaning. Remember that, my children, each time your mother has a birthday or celebrates Mother's Day. Make your celebration of Mother's Day into a celebration of life and of the life of your mother and of the Torah of life. My synagogue recently honored me with this year's *Ner Tamid* award. Among those whom I specifically thanked was my wife, your mother and grandmother: I thanked her for teaching me the meaning of goodness, which is the meaning of life.

Which brings us back to the question of the relation between life and the good, between choosing life and choosing the Good that has already chosen us. Tied to the Eternal, the Good is made of the Light that constitutes the Torah, the Divine Name, and the soul. Hence the Zohar teaches that the letter *tet*, the first letter in *tov*, "signifies in all places the Light of Life; therefore the word 'good' (*tov*) begins with this letter." As the Light of *Life*, the Good is the substance of all of these eighteen words that sustain a life. Indeed, according to a mystical method of interpretation that I have already mentioned, the method known as *At-Bash*, *tov* is *nefesh*, meaning "life" or "soul." Only where the Holy One, who is the Light of Life, abides can goodness be found, and only where there is goodness can the soul have life.

Finally, let us elaborate just a bit more on the relation between choosing life and saving life with a story from Steven Spielberg's film *Schindler's List*. There is a scene in which Itzhak Stern, the Jew who assisted Schindler in drawing up the list of Jews to be saved, asserts, "The list is life." The measures that Schindler takes to save lives do not arise from personal inclination or self-satisfaction. Contrary to acting out of self-interest, he acts in a moment of forgetting himself, in spite of himself; he is able to save those lives because he regards his own life not as an end but as a *means* to that end. Further, he does not *choose* to behold the sanctity of the other human being—he is overwhelmed by it, both from within and from beyond. Thus he is summoned to save lives, in such a way that he cannot do otherwise. We do not decide whether this life is at work within us and beyond us any more than we decide whether our heart shall beat. We are healed by the help we offer, saved by the salvation we bring. And so he comes alive by doing good. Something alive takes hold of Schindler; he is like a man possessed. What lays claim to him? It is life itself, which is the life of the Good: it is the God who is Life.

How to heal the wound that arises when, God forbid, we inflict a wound upon God or our beloved fellow human being? Through forgiveness and *teshuvah*.

Forgiveness

My children, just as I began my reflection on gratitude by offering you my thanks, so I begin this reflection on forgiveness by seeking your forgiveness. Please forgive me for the harm I have done to you through my words or my silence, through my actions or failures to act, through my insensitivity or thoughtlessness. We have seen that relationship is the foundation of our humanity and our identity, that meaning in life rests upon a living relationship, and that the soul draws its breath from the midst of a relationship. When a relationship has been wounded, a piece of who we are is wounded as well. When a relationship has been wounded, the soul has trouble breathing. Only forgiveness can heal a wounded soul and restore who we are; only forgiveness can return us to a relationship of meaning.

Because the meaning restored through forgiveness inheres in a relationship, we receive forgiveness only in the measure that we offer it to another. Like the life of the soul, forgiveness abides between two. When someone comes to us and sincerely asks for forgiveness, we must grant him or her that forgiveness, else we can never receive forgiveness, either from God or from a fellow human being. And only the one whom we have harmed can forgive the harm we have done. There is no forgiving a people or a culture, no forgiving the Nazis, for example. We cannot forgive suffering inflicted on a third party. A mother cannot, dare not, forgive one who has inflicted suffering upon her children. From a Jewish standpoint, the very notion is unintelligible. And some crimes are beyond forgiveness.

Part of our preparation for Yom Kippur, the day when we seek forgiveness from God, lies in first seeking forgiveness from our fellow human beings. For only when we have thus healed the human-to-human relationship can we ever hope to heal our relationship to God. What do we seek forgiveness for? For the suffering we have caused to another, whether human or God. The greater the love that another has for us, the greater the suffering we cause to him or her. Because God's love for us is infinite, his capacity for suffering is infinite. And so we spend the Ten Days of Awe from Rosh Hashanah through Yom Kippur seeking forgiveness for the suffering we have caused God, in awe of the his infinite capacity to forgive. As Yom Kippur approaches we seek forgiveness from the people whom we have harmed, because the greatest suffering we inflict upon God comes not from a lapse in our prayers or Sabbath observance but from the suffering we inflict upon his children.

Because we are commanded to love God's children, seeking their forgiveness for the suffering we have caused them is an act of love: the commandment to love is a commandment to forgive. There is no loving without forgiving, no forgiving without loving. If the Second Temple was destroyed because of the gratuitous hatred of brother against brother, it was destroyed due to the absence of forgiveness. Where forgiveness is absent, God is absent. The key that unlocks the gate of his entry into this realm is forgiveness, the forgiveness that each of us offers to another with open arms: where there is forgiveness, there is embrace. Where there is embrace, there is a certain exposure to being wounded: forgiveness, both offered and received, comes with this vulnerability.

Faced with this vulnerability, we often cling to the illusion that is the ego, which lives in fear of being wounded. We grow afraid of offering forgiveness to another, because, in doing so, we would have to shed our armor and open our arms to another. In our ego's drive to dominate others, we must see to it that they remain forever in our debt; and yet, the more we persist in such an attitude, the deeper we sink into the quicksand of righteousness indignation, so that our own need for forgiveness exceeds any forgiveness we might offer. Entrenched in the ego, we erect around ourselves walls of resentment and bitterness. Just as the illusion that is the ego is the biggest obstacle in our relation to God, so is it the biggest obstacle in our relation to the other human being. And yet, the only way to remove the obstacle of the ego is through the very forgiveness that we fear to seek and to offer. There is no room in the heart for both ego and forgiveness. Filled with the ego, the heart is filled with emptiness and darkness. Filled with forgiveness, the heart is filled with life and light.

Wherever we assume the stance of "Here, look how gracious I am to forgive you," there is no forgiveness. Indeed, such posturing further increases our debt to the other. The forgiveness we offer, like the forgiveness we seek, must come with a measure of *bitul hayesh*, with a certain abrogation or forgetfulness of the self. Not only is the self the opposite of the soul—it is poison to the soul. And if the soul is to find healing in the forgiveness offered and received, then it must be purged of that poison. Such a condition often takes the form of self-pity or insisting that others owe us an apology, viewing ourselves as victims, and not as victimizers. It is often steeped in a flight from responsibility into a stance of self-justification in the face of what we know to be unjustifiable. And so we sink into the quagmire of an attitude of excuse, hiding, as Adam hid, from the One who puts to us the primal, perennial question: "Where are you?" Which means: "Where is your forgiveness?"

It happens that the only thing more difficult than offering forgiveness is seeking forgiveness. For in order to seek forgiveness, we must look into the face of the one we have harmed—the face that forbids all wounding—and say, "Please forgive me for hurting you so. Please." Such a move can be overwhelming, because when we are lost in the labyrinth of the illusory self, we come to hate the one whom we have wronged. Why? Because the one whom we have wronged robs us of our purity, of our righteousness, of our excuses, and turns us over to an irreparable indebtedness. The Mishnah tells us that even if we have paid compensation for the suffering we have caused the person whom we have injured, the offense is not forgiven until we come before that child of God, look him in the eyes, and plead for his forgiveness. Compensation does not mend the relation. Forgiveness is not a business transaction. The same Mishnah teaches that if the injured party should refuse the forgiveness that we sincerely seek, then he or she is deemed a *cruel* person. Note well: Cruelty lies not only in the suffering inflicted but also in the refusal of forgiveness for that suffering. Why? Because that refusal redoubles the suffering. And it works both ways.

Once again, forgiveness comes to bear only within a relationship in which loving the other child of God comes to bear. Just as the clichés concerning the importance of loving yourself in order to love others are sheer wind, so is the deception about how you must forgive yourself in order to forgive others. It is not for me to forgive myself, as if that might make things all better; no, only the other, whether human or God, can forgive me. If forgiveness is a movement of embrace, how do you embrace yourself? Who is forgiving whom? And for what? For harm done to another? How can you forgive yourself for that? True, harm done to another is harm done to yourself: as I have said, the soul suffers what it inflicts. True, once you have sought and received forgiveness, you should stop pounding your breast and move on to the task at hand, which is to bring healing to the other human being. You cannot do that while you are beating yourself up. Do not get stuck in the quicksand of excessive remorse. That, too, is one of the dangers of the ego's thirst for self-righteousness. It is the flagellant complex: the self becomes so preoccupied with its self-flagellation and phony repentance that it loses all capacity to offer or receive forgiveness.

Forgiveness requires a good memory—not for what we have suffered but for the suffering we have caused. Indeed, it is said that God remembers what we forget. Forgiveness requires a memory of what matters and of what is at stake in the human and in the higher relationships. With the coming of Yom Kippur, after we have sought forgiveness from others, we ascend into the Day of Atonement. Each portion of the prayers we utter on that momentous day takes us to a higher level of the upper realms, and memory is the key to this ascent. The words that appear most frequently in those prayers relate not to forgiveness but to remembrance, to our remembrance of God and his remembrance of us, to our remembrance of those who have come before us and of those who are yet to be born. It is a remembrance of the legacy we inherit and of the legacy we leave behind. And of the legacy we have betrayed. If, as my teacher Elie Wiesel once said, faith does not mean that one day it will come but that one day it was there, then the remembrance that is essential to forgiveness is a remembrance of the way back, which is, in turn, is essential to *teshuvah*, the movement of "return."

The movement of forgiveness is a movement of *teshuvah*, of a "return" to a relationship, through a healing of the relationship. Forgiveness and *teshuvah* are of a piece. More than an attitude, a feeling, or a state of mind, forgiveness is a *movement.* Forgiveness requires *doing* something. What is the sign that we have been forgiven? It is this: we sin no more. Forgiveness, then, is a response, which is another meaning of *teshuvah*, a response to an outcry that comes both from within us and from beyond us. While repentance might be at work, *teshuvah* is not reducible to repentance, which is, indeed, an attitude or a state of mind and heart. "Repentance" is different word: *charatah.* It is an inner condition. The *teshuvah* that belongs to forgiveness is a movement outward, a reaching out to another.

"Great is *teshuvah*," says the great Talmudic sage Rabbi Meir. "For thanks to one who does *teshuvah*, the sins of the world are forgiven." Because all of creation is at stake in every action of every one of us, it just takes *one* of us to bring about a transformation of creation itself. We have seen that each of us is responsible for all, and I more that the rest. Each of us, therefore, has a messianic responsibility to all, for the sake of all of creation. Seeking forgiveness from another, we seek forgiveness from creation itself. For harm done to another soul is harm done to all of creation. Thus each movement of return has the potential to return all the world to the higher relationship that sanctifies the human relationship. And so we have a faint hint of what is at stake in our offering and receiving of forgiveness.

Recall the teaching from the Talmud: "Seven things were created before the world was created, and these are they: The Torah, *Teshuvah*, the Garden of Eden, Gehenna, the Throne of Glory, the Temple, and the Name of the Messiah." What does it mean? Why did these seven things precede the creation of heaven and earth and all of creation? Because heaven and earth and all of creation rest upon these seven things, each of which is tied to the other to form a foundation for all there is from beyond all there is. Yes. When forgiveness leads us to *teshuvah*, it leads us in the direction of redemption, in the direction of the garden of Eden, a path charted by our Torah. As each soul emanates from the Throne of Glory, so is each soul is summoned to this messianic mission, bearing in its own name a trace of the Name of the Messiah. The Temple was built on the Temple Mount—where the dust of Adam was gathered, where Jacob had his dream of the ladder connecting heaven and earth, where Abraham raised the knife over Isaac. From the Temple shines the light of the first utterance of creation: "Let there be light." Thus from the Temple radiates the light unto the nations, its windows designed not to let light in but to let light out. And Gehenna? Among the upper realms it is the realm of healing, the healing not only of the soul that through its transgression has wounded itself but also the healing of the relationships essential to the life of the soul. Here, in Gehenna, the ultimate forgiveness, the ultimate *Teshuvah*, is realized.

According to the Talmudic sage Rabbi Abbahui, the place occupied by those who seek forgiveness in a movement of *teshuvah* cannot be attained "even by the completely righteous." Why? Because *teshuvah* takes us into a realm that preceded creation. Because, while the "completely righteous" have all forgiveness to offer, they have no forgiveness to seek, no movement of return to make. Still, even the *tzaddikim* show up on Yom Kippur, as does God himself: yes, God himself seeks a path of return, of *teshuvah*, to his children. "Return, O Israel, and I shall return," God desperately cries out through his prophet Zechariah. On what day and at what hour are we to undertake the movement of forgiveness, of *teshuvah*? According to Rabbi Eliezer, one of the greatest of our Talmudic sages, we must seek forgiveness and make the movement of return one day before our death. Which means: it we must do it *now*, since none of us knows the day or the hour of our death. And yet, when it comes to seeking forgiveness and making *teshuvah*, we are always late for the appointment, whether we seek the forgiveness of our fellow human being or whether we seek God's forgiveness. And God? What about him? If he, too, undertakes a *teshuvah*, does he, too, seek our forgiveness?

We live in the aftermath of the Shoah. We live in a time of great suffering and evil, from the MD Anderson Cancer Center, to the halls of St. Jude's Hospital, to the killing fields of Iraq, Sudan, and Central Africa. Some of us, then, may have a problem with forgiving the God from whom we seek forgiveness. How can he, the One whose hand is in all things, be forgiven for his creation of such a world? How can he be forgiven for what looks like his betrayal of the Covenant, which promises that, if we abide by the Torah, he will uphold his promise "as long as the heavens are above the earth?" Perhaps there are times when the heavens are no longer above the earth, as when the heavens were transformed into a cemetery. Perhaps there are times when it seems that the Messiah has tarried too long. And yet, if the Messiah tarries, it is because we ourselves have tarried too long in our movement of return.

I used to have this conversation with one of the greatest of my teachers, with Rabbi Levi Klein. I would point out to him the teaching from the Talmud, according to which everything is in God's hands, except the fear of heaven. "That leaves room for a lot of things to go very wrong," I would say to him. And he would answer, "Yes, the responsibility for creation is in our hands. But don't let God off the hook."

A story: One Yom Kippur more than two hundred years ago, when Jews of Eastern Europe were undergoing horrific persecutions, the faithful of Berditchev gathered in the synagogue to offer up their confessional prayers and seek God's forgiveness. Rebbe Levi Yitzchak happened to be standing next to a humble tailor named Yankel and overheard the penitent's desperate plea.

"Our Father, our King," Yankel prayed with his usual fervor. "I humbly beg Your forgiveness for my sins. I have perhaps kept a bit of cloth paid for by another. I have, on occasion, overcharged a customer. . . . But what about You, O Lord? You have taken husbands from their wives, wives from their husbands, and, God forbid, children from their parents. I'll tell you what: if You forgive me, I shall forgive You."

To which Levi Yitzchak whispered in his ear, "O Yankel, Yankel, you let God off way too easily!"

Why did the rebbe speak such words of defiance, words that to some ears sound heretical? Because when it comes to forgiving the God of the Covenant, we must stand firm and insist that he live up to the Covenant that he has made with Israel. We must insist that he remember and watch over us, *zachor v'shamor*, his children who are most profoundly devoted to him. "Who am I," you may think, "to place such demands on God? After all, I am not the Rebbe Levi Yitzchak." But, I would ask in turn, who do you have to be? You, too, are a child of God, a child of the Covenant with God. Of course, in order to be in a position to pose such a challenge to the Holy One, we must be faithful to his Covenant. There's the rub. As my teacher Emil Fackenheim points out, the Jews of Europe were marked for extermination not because they abandoned the Torah but because their grandparents refused to abandon God and his Torah. For the Nazis defined the Jew as anyone who had a Jewish grandparent, and the grandparent was deemed Jewish by virtue of belonging to a synagogue. Nazi Jew hatred, as the Nazis themselves affirmed, was not about race.

Another story: One day in Auschwitz the inmates congregated in a block of death and summoned God himself to stand trial for betraying his Covenant with the Jews. After all, these Jews even in their affliction, remained devoted to God. Had they not lined up to take turns laying the *tefillin* retrieved from one of the dead? As Elie Wiesel has related, they laid the *tefillin* and said the prayers, but they said them with a tone of defiance. On the unprecedented day of that trial, broken and emaciated, dressed not in the robes of the court but in the stripes of the camp, the Jews who had seen their families slaughtered before their eyes, who had looked on as their parents, wives, and children were led off to the gas chambers, called the court to session.

Arguments were presented by attorneys for the prosecution and by attorneys for the defense. Said the attorneys for the prosecution: "The most afflicted of Your children have been the most faithful to You. They rushed into synagogues to rescue Your Torah from the flames. They cried out the *Shema* as they entered the gas chambers. Is this their reward for their last dying devotion to Your Torah?"

In the face such arguments, the defense attorneys were all but at a loss. "Whatever dedication God may have to His Torah," they argued, "what might we become without our own dedication to it? If the enemy should slay us as Jews, shall we become an accomplice to that murder by turning away for the One who has created us as Jews? Shall we join hands with our murderers, who aim is to annihilate God and His Torah through the annihilation of His witnesses?"

Still, things were not going well for the Holy One, the Creator of heaven and earth. Just as the judges were about to pronounce God guilty, one of the inmates rose and said, "We must stop now. It is time for the afternoon prayers." And so the Jews, both for the prosecution and for the defense, left off with the trial and fervently prayed to the God whom they had accused. For without their prayers, without their loving allegiance to Our Heavenly Father, their accusations were empty and self-serving. And as they prayed the afternoon prayers, the flames of the crematoria rose up into the heavens, casting the ashen body of Israel to the winds, so they prayed knowing that they, too, were destined for the flames.

One more story: It was a Shabbat in 1944, the one day of the week when the Holy One enters this realm, that day now eclipsed by the entry of the Evil One. As he was being ushered onto the sealed train from Sighet to Auschwitz, the Rabbi of Kretchenev consoled his disciples. "It is written," he said to the Jews who joined him, "that when the Messiah will come, God, blessed be He, will arrange a *makhol*, a dance, for the Just." And he added: "*Makhol* comes from the verb *limkhol*—to forgive. There will come a time when the Just Men, the *Tzaddikim*, will forgive God, blessed be He"—by dancing a dance of forgiveness.

There is a scene from *Zorba the Greek* by Nikos Kazantzakis, himself a Greek who loved Jews and Jewish tradition. Zorba, known for his dance, relates the tale of when his little three-year-old boy was stricken by an illness and passed away. The people of his village carried the tiny coffin to the burial site, and as his little one was laid into the earth, Zorba began dancing around the open grave. "Zorba has gone mad!" the villagers cried out. "Zorba has gone mad!" Then Zorba responds: "And ye, if at that moment I had not danced, I would surely have gone mad!" The Just Men will dance a dance of forgiveness, a dance made of an anguished outcry, else they will go mad.

To forgive is to dance. Why? Because when we break free of the ego, the otherwise firm ground starts to shift from under our feet, especially when it comes to forgiving God. What can it mean to forgive God, the Creator of heaven and earth? Perhaps it means forgiving him for his Creation, for creating a world in which three-year-olds are laid into the earth or consigned to the flames, a world in which the wicked prosper and the righteous suffer, like Job did. Or did he?

"I was preoccupied with Job," Professor Wiesel once said, "especially in the early years after the war. In those days he could be seen on every road of Europe. Wounded, robbed, mutilated. Certainly not happy. Nor resigned. I was offended by his surrender in the text. Job's resignation as a man was an insult to man. . . . He should have said to God: Very well, I forgive You, I forgive you to the extent of my sorrow, my anguish. But what about my dead children, do they forgive you? What right do I have to speak on their behalf?" Job cried out to God in his pain and outrage over the injustice of creation, over the deaths of most innocent of the innocent. In the end, even after rebuking Job, God declared, "My servant Job has spoken rightly." And yet Job remained silent over his dead children, even as they looked down upon him from on high, as the dead gaze upon us from the skies over Auschwitz. The dead and God. As Professor Wiesel has written, "These Children have taken Your countenance, O God."

God

AMONG THE EIGHTEEN WORDS that sustain a life, this word is unlike any other, for this word is made of many words. Made of many words, it is the most elusive of all words. It resists definition, because to define is to confine, and this word exceeds all such attempts to circumscribe it. It transcends every metaphor, every simile, and all comparison because, as it is written, *Ein k'mokha*, "There is nothing like You." And yet, this word is the most essential of all words, essential to every word, to every bond between word and meaning, to every human relationship, to every expression of gratitude, to every saying of "you" with all our heart and soul. It is a word essential to the very life of the soul. It is, in a word, the source of all words. The Baal Shem Tov, you recall, teaches that within every word lives the letter *alef* (yes, *lives*), the letter that consists of three letters: a *yud* above, a *vav* in the middle, and a *yud* below. The numerical values of these three letters, 10-6-10, add up to 26, which is the value of the Ineffable Name, the *yud-hey-vav-hey*, 10-5-6-5. So God, who at every instant creates heaven and earth through the word, abides in every word, as does the silence of the *alef* that preceded the *beit* of the first utterance of creation. This word subsists in the silence of all tongues.

In the Jewish tradition God is first and foremost the Creator of the letters and words through which all things come into being, the One who "creates through the twenty-two letters," as it says in the Midrash. It is he who "forms the light and creates the darkness," as we affirm the words of the prophet Isaiah each day in our prayers. All of creation is made of his Ineffable Name. All of Creation whispers his Name. The first word in the opening line of the Torah is *bereshit* or "in the beginning . . ." It does not refer to the first in a series of events but rather designates the most important truth of all truths: the first principle of any understanding that we may have of our lives and of God is rooted in the truth that *Bereshit bara Elokim*, "In the beginning God created," that God is the Creator, whose movement of creation is a movement into a relation. In an act of infinite love the Creator summons us into being and through that summons commands us to love.

The Christians say that God is love. The Jewish formulation is a little different: God is the *commandment* to love. God, as we have seen, lives *in* the commandment, in the *mitzvah*, beginning with the commandment to love. If, as God says, we are to be holy as he is holy, it means we are to love as he loves. There, in the movement of loving, lies God.

And yet there are times when we may wonder: Where is God's love? There are times when God, who is present everywhere, seems infinitely distant from us. A Hasid once asked his teacher: "Why is it that the God who is so close to us sometimes seems so far away?" His teacher answered: "Have you ever noticed how a father will step back from his little one to get the toddler to walk to him, so as to teach him to walk? So it is with God. There are times when He is teaching us to walk on our own, to walk toward Him." And God rejoices when he sees us take our first steps toward him, our arms outstretched, as any father or mother would rejoice. Even in his absence he is present: he is present precisely *as the One who is absent.*

There are times when we are angry with God, and there are times when God wants us to be angry with him, not in the whine of "Why me?" but in the outrage of "Why the children? Why the suffering of humanity? Why all the evil?" Therefore, the Zohar teaches, the word *barukh*, which means "blessing," can also refer to an anger or an outrage that is blessed. We look around and behold the suffering of humanity, and we erupt in a cry of "Why?!" As this *Why* is essential to the life of the soul, so is it essential to approaching God. It is a cry of "Where are *you*?!" as when God cried out to Adam. If we have no sense of *where* God is, then we have no sense of *who* he is, and without the *Who* of God there is no *Why* of creation: the *Where*, the *Who*, and the *Why* of all things come together in God. If we are ever to have any understanding of the *Why* of Creation and the *Who* of God, we must move toward that *Where*, toward the *Makom* or "Place," from which God reaches out to us, pleading, "Come to Me," like a father teaching his toddler to walk. Therefore *Makom* is among the many names of God. Without this Place—without this Why—we have no direction, no meaning, no mission, no life. We cannot walk.

When from the depths of our heart we cry out to the Holy One, "Why?!" and "Where are You!?" it is the Divine spark within us that raises the outcry. Only where there is a Why can there be presence. God is presence. God is the Why, especially when we cannot fathom it. There are moments when we can sense that presence, as when we gaze into the eyes of our infant child. It is the living presence of the One who is absolutely Other to the pretentions of my illusory I-saying ego. Hence the teaching that only God can say "I." God's I-saying is a cry of "you," of the word of relation, for presence happens only in the midst of the relationship between

I and you. And so God summons us to be present, to declare, "*Hineni!* Here I am for You!" Only where we are present for the sake of another is God present. God is the one who can be both absent and present in the same moment, eloquent and silent in the same instant. When God seems most distant, in that very hour we must walk toward him by reaching out to another, no matter how distant or how silent he may seem. That is how you seek God. That is how you may come to know God. Seek God, my children. Seek him by seeking what must be done. Seek to know God, for to know God is to know what must be done.

Who is God? What shall we call him? When Moses asks for his name, he identifies himself as "I Am Who I Am" or "I Shall Be As I Shall Be": *Ehyeh Asher Ehyeh.* Therefore Moses is to tell the children of Israel that I Shall Be has sent him. But what sort of name is I Shall Be? How is such a name to be understood? With the revelation of the *Ehyeh* in the future tense the *yet* that instills existence with meaning comes into being. It situates God in the eternal future, or in a future where the Eternal is forever yet to be revealed. Open-ended and replete with possibility, the Divine *Ehyeh* reveals God as the One who has no limit, no horizon, infinite and eternal. Abraham Abulafia interprets *Ehyeh* to mean "I shall be whatever you will be," suggesting that who God is depends upon what we make of ourselves through the works of our hands. *Yes!* The ephemeral *essence* of the Holy One lies in our *hands*! The heart may be the favorite dwelling place of God, but he comes to life in our hands. God is the shadow of man, says the Baal Shem, which means God imitates our every move. As we show loving kindness toward others, so God takes on the aspect of loving kindness. Where we are cruel, God appears to be cruel. And if we come to God empty handed, we encounter him as emptiness.

"Situated" in an elsewhere or in a "realm" that is otherwise than all there is, the One who is *Ehyeh* is *more* that all there is, *prior* to all there is, *beyond* all there is, and therefore *determinate* of all there is. The revelation of the God as *Ehyeh* precedes the revelation of the four letters of the "proper Name" of God. And yet, I Shall Be bears many names, many *kinuyim*, to use a Hebrew term for "names of God." Signifying a "name" or a "name of God," the word *kinui* has as its root the word *ken*, which means "yes": taking on a name, the Nameless One says yes to creation. And he is present wherever we say yes to life. If you would know God, my children—if you would know His Name—learn to say yes to life unconditionally, just as the Torah is a saying of yes to life, beginning as it does with the creation of life.

Not only does the Name of the Holy One impart meaning to every name, but the Name of the One who created through the utterance of his Name makes possible every utterance. What does he speak in the utterance of his Name? Torah. Hence in the Zohar it is written: "For the Torah is the Name of the Holy One, blessed be He. As the Name of the Holy One is engraved in the Ten Words (creative utterances) of creation, so is the whole Torah engraved in the Ten Words (Decalogue), and these Ten Words are the Name of the Holy One, and the whole Torah is thus one Name, the Holy Name of God Himself." Whatever else might be said of the names of God or the meaning of the word *God*, this point is crucial, because it reveals two fundamental features of the very life of God: (1) God is the living ground of all that exists, and (2) God's Name conveys a commandment, through which he sanctifies our lives with meaning. God imparts meaning to creation because creation is born of that Name. As God creates, God commands. To know God, my children, is to know you are commanded, with love.

According to our tradition, there are seventy words for the word *God*. Don't worry. I shall not go into all of them now, but maybe a few. These seventy names of God, says the Zohar, are gathered into the single name *Shema*, which begins the prayer "Hear, O Israel, the Lord our God, the Lord is One." It is as if the prayer were saying, "Hear, for that hearing of God *is* God." When we hear, God hears. God is manifest in the movement of his witness, which is a *hearing*, a *heeding*, and a *healing* of the soul. That movement is his movement. And his movement is his Name: *God* is a verb. In the Midrash God declares, "You wish to know My Name? I am called according to My deeds." And so the names of God derive from his actions: *who* God is lies in *what* he does. And in what we do: the meaning of the word *God* lies in the meaning of our deeds. So what will our deeds be like? Will they be deeds of love, as commanded by God, or will they be deeds that attest to the world's nihilism that would obliterate God?

One essential response to the meaninglessness of the nihilism that surrounds us is the remembrance and observance of the Sabbath: remember and observe the Sabbath, and you will know the meaning of this word that sustains life—*God*. Remember and observe the Sabbath even in the smallest ways. Light a candle. Say the *Kiddush*. Bless your children. And you will come to know the meaning of this word that sustains a life, above all other words. You will come to know *HaShem*, the Name. For *Shabbat* is among the seventy names of God.

To refer to God as *HaShem* is to affirm that all that is formed and all that is spoken—all that is real and meaningful—emanates from one Name. There lies the oneness of the God who is One. When God speaks and thus summons the world into existence, he speaks His Name. While language contains names and nouns, it does not contain the Name; rather, the Name contains language. The Name, therefore, is not something we use to call upon God—it is how God calls upon us *by name*. *HaShem* is the One who is "there," who is *sham*, not as a blind principle or an abstract essence—not as an indifferent it—but as a loving he or she, calling out from within every he or she, from within every you. Where is God? How are we to know God? By helping another, a he or she or you, the one who is right here before us, reaching out to us. The One who is *HaShem* is One who listens and calls out, not a logos we derive, a phenomenon we observe, or a concept we contrive but One with whom we enter into a relation. Recalling that *shamah* means not just "there" but "to there," we realize that *HaShem* is the One we move *toward*, so that the Name is also a movement, the noun one with the verb.

As the Name that permeates being from within and beyond being, God is also known as the *Shem Havayah*, or the "Name of Being." Which is to say: God is the *meaning* of being. Being has no inherent meaning or name; being is simply *what* is there, not *who* is there. Every *who* is a breach of being. Neutral and indifferent, being is deaf and mute, an "it" whose silence is but a rumbling and whose rumbling is just a noise—until God enters. For the philosophers of being, God is not the Creator but is, at best, the Supreme Being, the Unmoved Mover, the First Cause, or the First Principle—all of which are utterly indifferent toward humanity and therefore utterly alien to Jewish teaching. It is the god, who, in the words of Aristotle, neither loves nor is in need of love. Cause, principle, and other "big bangs" are not called by name: we do not cry out "Father!" to a concept or to some primal event in the past. Nor does such being, however perfect or supreme, ask what God asks Adam and each of us: "Where are you?" It is not for nothing that the philosophers of being, the beloved of the intellectuals, are the philosophers of nihilism and nothingness, who would proclaim with pride the death of God. Thus when Pascal died in 1662, there was found pinned inside his waistcoat a slip of paper that read, "The God of Abraham, the God of Isaac, the God of Jacob, *not* the god of the philosophers!"

God opens the revelation at Mount Sinai with the word *Anokhi*, "I." The I-saying of God, which is the ground of all I-saying, comes from beyond being, which is to say: he is not perfect—he is *holy*. As the Holy One, God bears an Ineffable Name because God is beyond essence; he harbors an Ineffable Name because he is more than he is: he is eternally *more* and therefore eternally *meaningful*. Only as the Name of Being calls out the name of the soul can the soul come into being to occupy space and time and thus take on a name and a meaning in a breach of being. The soul is not a subject who imposes its will on the world; rather, the soul is the object of God's creation, entrusted with his creation. That is why human I-saying, when it means "I who am here for You," reveals a trace of the Divine utterance of I.

God is the One who *cares* about every detail of all there is, so that through our attention to detail we pay attention to God. Only because God cares can we enter into an argument with him—which brings us to another meaning of *Havayah*: it is "argument" or "dispute." The Name of Being, God is revealed as the Name of Argument, the One in whose name we enter into argument, sometimes with God himself, as when Abraham challenges him, saying, "Will the Judge of all the earth not do justice?" With whom are we to argue, if not with God? Without God all argument over the justice or injustice of Creation is vain and vacuous, like arguing with a wall. The Talmud teaches that God likes to be defeated in such arguments, for to know God is to argue with him, to wrestle with him, as the very name of *Yisrael* commands us: "Strive with God, wrestle with God." The question that Abraham puts to God comes in their first encounter after the Covenant is sealed; it is precisely the sealing of the Covenant that makes such a questioning possible. The Covenant is made not with mute being but with One who speaks and listens and cares—who calls our name with love, like a mother, and whose Name we seek and long to know: in the words of Miguel de Unamuno, "Tell me Thy Name!" means "Save my soul!"

Engaging God in an argument is not only possible—at times it is *required* in order for God to be God, in order for this word *God* to have any meaning. Entering into a Covenant is like entering into a marriage. The human being here becomes to God what Eve was to Adam: an *ezer kenegdo*, a "helper against him." The Name of Being, the Name of Argument, longs for the disputation undertaken for the sake of the Name. Because it is not good for either God or the human being to be alone, the One who is like no other enters being to *engage* the human being in an argument, for the sake of the human being. Think of it! There is a Midrash that reads the verse in Exodus 15:11, *Mi k'mokhah b'elim*?, "Who is Like You among the mighty?" as *Mi k'mokhah b'ilemim*?, "Who is like You among the mute?": that is, how long will you stand by silently while your children suffer? Where is God when, in our outrage and our pain, we wish to confront him, as Job did? He is in the anguished outcry itself.

God is the *Mechuyav-HaMetziut*, the One who "Affirms Reality" or "Obliges Reality"—or better, who affirms the dearness of reality by infusing reality with "duty," with *chovah*, a cognate of *mechuyav*. Significantly, the phrase *Mechuyav-HaMetziut* also means "necessary" or "vital," indicating what is necessary to the affirmation of life; indeed, the noun *chiyuv* means both "affirmation" and "obligation." The life we affirm obliges us in our very affirmation of it. The life we affirm is the *Chei HaOlamim*, the "Life of the Worlds" or the "Life of the Eternal," which is yet another meaning of *God*. Being is not simply *there*—it is *alive*. Because it is alive, all that unfolds within being does so according to a certain wisdom or intelligence; thus we have the phrase *HaSechel HaPoel*, denoting God as the "Intelligence at

Work." This expression tells us, once again, that God *is* what he *does*. It tells us that his wisdom is manifest throughout creation; it tells us that the Life of the Worlds is precisely the Intelligence at Work all around us all the time in a constant renewal of creation.

Another name for God is *Elokei Kedem*, which means the "Ancient God" or the "Eternal God," eternal because ancient, where ancient refers not merely to a time long ago but to what is eternally *already*, what I have described as the immemorial. The situation does not determine the good; rather the Good judges the situation from a position that is always *prior* to the situation, eternally *kodem* or "before." Meaning in life derives from this "before." For it contains the movement "forward," *kadimah*, into the future, which is the realm of meaning, the realm of God. Recall Abraham Joshua Heschel's remark: "Time is God in the realm of space." Here we understand this truth on a deeper level: the presence of God in the realm of space is the presence of meaning in the realm of life.

This brings us to yet another expression for God: *Atik-Yomin*, the "Ancient of Days." The ancient God is not really, really old; rather, he is the One whose antiquity signifies the ever renewed eternity that is always *already*, the *alef* that already precedes the *beit* of the beginning. The *Atik-Yomin* is the God who constitutes life time by imparting meaning to the days of our lives before the day begins: older than the sum of days, the Ancient of Days fills our days with destiny. And so the Ancient of Days takes hold of us as we seize the day. It is the Ancient of Days who renews our days as in the days of antiquity; he gives us a future by making us contemporary with our forebears. The Ancient of Days is he who commands us "on this day," *hayom*, to lay the words spoken at Mount Sinai upon our heart. The ground may shift, but the *already* is certain. Even when we are confused about which path to follow, we have no doubt that one path is better than another. Though the ground under our feet may crumble, we must still tread a path.

In God alone lies any certainty we may have in life. He is, therefore, the *Tzur Yisrael*, the "Rock of Israel." This certainty, this security, is not the security of arms and ramparts. Rather, it is the security of meaning, of what lies beyond all concern for security. Like the path that remains even when the ground is gone, this security is an assurance that exceeds safety. It is the security of having something to live for and thus something—or better, some*one*—to die for. It is the security that we do not live and die in vain, that in our life, as well as in our death, we have a mission to accomplish. Here, too, my children, we discover the meaning of the word *God*. The *Tzur Yisrael* does not protect us from death; he protects us from *meaningless* death, from a life lived and a death endured *for nothing*. For there is no terror greater than this terror over empty and meaningless suffering and death.

God does not protect us from suffering; he protects us from this terror, so that we have a refuge in God without having to transform our home into a fortress that inevitably falls. For suffering and death breach the walls of every fortress. The Rock of Israel is the rock not of the firm ground but of the good deed, which endures beyond the death that besieges us, unto the thousandth generation, as it is written.

The God who is the Rock of Israel is the *Chakham HaRazim*, or the "Sage of the Secrets," that is, the One who knows all that is hidden and fathoms every mystery. God is far more than One who knows our every thought and deed, as if God were a kind of super spy. Beyond his knowledge of what we ourselves secretly know and are afraid to admit, God knows all that we do not know and can never know, even about ourselves. Precisely what lies beyond our knowledge gives meaning to our knowledge; it is the mystery beyond the horizon of our understanding that summons us to draw nigh unto that horizon, even though it recedes as we approach it. Without mystery, knowledge is nothing more than information and power; and if knowledge is nothing more than power, then it is meaningless. Mystery is not about ignorance; rather, it is a mode of understanding that exceeds knowledge, something we sense when we gaze at the heavens above, peer into the eyes of our beloved, or look inward to our heart.

In every thought the One who transcends thought is revealed. When we think in terms of Torah, God thinks through us. We do not study Torah—Torah studies us. In our study of Torah God studies us, measures us, questions us through the questions we put to Torah. To ask of a passage in Torah, "What does this mean?" is to ask "What do I mean?" Or better: God asks us, "What do you mean? What is the meaning of your life?" It is a question concerning our righteousness. And so God is known as the *Neveh Tzeddek*, the "Dwelling Place of Righteousness." This phrase is also used to refer to the Temple, whose light emanates from its windows to transform the land into a dwelling place, making it into the *Holy Land*, and not just a piece of real estate or a slice of geography. The land of Israel is the Holy Land because it is the dwelling place of the Holy One: it is holy not because of what has transpired there, but rather what has transpired there has happened because it is holy—*already*. Anyone who has set foot in Israel has experienced this truth. Only where the Holy One dwells can there be a dwelling place for the human being. And only as long as Israel is the Holy Land—a dwelling place for the People of the Covenant—can humanity hope to dwell in the world.

Here we come to another dimension of the word *God*, expressed in the phrase *Tzaddik HaOlamim*, the "Righteous One of the Worlds." The implication is that God is not only the foundation of righteousness but that creation itself—all of reality, in this world and all worlds—rests on righteousness. Righteousness is not a cultural invention; rather, it makes culture possible. Upheld by righteousness, everything that exists has both value and design. Nothing is merely "there," neutral and value free. Nothing is accidental. This truth brings to mind the legend of the *Lamed Vavniks*, of the thirty-six righteous people in each generation whose righteousness sustains all of creation. Nothing physical—*nothing existent*—sustains existence. This bears repeating: *Nothing existent sustains existence.* The world, rather, rests on something *above* it, on something it never touches but that is nevertheless in its midst. That is why pursuing a path is not the same as clinging to the firm ground. And there is no pursuing a path without storytelling: the path laid out by God lies in the tale. God created us because he loves stories, as you love stories, my children.

Because the events of the world belong to a design, they form a kind of narrative: they are about something in the way that a story is about something, transmitting a message that is not subject to lectures or sermons. Recall what is written in the *Sifre* about *Aggadah*, or the tales of the tradition: "You wish to recognize the One who spoke and brought the world into being? Learn *Aggadah* for in *Aggadah* you will find God." The tale that constitutes tradition is part of the tale that constitutes creation, and the tale of creation is the never-ending story of God. How does God create? By telling a tale. How do we teach and transmit a legacy? By telling stories. Hence the prominence of tales in this ethical will.

Just today, my children, I was studying a Mishnah with my friend and teacher Alan Rosen. It concerned the giving of tithes to the Levites, the priests, and the widow, orphan, and stranger. We noted in this sequence a movement of ascent, where the highest, the Holy One, was to be found in the widow, the orphan, and the stranger, those who are most vulnerable and most in need, those in whom we encounter the need of the Holy One Himself. Therefore God is known as the *Avi Yetomim*, the "Father of Orphans," and the *Dayan Almanot*, or the "Protector of Widows." More than painful, the loss suffered by the widow and the orphan is meaningful. It is meaningful because our relation to the widow and the orphan rests on the commandments of their protector, who requires us to act as a protector. The urgency of caring for one who has no protector—the widow, the orphan, and the stranger—therefore, does not rest on anything so flimsy as human compassion; rather, it arises from on high. Caring for the other human being is a question of justice, not merely a question of kindness, where justice is understood, once again, as a giving, not as a balancing of the scales. For God is also the "Judge of Widows," in the sense that he judges our treatment of them: he judges *on behalf of* the bereft. Who is the widow? Anyone, man or woman, in need of a protector.

In the realization that God as Protector summons us to provide protection we come to another realization: we must be for the other person what God is for us. In this task imposed upon us we find a certain comfort—not in the help we receive but in the help we offer. And we understand why God is referred to as the *Baal Nechamot*, or the "Comforter." It is not that God pats us on the back when we are feeling low; nor is it that God loves us even when we are unworthy of love. Rather, God is the One who comforts because God is the One who commands. Our comfort lies in our performance of *mitzvot*, because that is where our redemption lies. To be sure, the word *nechamah* means not only "comfort" but also "redemption"; like redemption, comfort comes through adhering to the commandments of Torah. Similarly, the word *nacham* means both "comfort" and "repentance." In our repentance we find both comfort and redemption because repentance lies not in feeling a certain way but in living a certain way. It lies in returning to a relation to the Holy One by entering into a deeper relation to the people around us. In short, we receive the comfort of the Comforter inasmuch as we offer comfort to another, as the Father of the Fatherless and the Protector of Widows commands us to do. In the comfort we offer to another the *Shekhinah* offers us her comfort. And the wholeness of the peace that comes only through her.

Peace

With this word we come to the eighteenth of the eighteen words that sustain a life. In the end, these eighteen words are gathered into this word: *peace*. I do not end with the word *God* because God ends in peace, as we shall see. Peace, *shalom*, is *shalem* or "wholeness." Wholeness lies in the wholeness of body and soul, of past and future, of creation, revelation, and redemption; it is rooted in the wholeness of thought and word, of word and deed, of confidence and care and the courage to care. Yes, courage: peace requires courage. Peace is not the absence of inner conflict or turmoil; indeed, there is a certain strife of the spirit born of a concern for the suffering of others that is the mark of peace. If Mother Teresa had an aura of peace about her, it was not because her soul was free of turmoil but precisely because her courageous soul was filled with a certain blessed strife of the spirit, a sense of what must be done, a sense of urgency. Where there is no sense of holy urgency, there is no peace. That turmoil is a blessing. It brings a certain peace or wholeness to the soul who knows what must be done and why. It leads a soul not to raise a hand but to extend a hand, not to take up arms but to open up arms. It leads a soul to speak, at times silently.

I recently read an article that justifies rioting and looting, claiming that it is the language of the disenfranchised. But violence is the opposite of language. Violence ensues when we run out of words. What has happened to the legacies of Martin Luther King Jr. and of Mahatma Gandhi? Their peaceful protests, protests that refused to raise a hand, were grounded in the faith that protesting in peace, refusing to engage in violence, could awaken the souls of the violent to a realization that they are destroying their own souls in the violence they do to others. It rested on the faith that they, too, are human. I have spoken about faith. Here we see another meaning of *faith*, not as faith in God but as faith in humanity. Each is bound to the other through peace. Without that faith, we have no peace. And where are we now? What have we come to? Why, concretely, do I end with this reflection on peace? Because it has concrete implications, as, indeed, all of these words do. The life sustained by these words is a life of flesh and blood, and peace is to be found only in such a life: apart from the flesh-and-blood human being, the word *peace* is meaningless. Albert Einstein said of Gandhi, "In future generations people will scarce believe that one such as this walked the earth." Have I set the bar too high? Nevertheless! In our own time among those who pass themselves off as "men of God"—men who have many admirers—are the purveyors of hatred, rage, and violence. You know who they are.

Inner peace, my children, lies in calmly focusing on how we must respond to the evils and injustices in the world. Indeed, that peace is what enables us to focus; when we are not at peace, we cannot focus, and when we cannot focus, we have no peace. Inner peace lies in the wisdom to discern between the trivial and the important, a difference that constantly eludes us. All too often, the first things we forget are the most important things. Most of the time, the things that anger us, the things that we allow to disturb our peace, are actually very unimportant. Yes, there are forces at work all around us that disturb our peace and leave us lying awake at night. We speak within our heart as we lie upon our bed, as the psalmist says, but we find it difficult to fall silent. These forces of evil have one thing in common: antisemitism. The antisemites claim that the Jews are the source of all evil, when it is the other way around: antisemitism is the source of all evil. Antisemitism is not a form of racism; rather, racism is a form of antisemitism. It is a hatred of the millennia-long Jewish testimony concerning the holiness of the other human being and the infinite responsibility that comes with that holiness. Here the four ancient sources of the oppression of the Jews continue into our own time: the Babylonian, the Persian, the Greek, and the Roman oppressors. The Babylonian oppressors are to be found among the Arab Jihadists, the Persian among the Iranian Jihadists, the Greek among the left-wing ideologues, and the Roman among the Christians.

How shall we deal with it? And what do these ancient and modern forms of Jew hatred have to do with peace? This I ask, because being at peace is very difficult when you are hated. My teacher Elie Wiesel once said that there comes a time for any human being when, in order to remain human, he or she must assume the Jewish condition, a condition not of victimhood but of testimony to the sanctity of the other human being. Only through that testimony, both in word and in deed, is peace to be found. The Jewish condition is a condition that refuses violence, or at least refuses the violence spawned by hatred. A story is told of Golda Meir, who was prime minister of Israel during the October War of 1973. After taking heavy casualties, the Israelis emerged victorious, whereupon Prime Minister Meir declared to the Arab nations that tried to wipe out the Jewish state, "We can forgive you for attacking us and starting this war. We can even forgive you for killing our children. But we will *never* forgive you for making our children kill your children." The refusal of forgiveness for *this* is essential to peace.

Arthur Miller's novel *Focus* tells us something about the meaning of *peace* and its relation to violence, about what it means to focus and thus to be at peace. Set in New York City in 1945, the novel relates the tale of a man named Lawrence Newman who, after acquiring a pair of glasses, is mistaken for a Jew, with all the antisemitic reactions that come with it. Newman then spends his days in a state of inner agony, denying he is a Jew; of course, he is not literally a Jew. But there is no escape for him. No peace for him.

One night four young hoodlums from the antisemitic Christian Front follow him on his way home from the movies. At first he thinks they are headed toward the shop of the Jew Finkelstein, and it gives him a fleeting moment of relief. It turns out, however, that they are not after the Jew Finkelstein—*they are after the Jew Newman!* They assault him outside of Finkelstein's store, when Finkelstein suddenly appears wielding two Louisville sluggers. He hands one to Newman and they fight off the attackers. After the skirmish, their faces bruised and bleeding, Newman helps Finkelstein back into the shop. Having once been repulsed by the touch of Finkelstein's hand when purchasing a newspaper, Newman now collects some ice and attends to Finkelstein's wounded face, the face that forbids violence and murder. Then he looks into a mirror; his own face looks back at him, now black and blue and oozing blood. Gazing into the mirror, his heart racing, a strange feeling of peace comes over him as he stares at the face that others had taken to be the face of a Jew. This peace, this *shalom*, is the *shalem* or "wholeness" of identity; it is the peace that comes only from on high, with the opening of the dimension of height and truth and goodness. It is the peace that comes with knowing who you are. After the attack Newman resolves to finally go to the police and report it. When the police ask if he and Finkelstein are the only Jews on that street, he answers, "Yes, we are," thus speaking a truth from which he had fled throughout the tale, the truth of Elie Wiesel's insight, the truth that brought him peace for the first time. Speaking this truth, he declared, "*Hineni!* Here I am!" For there is no peace apart from this cry of *Hineni!*

The peace that came over Newman and ran through his soul arose from the realization of who he is *in truth*. The Bahir, an ancient Kabbalistic text, teaches that *shalom*, "peace," is a synonym for *emet*, "truth." Here the wholeness of the Holy Tongue, which brings us peace through its truth, can be seen in the word *emet*, consisting of the first, middle, and last letters of the Hebrew alphabet: *emet* contains the whole alphabet and every Hebrew word made of Hebrew letters. Wholeness—the *shalem* that is *shalom*—lies in *emet*, in truth. The wholeness of *shalem*, moreover, lies in the wholeness of the God who is One and whose Name is One. To be sure, *Emet* is one of the names of God, as it contains all the letters that form all names, and all names issue from God. Newman came to understand that peace lies in knowing who he is, in knowing his name. He came to realize that we spend our lives learning our names, seeking the truth of our true identity, for only in that truth is peace to be found. That is why, when we lie in our graves at the end of our lives, the Angel of Death asks us our name in order to determine whether we are able to enter into the presence of the Holy One. Only in the presence of the God who is Truth—only as we become present—can we ever attain the wholeness that is peace. Newman affirmed that he was a Jew in a moment of affirming the truth of who he is as a human being created in the image and likeness of the Holy One, and in that affirmation of the truth he found peace—or rather peace found him, came over him, like a living presence or a breath of life.

The fifteenth-century sage Don Isaac Abarbanel teaches that *peace* is a synonym for the Good. Simply stated, you cannot be at peace—you cannot be whole—without being good. And I know all of you to be good, my children. Goodness is grounded in truth, and truth is grounded in peace. Just as *peace* is a synonym for *truth*, so is it a synonym for *good*: there is no peace to be found, either within or without, in the absence of goodness. As the Jews affirm three times each day in the last of the Eighteen Benedictions, it is a peace that comes only from God, *HaEl HaTov*, the "God who is the Good." Yes, Newman engaged in violence when it was necessary to do so; his friend Finkelstein engaged in violence only to come to Newman's aid as he was being attacked. At times violence becomes necessary, God help us, when we must prevent violence done to another through the shameful use of violence. The Torah teaches us, therefore, that we cannot stand idly by our brother's blood. As I have said, death is not evil; standing by while others die is evil, so that opposite the wholeness that is good we have the brokenness and woundedness that is evil.

If the wholeness of peace belongs to truth, the brokenness of fragmentation belongs to the lie, and evil thrives on the lie. If you would be at peace, do not lie, my children. All too often, our lies are what disturb our sleep. But then you already know that. We have all told a lie, however "white." And we have all known the sleeplessness that comes with the lie. When you crawl into bed, speak the truth within your heart, and then rest silently in the welcoming arms of peace.

If peace, *shalom*, is tied to wholeness, *shalem*, then the opposite of peace is not the absence of strife, upheaval, or even violence. No, the opposite of peace is the fragmentation of despair, which, to be sure, can lead a person to do violence to himself and to others. In fact, despair is the most common source of violence, whether in word or in deed. Peace comes not with a withdrawal from discord but with a movement toward mending, a movement of *tikkun*. Thus in the Eighteen Benedictions we pray not just for healing but for a *refuah shlemah*, which is not just a "complete healing" but a "whole healing," that is, a "healing of wholeness," body and soul, word and deed, to be found only in peace. It is a healing and a wholeness that, as I have said, can be attained only through the strife of the spirit manifest in our loving concern for another, whose suffering breaks our heart. A broken heart is like broken bread: it is broken in its offering, and yet, only in its offering, may it become whole. Bread is not bread until it is broken and shared with another, and the heart cannot break over one's own suffering. No, a heart breaks over the suffering of the other person.

That is where the human being becomes a human being: through the brokenness of a broken heart. There is no being human, no being at peace, without a broken heart. Hence the teaching of the Baal Shem Tov that there is nothing so whole as a broken heart. If the Holy One is revealed in the disturbance of the witness, which is a manifestation of his own broken heart, then the peace that belongs to the life of the soul lies in a disturbance over the plight of the other human being. This disturbance that is essential to peace is an eternal laboring to heal what has been wounded, to mend what has been torn. In that labor in the midst of time, the soul comes into contact with the eternal. And in a world of ephemeral thrills and fleeting pleasures, the eternal is precisely what is needful: in the eternal there is peace. Rooted in the eternal, peace takes us beyond the confines of time, even as we seek healing in the midst of time. Time is made of this seeking, without which we have no peace. In the peace that comes with this seeking and striving the eternal is manifest.

I have said that there is nothing more mystical, nothing more wondrous, than the mundane. It shines through the simplest of actions, as when we greet another, saying, *Shalom aleikhem*, "peace be upon you," and the other returns the greeting with *V'aleikhem shalom*, "and upon you peace." By now you can see the profundity that this simple greeting harbors. It is like a prayer. It tells us that we can never attain peace without conferring peace upon another. That is why the Talmud teaches that when we encounter another, we should be the first to greet him or her with *Shalom aleikhem*. That is why the Talmud urges us to greet another with a face full of joy. In joy there is wholeness. Only in joy. There is no peace without joy. With joy we greet the angels who visit us on Shabbat, saying *Shalom aleikhem* to the *malakhei ha-shalom*, the angels and messengers of peace who bring with them the peace of the Shabbat, in which time itself finds its wholeness with the entry of the eternal, who is the Sabbath Bride. The Sabbath is not a day of rest—it is a day of peace, when we are delivered from a time of unrest and insanity. And so among the Sabbath prayers is Psalm 34, which David composed on the occasion of feigning madness when he had been captured by the Philistine king Avimelekh. During the six days of the week we pretend to be mad, so as to make our way in an insane world. But on Shabbat we regain our sanity and our identity and are at peace.

We pray for the peace of Jerusalem, for the wholeness of Jerusalem, in which the wholeness and the oneness of the Divine Name is realized, for Jerusalem is one of the Names of the Holy One. As the Sabbath is the entry of the eternal into time, so is Jerusalem the entry of the eternal into space: what the Sabbath is to time, Jerusalem is to space. In both we discover the meaning of *peace*. There can be no peace for humanity, either within or without, until we have attained the peace of Jerusalem. I have taken groups of students to Jerusalem, almost all of them non-Jews. They, too, sense the peace, the wholeness of the soul, that is to be found only in Jerusalem. They sense the truth that their own souls emanate from the Holy City. They experience the truth that the dust of Adam was gathered from the Temple Mount. During its long history, Jerusalem has been attacked fifty-two times, captured and recaptured forty-four times, besieged twenty-three times, and destroyed twice. Few cities have been less at peace than Jerusalem. Why? Because it is the city most essential to peace, to the peace of humanity and to the peace of the soul. What I have said about the Holy Land applies even more so to the Holy City: it is holy not because of what has transpired there, but what has transpired there is because it is holy—*already.* For the Torah goes forth from Zion and the Word of God from Jerusalem, both of which are essential to the wholeness of peace.

We face Jerusalem even as we pray for the peace of Jerusalem. The sages are agreed: we must face the Holy City, our gaze turned to the *Har HaBayit*, the "Mount of the Holy Dwelling Place," when we pray. For peace is essential to dwelling, both for God and for humanity. In the Talmud, however, they ask: when we pray, should our eyes be turned upward, toward the Most High, or downward in humility? The answer is: both. When Abraham journeyed to Mount Moriah, which is the Temple Mount, he stood on a high hill, turned his eyes upward, and saw the Place, the *Makom*, that God showed him. But if we look at the topography, it turns out that the place where Abraham stood and looked up is at a higher elevation than Mount Moriah: *up* is not a direction in space but the dimension of the holy.

To pray not only *for* peace but *in* peace is to attain this wholeness of above and below, of inward and upward. Rebbe Nachman of Breslov taught that there is no peace, no *shalom*, and no wholeness, no *shalem*, without the wholeness of above and below, of the Most High and the most humble. True height is to be found, my children, only in humility, and true peace issues only from the attainment of this wholeness. There are many illustrations of this in our tradition. The commandment of *tzitzit* or "fringes" on our garments, for example, teaches us to *look* at the fringes hanging down, at the *tzitzit*, a word with a numerical value of 600; add to that the eight threads and the five knots of the fringes, and we have 613, so that we may remember the 613 commandments of Torah. Therefore this looking down is a looking up. Indeed, the word *tzitzit* is a cognate of *hetzitz*, which is to "look at very closely." The *tzitzit* are to have a thread of a special blue color called *tekhelet*, from a dye made of a rare snail; *tekhelet* is the same color as the Throne of Glory on high, which is the origin of every soul, so that we may know that the soul within is bound to the Throne above. The movement below stirs the movement above. In this wholeness that is peace, in this *shalem* that is *shalom*, we have the wholeness of these eighteen words that sustain a life and the peace that, hopefully, is my legacy for you my children.

And so let me leave you with a story from the Hasidic tradition that beautifully illustrates this teaching and this legacy. Like many Hasidic tales, this one has several variations. The version that has become the most famous is the one we have from the great Yiddish writer Isaac Leib Peretz.

The hero of the tale is the unnamed rabbi of Nemirov. It takes place during the time of *Selichot*, the Penitential Prayers leading up to Rosh Hashanah, the Days of Awe, and Yom Kippur, the day of judgment and atonement. Each year during those weeks of the month of *Elul* the rabbi would disappear in the early hours of Friday morning; he was nowhere to be found, neither in the House of Prayer nor in the House of Study, which was very unusual for the Nemirover rebbe. "Where could he be?" the Hasidim would ask. "Why, where else?" they answered: he had ascended to the uppermost realms of the uppermost worlds to come before the Most High, the Holy One Himself, and plead the case for Divine Mercy for the Jewish people.

A Litvak Mitnagged, one of those who opposed the mystical madness of the Hasidim, happened to be passing through Nemirov one year during *Elul*. He was, of course, skeptical about this business of the rebbe's ascending into the uppermost realms. Determined to expose the rabbi of Nemirov as a fraud and the Hasidim as fools, the Litvak sneaked into the rabbi's room one Thursday night, hid under his bed, and waited. It is no small matter to lie quietly through the night beneath the bed of a *Tzaddik* such as the rabbi of Nemirov. But the Litvak was determined to find out just where the rabbi disappeared to. When the rabbi rose in the wee hours of the morning, he dressed himself in peasant's clothes, with a rope dangling from his coat pocket. He quietly went out from his room, picked up an ax from the kitchen, and set out into the darkness of the early dawn, with the Litvak following behind.

Careful to remain in the shadows, the rabbi stole his way to the outskirts of town and into the woods. There the Litvak saw him fell a small tree and chop it into logs and the logs into sticks. The rabbi then made a bundle of sticks, wrapped the rope around the bundle, and returned to the edge of town. With the Litvak watching all the while, the rabbi stopped at a broken-down shack where a sick old woman lived. He knocked on the door. In a weak voice she asked, "Who is there?" And he replied, "It is Vasily, a poor Russian peasant selling wood." She told him she had no money, but he persisted: "No matter. I trust God to provide, I can trust you for a few kopeks." And the rabbi entered the shack.

The Litvak continued to spy on the rabbi. He heard and saw everything, as he peered through the window of the sick woman's shack. Disguised as the Russian peasant Vasily, the Rabbi proceeded to make a fire and, while doing so, uttered the first of the Penitential Prayers. As the wood burned, he recited the second portion of the prayers, and then the third, the Litvak looking on all the while. He then prepared food for the ailing old woman and comforted her with loving words of kindness. Then and there the Litvak resolved to become a disciple of the rabbi of Nemirov. From that moment onward, whenever the Litvak heard one of the Hasidim of Nemirov declare that the rabbi had disappeared into the uppermost realms to plead the case for the Jews, he simply nodded, smiled, and declared, "Yes, if not higher."

In those heights, peace and all that sustains a life are to be found. So I leave you, my children, with a blessing:

> May *HaShem* bless you and keep you
>
> May *HaShem* shine His face upon you and show you favor
>
> May *HaShem* lift up His face and give you peace

Look up, as God himself lifts up his face, and you will find peace, my children, from on high, as told in this tale of what is even higher than the Most High.

Jerusalem
11 Av 5782
8 August 2022

About the Author

David Patterson holds the Hillel Feinberg Distinguished Chair in Holocaust Studies in the Ackerman Center for Holocaust Studies at the University of Texas at Dallas. A winner of the National Jewish Book Award and the Koret Jewish Book Award, the Hadassah Myrtle Wreath Award, and the Holocaust Scholars' Eternal Flame Award, he has published 250 articles and chapters on philosophy, literature, Judaism, and Holocaust studies. His writings have been anthologized, and his more than forty books most recently include *Judaism, Antisemitism, Holocaust: Making the Connections* (2022), *Shoah and Torah* (2022), *Portraits: Elie Wiesel's Hasidic Legacy* (2021), *The Holocaust and the Non-Representable* (2018), *Anti-Semitism and Its Metaphysical Origins* (2015), *Genocide in Jewish Thought* (2012), *A Genealogy of Evil: Anti-Semitism from Nazism to Islamic Jihad* (2011), *Overcoming Alienation: A Kabbalistic Reflection on the Five Levels of the Soul* (2008), and *Emil L. Fackenheim: A Jewish Philosopher's Response to the Holocaust* (2008).

www.ingramcontent.com/pod-product-compliance
Lightning Source LLC
LaVergne TN
LVHW050957080826
845145LV00009B/2333

* 9 7 8 1 6 6 6 7 5 0 9 3 5 *